SPORTS JUSTICE

ROGER I. ABRAMS

SPORTS JUSTICE

The Law &
the Business
of Sports

NORTHEASTERN UNIVERSITY PRESS
  Boston
Published by University Press of New England
  Hanover & London

NORTHEASTERN UNIVERSITY PRESS
Published by University Press of New England
One Court Street, Lebanon NH 03766
www.upne.com
© 2010 Northeastern University
All rights reserved
Manufactured in the United States of America
Designed by Eric M. Brooks
Typeset in Arnhem and The Sans by
Integrated Publishing Solutions

University Press of New England is a member of the
Green Press Initiative. The paper used in this book meets
their minimum requirement for recycled paper.

For permission to reproduce any of the material in this
book, contact Permissions, University Press of New England,
One Court Street, Lebanon NH 03766; or visit www.upne.com

Library of Congress Cataloging-in-Publication Data
Abrams, Roger I., 1945–
Sports justice: the law and the business of sports / Roger I. Abrams.
p. cm.
Includes bibliographical references and index.
ISBN 978-1-55553-700-5 (cloth: alk. paper)
1. Sports—Law and legislation—United States. 2. Athletes—Legal
status, laws, etc.—United States I. Title.
KF3989.A934   2010
344.73'099—dc22   2010021932
5 4 3 2 1

CONTENTS

This is a book about rules: the rules of the game, which ensure a level playing field within sports, and the rules of law which apply to the business of sports. It is a book about the authoritative institutions that apply those rules: the courts, labor arbitrators, agencies, and private associations. It is also a book about the men and women who were involved in ten of the most important legal controversies in sports.

For over a decade, I have focused my research on one sports business, our national game of baseball. The law, economics, and social history of baseball teach us much about ourselves and our social norms, where we have come from and where we are now. Although baseball is discussed in the concluding chapter, this book includes a broader spectrum of sporting activities — from golf and gymnastics to football and basketball. They provide the context for our analysis of how legal rules apply to the business of sports. As philosopher Michael Novak has written: "Sports are at the heart of the matter."

First, we focus on defining our subject matter: what are the essential characteristics of sports and how do we distinguish this human activity from other contests and entertainments that consume the public's attention? What exactly is sports justice as opposed to injustice? At the same time, we try to answer a more basic question: why do we care so much about sports?

Along the way, we will meet some really interesting and talented athletes: Jeremy Bloom, the world champion mogul skier who was barred by the NCAA from playing amateur football for the University of Colorado because he had modeled clothes for Tommy Hilfiger; John Mackey, the greatest tight end in the history of the National Football League, who became the president of the Players Association and sought freedom for professional football players in court; and Terrell Owens, the spectacular wide receiver who has not played well with others. There is also one non-athlete:

Al Davis, the renegade owner of the Oakland–Los Angeles–Oakland Raiders, who—in an effort to gain the respect he felt that others had denied him—used antitrust laws to defeat the National Football League cartel.

All of the cases on which we focus involve someone who was powerless in the face of the institutions of sport. Some sought access to play—such as Casey Martin, Renee Richards, Jeremy Bloom, and the young gymnasts from Brown University—but needed judicial intervention to achieve justice (not always successfully). Al Davis and John Mackey used the courts to compel the powers of the National Football League to accede to their demands. Club owners, in turn, used the private tribunal of labor arbitration to declare and acknowledge their rights against Brian Shaw in basketball and Terrell Owens in football. Others would have preferred keeping their matters private, but were forced to deal with the public authorities, like hockey players Ted Green and Wayne Maki after their stick-swinging bout on the ice.

The interplay of sports, business, law, and legal institutions makes for some compelling narratives. Renee Richards' internal battle with her sexual identity, Casey Martin's race against his progressively degenerating right leg, John Mackey's victories and defeats on the gridiron, at the negotiating table, in federal court, and then eventually with the physical impact of his football career on his body and his mind—all are part of the stories of sports justice.

There are many people to thank for their help and assistance in completing this project. My wife Fran read the chapters and pointed out my numerous errors. She claims that this text is the best of my five books. If it is so, it is because of her work. Associate Dean Marie Melito of Rutgers Law School once again proofed the finished manuscript. She is a marvel and a dear friend. My research fellows, Sofia Lingos and Lindsey Owen, provided valued editing and indexing assistance. My colleagues in sports law read many of the chapters and offered valuable advice. Every book is a team project, and I was fortunate to have a stellar squad helping me.

SPORTS JUSTICE

SPORTS AND THE LAW

Sport is where an entire life can be compressed into a few hours, where the emotions of a lifetime can be felt on an acre or two of ground, where a person can suffer and die and rise again on six miles of trails through a New York City park. Sport is a theater where sinner can turn saint and a common man become an uncommon hero, where the past and the future can fuse with the present. Sport is singularly able to give us peak experiences where we feel completely one with the world and transcend all conflicts as we finally become our own potential.

GEORGE A. SHEEHAN

[Sports] are good because they encourage a true democratic spirit; for in the athletic field the man must be judged not with reference to outside and accidental attributes, but to the combination of bodily vigor and moral quality which go to make up prowess.

THEODORE ROOSEVELT

• • • There is no easy way to explain the hold that sport has on our psyche and everyday lives. It is, for many of us, just part of what we are, perhaps the most important part of our inner lives. Playing sports can be beautiful, fun and therapeutic. Hippocrates wrote: "Sport is a preserver of health," at least when done in moderation. Watching others compete in sports can also be enjoyable, especially when those athletes are among the very best at their game. Sport, therefore, can be entertainment and a diversion, but it is more than that.

We live for sports; we die, at least figuratively, with the failure of our teams, exalt in their victories, and spend days consumed by talk and thought about sport. Sports are not mere pastimes, like a good book, a cold beer, or a conversation with a friend. Sports are an essential part of human life and health; for some, they seem to be life itself. Sports are amalgams of myth, entertainment, wonderment, passion, and exaltation; they are quintessential human experiences and nothing less.

If this sounds overly dramatic, consider the evidence, as a lawyer might say. Psychologists have studied the impact on public mental health of a loss by the home team in an important game. It can result in a generalized depression in a community. Most recover in fairly short order, but for others the misery of defeat lasts until it is replaced by the thrill of victory. Cities with professional clubs that are perennial losers suffer continuously. Mediocrity is a cancer without a cure. A game is not only for now, but also is part of a sequence of contests that spreads back over time.

A study released in 2009 of death rates on Super Bowl Sunday showed that a loss by the home team was related to a spike in the death rate, due mostly to an increase in heart attacks. On the other hand, a Super Bowl victory was correlated with a decrease in death rate. The research recommended the use of "pharmacologic agents" or relaxation techniques such as deep breathing for those persons with cardiac risk factors. Deep breathing, of course, will not lead your team to victory.

But when our favorite teams win, sports fans experience a tangible lift. According to President John Kennedy, a great sports enthusiast: "We are inclined to think that if we watch a football game or a baseball game, we have taken part in it." After a victory, we all are champions and act as such, exhibiting triumphal behavior and a positive self-image in our interpersonal dealings, especially toward those who favored the team that our club has conquered on the field of play. We share in a communal euphoria. These are primal emotions that translate into civic pride, even if not one of the players on the winning team came from our town.

Economists have measured the effects of sport victories and defeats. Communal self-esteem fostered by sports triumphs enhances productivity, creativity, and commerce. At the other end of the spectrum, entire regions suffer self-doubt and feelings of inferiority caused by losses at sporting contests; they might even experience declining economic indicators. On the college level, a dramatic success in a critical football or basketball game — Doug Flutie's famous "Hail Mary" touchdown pass for Boston College in 1984 or Christian Laettner's half-court shot for Duke to win the 1992 eastern regional basketball championship come to mind — engenders an increase in admissions applications at the schools that prevailed. Who would not want to be part of a winning sports tradition? By the simple acts of matriculation and tuition payment, a student becomes the beneficiary of ages of sports victories.

Failure, of course, is inevitable; it is the default position of all sports endeavors. Most of the time, a seventy-yard pass will fall harmlessly to the ground and a turn-around shot from half court will miss the basket. The amateurs on the 1980 U.S. Olympic hockey team will lose to a squad of Soviet professionals ninety-nine times out of a hundred. And only in 1969 will the "Miracle" Mets defeat the Baltimore Orioles to win the World Series. Each season, in each sport, there are many losers but only one champion. While these long odds make success even sweeter, its rarity makes most fans losers most of the time. But there will always be another season, and hope springs eternal in the hearts and souls of sports fans.

Some may think that the connections among sports, life, and death are overstated. The evidence suggests to the contrary. The great Dutch soccer club, Ajax Amsterdam, was merely the first to build a cemetery for their most dedicated fans. Germany's Hamburg HSV offers their supporters the opportunity to be buried in club colors adjacent to their team's arena while the band plays the club's anthem: "Hamburg, My Pearl." In 2008, the Boston Red Sox announced that—because they had received too many requests—they would no longer allow deceased fans' ashes to be scattered at Fenway Park.

Some people, of course, miss out on all the action. They denigrate those of us who enjoy such plebian pursuits as sports. They do not feel the spirit, the attraction, or the fascination—let alone the very compulsion—of athletic games. They are amused by those of us who would take seriously what they see as simple blue-collar diversions. Essayist Fran Lebowitz, for example, wrote:

> When it comes to sports, I am not particularly interested. Generally speaking, I look upon them as dangerous and tiring activities performed by people with whom I share nothing except the right to trial by jury.

Folks like Lebowitz may be fortunate because they do not suffer with the inevitable failures of a team. They feel no psychic connection. They do not waste time away from their quotidian tasks or their work to rehash the "what ifs" of the most recent contests. They bring their fact-based perspective to all aspects of life: what kind of sentient being could care about games played with pucks or balls of various shapes and sizes?

However, those who chose not to watch, care, or participate also miss out on the exultation. They do not share the redemption of a sweet triumph, the hope of the next contest. They do not experience the very human feeling of misery and despair that comes from losing. Every club triumphs sometimes, if not in the ultimate match for the championship, then in an every-day game during the season. Fans have long memories, and ultimately there will be redemption for all adherents. Remember, the best baseball club only wins two out of three games, while the worst wins at least one out of three. Those who would refrain from sports live the safer life, avoiding the risks to their self-esteem that participating as a fan provides, but missing, in the process, part of our culture. Even losing is worthwhile, because it means you tried, and it makes success all the sweeter. What a shame to waste a life without taking that risk.

Sports have moved many to rapture. The Duke of Dorset, a brilliant athlete before assuming the British ambassadorship to Paris, wrote in *Ladies and Gentlemen's Magazine* in 1777: "What is human life but a game of cricket!" U.S. Supreme Court Chief Justice Earl Warren vowed that each morning he would "always turn to the sports page first. The sports page records man's accomplishments; the front page has nothing but man's failures." This jurist, who led the greatest peaceful legal rights revolution of all time, was a devoted sports fanatic. And in the third season of *Seinfeld*, Jerry and George have a brief, but meaningful, exchange while waiting in line for the movies:

> GEORGE: All I know about is sports. That's it. No matter how depressed I get, I could always read the sports section.
> JERRY: I could read the sports section if my hair was on fire.

If you don't appreciate the phantasmagorical pull of sports, how do you explain the opening section of the Supreme Court's 1992 decision in Curt Flood's unsuccessful antitrust suit against Major League Baseball? Justice Harry Blackmun starts his opinion with a paean of praise for the game of baseball, relating baseball frippery and mythology. He reviews the historical highlights of the National Game in a footnote, then lists in the body of his opinion the names of baseball players "celebrated for one reason or another, that have sparked the diamond and its environs and that have provided tinder for recaptured thrills, for reminiscence and comparisons, and for conversation and anticipation in-season and off-season." The case was about antitrust law, interstate commerce, and jurisdiction, but for Justice Blackmun it was first and foremost about baseball.

There have been some notable sports rejectionists. George Orwell blamed sports for catalyzing social antipathy and even hostility. In December 1945, he wrote in *The Sporting Spirit* that sport "is bound up with hatred, jealousy, boastfulness, disregard of all rules and sadistic pleasure in witnessing violence." Sport, he offered, was the cause of war, not a substitute for it. Sports enthusiasts can only pity dissenters like Orwell. They are outvoted by the weight of public opinion which values sport as a genuine measure of a society's richness and culture.

Orwell's characterization of sport should not be dismissed out of hand, however. Recognizing the value of the sports experience should not blind us to its darker side. Even if sports were pure (and they are not), they consume an enormous amount of society's time, passion, and energy that might be better spent elsewhere. It may be impossible to calculate how much a nation's productivity is sapped by a sports obsession. The risks of injury to self and psyche can also be immense.

President Theodore Roosevelt often preached that participation in athletics, at least when the activity was done in moderation, might improve health, discipline, teamwork, and self-esteem. At the same time, the rules of every game have always been inviting targets for those devious (or clever) enough to find loopholes. Cheating, sports teaches us, is as American as apple pie. Whether it is an athlete taking performance-enhancing drugs or a coach ordering the videotaping of an opposing team's signals, sports produce a mixed bag of values, a morality play of dubious purity, not unlike the rest of the social and economic life of America.

How then do we explain the hold sport has on the public psyche? Are sports a basic and innate human instinct, like the will to survive and to procreate? We need food, but do we need football? It is human nature to flee from danger in order to survive, but sports fans face psychic dangers every time their teams take the field. While they are not typically threatened with actual physical harm, fans have always invested themselves in the game's outcome, and as a result they place their sense of self-worth at risk.

IN THE BEGINNING

Sporting activities were conceived by primitive societies to prepare warriors for the hunt and, if necessary, for battle against rival tribes. Survival in the struggle for life depended upon perfecting eye-hand coordination. Engaging in competitive sports enhanced both the ability to fight and the ability to obtain food. They were competitions, but within limits. It made no sense to lose your warriors on the practice field.

Perhaps sports are a modern artifact of our primitive origins. The skills of sport mirror many of the skills of living. Those spectators who watched the hunters preparing for the hunt knew that their lives were on the line as well. An unsuccessful hunt meant starvation. Thus, group loyalty and the perfection of skills are intensely human survival traits.

It is not surprising to find that sports remain a part of all civilizations. Spectators no doubt enjoyed watching their heroes perform the skills essential for community continuity, and that pattern has continued even though community survival is no longer the primary goal. Defeat in prehistoric times meant literal death, and we teach our children, who carry our genes, to win at the games that are a preparation for life. Improved eye-hand coordination kept proto-humans alive on the plains of Africa. Although we rarely wrestle with lions today, we continue to wrestle with each other. Modern sport is basic human training, not a mere escape from our quotidian tasks. It is fundamental to life itself.

During the nineteenth century, some notables waxed eloquent about the benefits of athletic activity that would take city dwellers outside to breathe fresh air instead of the musty contaminants of the tenements. Factory workers who served as cogs in the machines of the Industrial Revolution also needed to develop their coordination and other skills. As Henry Wade Rogers, the president of Northwestern University, wrote in 1893:

> [Athletics] teach self-mastery, the ability to control one's temper, and to work with others. They demand steadiness of nerve, coolness, self-reliance, the subordination of animal impulses.

Idealized conceptions such as this one made athletics part of the American myth. Through this shared culture, sports acted to hold together a heterogeneous society of natives and immigrants, farmers and city folks, workers and traders. Professional sports have always been an entry point into the nation's socioeconomic life for children of new immigrants. Sports teams represent places, cities, and regions of which each individual is a part. As the population in urban centers grew dramatically in the nineteenth century, the games of the city flourished. They still do. Sports fans did more than simply observe the games; they participated in them by rooting, caring, and risking their inner emotions. They identified with their teams, sharing the joys of winning and the pain of losing.

SPORT AS OUR SECULAR RELIGION

Is it possible that sport has had a treasured place within society because it plays the role of a secular religion? Religion centers us within the universe of unknown and unknowable forces that control our comings and goings from birth to death and beyond. It teaches us context: who we are and why we are here. It identifies those elements that are sacred and special. Might sport play this same role across an entire population?

Amos Alonzo Stagg, head football coach at the University of Chicago from 1892 to 1932, had wanted to become a Presbyterian minister. Instead, this patriarch of early twentieth century football was among the first to unite sport and devout religious principles. A college football coach for seventy-one years, he viewed the football huddle (which he developed) as a kind of religious congregation on the field.

Michael Novak, in his classic and important 1976 book *The Joy of Sports*, explored how the elements of organized religion were mirrored in sports. Much like religions, he explained, sports are structured activities with ceremonies and heroic forms, carried out with intense concentration in spaces that inspire awe and reverence. Think of the intense emotion a spectator feels after emerging from beneath the stands and seeing—for the first time—a baseball diamond in an amphitheater of placid green. Like religious parables, sporting events convey danger, contingency, chance, and fate. Religion and sports celebrate the ages of man with chants and songs performed by groups of people joined in common purpose.

For Novak, sports are more than entertainment. They are secular religious experiences in which the fans play an essential role; they are the chief communal ritual of citizens. Athletes demonstrate more commitment, discipline, and dedication than are necessary for mere entertainment. People care about athletes and sports in a way quite different from the way they care about celebrities or politics. They invest great passion in their heroes and their teams: "Defeat hurts like death," Novak suggests, and victory leads to exultation.

Some may consider that equating sports with religion is blasphemous and understandably so. Sports are accessible and commonplace; the world of true faith, by comparison, is celestial and transcendent. Divinity is debased by comparing it to a soccer match. Sports are, at their best, ersatz life performances; by comparison, religion—to many people—offers the genuine article. Aspects of sport might mirror aspects of religion, but sporting experiences are not religious ones. On the other hand, for some adherents sport comes very close to rapture. In his book *Under the March Sun*, Charles Fountain explains: "Red Sox spring training fans are like pilgrims at Lourdes, convinced that their lives have been touched by something spiritual and life affirming."

Even if the comparison to religion is inapt, Novak was on to something profound. There is certainly something about sports that set them apart from other human activities, something we need to understand in order to explore the realm of sports justice. Like other people, judges and arbitrators are affected by the distinctive nature of the sports enterprise. When not adjudicating disputes, they may be participants in the rituals of sport. Whether they rule for or against the established institutions of sport, the fact that a case involves sports certainly affects their decision making.

On the other hand, neuroscientists might offer a catalytic explanation for sports. Participating in sports as a devoted fan provides occasions for the brain to secrete dopamine, the neurotransmitter that regulates all of our emotions. The expectation of success might create positive dopamine effects. Conversely, a defeat might generate electrical signals of disappointment in the anterior cingulate cortex. Maybe sports are just chemicals in action.

WHAT IS A SPORT?

To discuss the principles of sports justice in operation, we should first define our terms. What is a sport? Don Murray succinctly explained the evolution of a chance activity into a sport: "You take a bunch of kids throwing rocks at random and people look askance, but if you go and hold a rock-throwing contest—people understand that." Rock throwing becomes a sport, but only if there are rules to the contest. Major North American sports such as baseball, football, basketball, hockey, golf, and tennis fit easily within this domain. But what about other human competitions, such as chess or poker? Or the ubiquitous, if occasionally staged, television reality shows?

At its core, a sport is an organized competitive and physical activity where participants interact in accordance with pre-established rules. Competition, rather than cooperation, is valued as the central mode of human interaction in sport, although cooperation is essential in team competitions. The rules of the game—its internal laws—provide the architecture for the "level playing field." For example, football matches between one team with eleven players and another with seven would not qualify as a sport. In baseball, a batter gets three strikes and four balls when playing for either the red team or the blue team. The rules of sport are administered on the field of play by designated officials — umpires and referees. Their decisions are the law as applied to any given play, although "instant replay" (in football and tennis, for example) has recently allowed an appeal in arguable cases. Institutional authorities are presumed correct because, according to the rules they enforce, their judgments are final. Their roles are critical in creating sport.

After applying this "organized competitive activity" test, both chess and reality shows would seem to pass. So perhaps we need further definitional guideposts. In addition to occurring on a level playing field, a sport is a competitive activity for which, before the contest begins, the outcome is uncertain. It is not just entertainment, like a play or an opera where performances always end in the same way. Hamlet always dies in Act V. While his sword-fighting with Laertes could approximate a sport — and certainly was intended to excite the groundlings standing in front of the Globe Theatre stage — the outcome is certain: Hamlet will die. Similarly, when the Harlem Globetrotters play the Washington Generals, we know the Trotters will prevail while demonstrating great athletic skill. (The Generals have won six of these staged contests, while losing more than thirteen thousand times.) With mere entertainment, there is no genuine risk of loss, no trial, no test. The Globetrotters' contests are not sport, although they are athletic entertainment. Do reality shows and competitive chess pass the undetermined outcome test? Yes, unless the fix is in. So we move on to a third criterion.

The final element that converts competition into sport is the requirement of physicality. Physical exertion and athletic skill are part and parcel of sport. This does not mean that all sports must end like the Boston Marathon, where participants sometimes collapse as they cross the finish line in front of the Boston Public Library, but there must be some perspiration involved. Thinking hard about your next chess move (or, more likely, your next five moves) does not involve physicality. Although you might physically move your pawn to queen's bishop 5 — and punch the time clock after each move — that is not physical exertion. The same argument applies to selecting and executing your menus on "Top Chef," or picking your categories on "Jeopardy" then pushing the button.

As a matter of clarification, however, sport is not simply exercise. Although members of the Knickerbocker Social and Athletic Club exercised in the evenings on Madison Square in New York in the 1840s, there was no competition—and thus no sport—until the club invited alumni to play a match game on the Elysian Fields of Hoboken, New Jersey, on June 19, 1846, in accordance with Alexander Cartwright's new rules of the game he called "base ball." (The Knickerbockers lost.) In sport, the object is to determine winners and losers. Perhaps that is why tie matches in soccer can be so disquieting. An exercise regime such as yoga or spinning, while certainly good for you, is not a sport.

Bart Giamatti, the great renaissance scholar and president of Yale University, who briefly served as baseball's commissioner late in the 1980s, understood the nature of the enterprise:

> Sport is about energy and action within rules, boundaries, codes. It has a vast body of internal law and regulations and officials to dispense judgment, if not justice, quickly and in public.

Numerous human activities exist at the boundaries of sport. Poker is a pastime pursued by many, but because there is no physical exertion, it is not a sport. This does not mean it is not fun or potentially lucrative. The winner of the annual World Series of Poker in Las Vegas earns as much money as ten Wimbledon champions. Other activities featured on ESPN— the National Spelling Bee, for example, or the annual hot dog eating contest on Coney Island—also do not qualify as sports. Competitive ballroom dancing, on the other hand, is a sport filled with physicality. But I will leave the rest of the sorting to you. In this book, we will discuss football, basketball, baseball, hockey, golf, tennis, skiing, and gymnastics—all of which fit comfortably under the aegis of sport.

The process of categorization, however, is useful for distinguishing sports from life's other activities. Beating out a competitor to sign a new client is not sport; it is work. Driving home on Interstate 5 or 95 may be sufficiently physical, but there are no winners—unless you award victory to everyone who survives the ordeal.

Categorizing activities as sports or non-sports also may have important legal implications. The state of Wisconsin has a statute that offers limited tort immunity for participants in sports that include physical contact. Under this law, they would be liable for injuries they cause to other participants only if they "acted recklessly or with intent to cause injury." The Wisconsin Supreme Court parsed this statutory language in 2009 in *Noffke v. Bakke*, a case that involved a cheerleader injured during a pre-game warm-up session. She sued her coach for negligently failing to spot her while she was practicing a stunt. The coach claimed the statute applied.

Does cheerleading include physical contact? Unwilling to limit the statutory coverage to aggressive sports like football and hockey, the court found that the foreseeable physical contact between and among cheerleaders was sufficient. There is significant physical contact "when one person is tossed high into the air and then caught by those same tossers." Using our analysis of what constitutes a sport, the element of physicality is met.

But what about our requirement that a sport be competitive? Does cheerleading meet that standard? In this case, the court relied on the dictionary definition of sport: "[a]n activity involving physical exertion and skill that is governed by a set of rules or customs." This definition does not require that there be competition, although there are an increasing number of cheerleader competitions, and many colleges give athletic scholarships to premier cheerleaders. If the court does not require some element of competition, however, the statute could be read to cover other amateur activities, such as band or dance squads, which are noncompetitive but physical in nature.

This is, of course, not the only statute or regulation that includes reference to sports. For example, Title IX of the Education Amendments of 1972 (which we will explore more fully in chapter 6) requires gender equity in athletic opportunities. Could a college meet its statutory obligations by dramatically increasing the size of its cheer squad, which typically is predominantly female? Leaving out competition omits the essence of sport. If cheerleading is a covered "sport," then gender equity is a mirage.

WHAT IS SPORTS JUSTICE?

Society establishes laws to govern the interaction of people and establishes institutions to administer and apply those laws. In the same way that the rules of the game make a sports contest possible, the laws of society allow individuals and entities to function productively and peacefully. Persons can enter into contracts because the law will, in most instances, enforce promises fairly made. A person injured as result of the wrongful conduct of another can obtain compensation in court without having to resort to revenge. Society protects itself against wrongdoers through the criminal laws. Congress and legislatures enact statutes to protect important interests and promote certain public policies, and courts enforce those enactments on a case-by-case basis. These fundamental principles of a system of law apply to all, including athletes, the teams for which they play, and the leagues in which their teams participate. Sports have their own internal rules of the game, but are also bound by external laws.

This book will examine the relationship between the business of sports and the authoritative systems which resolve the disputes that arise within the business. Some of these systems, such as courts and administrative agencies, are established by governments to resolve all types of disputes, not simply those involving sports. Others, such as labor arbitration tribunals, are established privately without governmental intervention under the terms of collective bargaining agreements between club owners and the unions representing professional athletes. Many disputes in sports involve decision making by league commissioners and individual club owners without the intervention of outsiders to the game.

The customary instruments and principles of the law are invoked to address issues that arise from the business of sports. Those aggrieved will resort to legal institutions for redress. Sometimes they will receive a sports-related version of the law in return, as with Blackmun's curious opinion in Curt Flood's case. In cases where judges sense an attack on the sport itself, the bedrock of the law may be contorted. Occasionally, sports disputes may cause judges to lose their logical compasses.

The business of sports is a multibillion-dollar-a-year activity, an economic giant larger than many other industries. Its organizations and operations are almost exclusively private. The entrepreneurs who create the enterprise may later refine and modify the product. Usually, those who invest their financial capital in a professional sports team must work with the union that represents the players, who bring their physical capital to the field. Ultimately, it is the spectators who decide whether they will purchase what the owners and players have to offer and whether they will invest their psychic energies as devotees.

What then is sports justice? The cases and controversies we will examine do not always result in outcomes that all would consider fair or just. When tennis player Renee Richards secures her right to participate in the U.S. Open as a women after sex reassignment surgery, and professional golfer Casey Martin is allowed under court order to use a golf cart in order to accommodate his disability, some will see these as just results in terms of being fair to people who differ from the norm or are disabled. But when the NCAA bans Jeremy Bloom from playing amateur college football because he endorsed products as a professional skier, we may see that outcome as unfair. Using the antitrust laws and the federal courts, Al Davis of the Oakland Raiders triumphs over his fellow football club owners and wins the right to relocate his franchise anywhere he wishes. Was that fair to the fans in Oakland?

Many of the narratives we will address involve people who would have been helpless in the absence of the courts or labor arbitrators. That does not mean that such people always prevailed. Terrell Owens lost his case because an arbitrator determined that he deserved the Eagles' discipline. Jeremy Bloom did not get to keep his endorsements while playing college football because the Colorado state courts were unwilling to set aside the decision of the NCAA. Each of the cases we investigate could have been decided differently, and we will explore those alternatives. The law is not a mechanical instrument applied without the exercise of judgment by the adjudicators.

For our purposes, sports justice is the product of the authoritative procedures used in the business of sports to resolve disputes and controversies. In the same sense that the decisions and actions of the Department of Justice are not always "just," the decisions of sports' adjudicators are not always objective, impartial, unbiased, equitable, fair, or dispassionate. In each of the following chapters, we offer a description of the participants and a narrative of how their claims were resolved. We will applaud some results as fair, criticize others as unfair, and try to explain our conclusions.

We also will explore how each dispute affected the lives of the people involved and the sports they represented. Dale Hackbart, Casey Martin, Renee Richards, Brian Shaw, Jeremy Bloom, Teddy Green, John Mackey, Amy Cohen, Al Davis, and Terrell Owens are all interesting people involved in the business of sports. They all sought help from either courts or arbitrators. Some prevailed; some did not. You must make up your own mind about the outcomes of their cases.

CHAPTER 1

STAY OUT OF MY COURT

Justice should not only be done,
but should appear to have been done.

LORD SANKEY

When you doubt, abstain.

AMBROSE BIERCE

I choose not to run.

JERRY SEINFELD

• • • The mellifluous Howard Cosell insisted that sport was only the "toy department of human life." He was wrong. Sport plays a far more central role in people's lives, from pre-adolescence to dotage. They are a point of self-identification for many people. Sport in its various forms may consume more time in a person's life than any activity other than work, including attending church and following politics.

Sports are voluntary activities, although social pressures may be brought to bear on those who would decline the opportunity both to play or to spectate. With the exception of high school gym class, one need not participate. Sports are a matter of choice. In the sixth season of *Seinfeld*, for example, Jerry decides not to offer a high school rival another opportunity to race, knowing that this time he would lose. He announced, memorably: "I choose not to run."

You can choose not to run, or to play, or even to watch, but what if you want to participate and are barred by those who control the sport? Exclusion can be both financially and psychologically damaging. Sport is a very lucrative profession for those with the skills to participate at the highest level. It is here where the availability of legal recourse becomes vitally important.

SPORTS, MONEY, AND THE LAW

By the middle of the nineteenth century, American entrepreneurs had discovered that spectators would pay to watch the very best athletes play sports. The first baseball game for which admission was charged occurred in the summer of 1858 at the newly opened Fashion Race Course in what is now Corona, Queens, not far from the site of the New York Mets' Citi Field. Two all-star teams of amateur players from Manhattan and Brooklyn squared off for a three-game match, and spectators paid a dime each to attend. Manhattan prevailed, as it would often do over the years when matched against rival Brooklyn. One exception, of course, was the 1955 World Series, heralded as divine glory in the City of Churches.

In the early days of professional sports, leagues made an effort to ensure that any conflicts were resolved in-house. The president of a league had authority to resolve disputes between clubs, or between players and clubs.

previous page
Dale Hackbart played professional football for more than a dozen years until Charles "Booby" Clark broke his neck during a game in Denver.
AP Photo / NFL Photos

In baseball's National League, William Hulbert first played that role, followed by Albert Spalding. With the advent of rival baseball leagues, however, purely private resolution became far more difficult. Disputing parties would head to court.

When called on to resolve disputes in the sports business, nineteenth-century courts applied general legal principles established by the common law. Judicial decision making, however, was never a mechanical or predictable endeavor. It was — and is — a very human process in which judicial objectivity and subjectivity combine to decide actual cases, preferably in a manner that upholds the integrity of the adjudicatory process and fulfills the legitimate expectations of the parties and the society within which they operate.

More than a century later, going to court remains the strategy of last resort for resolving disputes in the sports industry. Business entities only sue when negotiations and economic pressures fail. The transaction costs of lawsuits make them a disfavored option. It is expensive to sue — win or lose. But in situations where resolution by consensus fails, a disadvantaged party will have no option but to bring suit. The court system may be the only way to protect the interests of players excluded from participation. For example, female gymnasts at Brown University sued because the college abolished their team and refused to consider reinstatement. On the other hand, some athletes — including hockey players Wayne Maki and Ted Green — have been summoned to the criminal courts to answer for their allegedly lawless actions while engaged in sports. They did not appear as a matter of choice; they could not say, as Jerry Seinfeld did, "I choose not to run."

In unionized professional sports, management and labor have created an alternate mechanism for resolving disputes. Labor arbitration is the greatest invention of the American labor movement, providing disputing parties with a cheaper and faster substitute for protracted litigation. In later chapters we will examine disputes involving basketball player Brian Shaw and football player Terrell Owens, which were resolved by independent and neutral arbitrators, consistent with what has become the common law of the labor agreement.

ABSTENTION AND THE DECISION MAKER

Courts and arbitrators cannot hear or resolve every issue that comes before them. Courts have limited jurisdiction; they can hear only specific types of disputes. For example, there must be a genuine "case or controversy," rather than a hypothetical problem. Certain issues — such as simple tort and contract matters — belong in state courts rather than federal courts unless the disputants are from different states and there is a significant amount of money at stake. In some instances, parties call upon the courts to resolve questions better suited for resolution through the legislative process. Similarly, an arbitrator's power is limited to the types of disputes the parties to a collective bargaining agreement have designated for resolution through that private tribunal.

A court may decide to abstain from hearing a dispute as a matter of prudence and discretion. The refusal to hear a case otherwise cognizable in court, however, requires a judge to offer a compelling rationale, a clear and convincing explanation for abstention. In 1977, a respected federal district court judge in Colorado, Richard Matsch, suggested in a provocative opinion that courts should abstain from resolving disputes involving injuries caused by the mayhem of professional football.

DALE HACKBART, CHARLES "BOOBIE" CLARK AND JUDGE RICHARD MATSCH

For thirty-six years, Judge Richard Matsch has been known in Denver for running a no-nonsense courtroom. He arrives at federal court promptly at 9:00 A.M., by which time the lawyers must be ready to proceed. The son of a grocer from Burlington, Iowa, and a graduate of the University of Michigan Law School, Matsch was appointed to the federal bench by President Nixon. In addition to an occasional sports-related case — most recently he handled the criminal accusations against basketball great Kobe Bryant — Judge Matsch presided over Timothy McVeigh's Oklahoma City bombing trial and the Denver school desegregation case. He is a well-regarded jurist, and therefore his thoughts about the relationship between sports and courts cannot be ignored.

The sports injury case heard in Judge Matsch's court involved the veteran safety of the Denver Broncos, thirty-five-year-old Dale Hackbart, who was brutally assaulted by an opposing player, Cincinnati Bengals rookie Charles "Boobie" Clark, during the first game of the regular season in Denver on September 16, 1973. Many years later, this was the way Hackbart described the incident in an interview with Los Angeles author Robert Janis:

It was just before halftime and the Bengals had the ball at around the 45 yard line going in. Boobie Clark came out of a split backfield and ran down the hashmarks. I was playing free safety so I dropped back to the center of the field. The ball went up in the air and I converged into the endzone. Billy Thompson, who was playing left corner for the Broncos, jumped in front of me and Boobie Clark and intercepted the pass. I tried to block Boobie and landed on the ground. When I came up on to one knee watching Thompson run the ball, Boobie came up from behind me and whacked me in the back of the head and drove me into the ground. My left arm went numb. At halftime in the locker room I couldn't take off my helmet, so I was packed in ice around my neck and helmet. Then I went out and played the second half.

Despite his injury, Hackbart, a true warrior of the game, played for two more weeks on the Broncos' special teams, then was released by the club. His doctors later determined that Clark's blow had fractured the C4, 5, 6, and 7 vertebrae of Hackbart's neck. Hackbart sued Clark and his club for one million dollars.

Hackbart had attended the University of Wisconsin, where he lettered in football, basketball, and baseball. He was considered a promising quarterback, and won the Badgers' starting slot by mid-season of his sophomore year. By his senior year, he was considered the best quarterback in the Midwest and a premier punt returner, placing seventh in voting for the Heisman Trophy. He led the 1959 Wisconsin team in rushing and passing. In 2008, *Sports Illustrated* would name Hackbart to the all-time University of Wisconsin squad at strong safety, the position he played for more than a decade in the pros.

Hackbart's professional career was typical of many athletes below the superstar level. He was drafted by the Green Bay Packers in the fifth round of the 1960 NFL draft. (Hackbart had let it be known that he intended to play baseball and not football, thus explaining his late selection. He would otherwise have likely been drafted in the first round.) He played first base and outfield for the Grand Forks (North Dakota) Chiefs, a Class C minor league team in the Pittsburgh Pirates' organization, where his teammates included future Hall of Famer Willie Stargell. Green Bay's legendary coach Vince Lombardi convinced Hackbart to move back to football: "Lombardi said that baseball players were wimps and that football players were real men. I took the advice and dropped baseball." One of those "real men" of football would later break his neck.

Midway through his second NFL season, the Packers traded Hackbart to the Washington Redskins. He injured his shoulder, and the Redskins cut him at the end of that season. He played with the Minnesota Vikings and the Canadian Football League's Winnipeg Blue Bombers in 1965. The Vikings traded Hackbart to the St. Louis Cardinals, and he retired after the 1972 season.

Hackbart moved to Longmont, Colorado, where a Wisconsin college buddy, Jim Holmes, had purchased a tire store and offered the footballer the opportunity to buy into the business. His friend suggested that Hackbart try to get the Cardinals to trade his contract rights to the Denver Broncos, figuring that it would be good publicity for their tire business. Hackbart became the Broncos' starting safety in 1973. Because his injury occurred during the first regular-season game, it turned out to be a costly bit of advertising.

After the injury, Hackbart returned to his hometown of Niwot, Colorado, a short drive from the tire store in Longmont. Medical specialists warned that if he did not have surgery to repair the damage to his neck and spine, he would lose the use of his left arm and shoulder and the muscles around the damaged vertebrae would atrophy. Hackbart had the surgery, but the Broncos refused to pay for the operation. Hackbart hired an attorney, Roger Johnson of the Denver firm of Johnson & Mahoney, who advised that he sue his assailant, "Boobie" Clark, and Clark's club, the Cincinnati Bengals.

Charles "Boobie" Clark was a chunk of granite at six foot two inches tall and 245 pounds. He would rumble like a rhinoceros across the line of scrimmage. An unheralded rookie, the 302nd player picked in the fourteenth round of the draft out of Bethune-Cookman College, he became a folk hero in Cincinnati by the end of the 1973 season. Bengals coach Paul Brown saw him as the second coming of Marion Motley, the Hall of Fame runner who played for Brown in Cleveland. The Bengals were impressed with Clark's 4.75 speed in the forty-yard dash, but his weight would become an issue, as Clark ballooned above 260 pounds during his years in the league.

As an NFL rookie selected late in the draft, Clark needed to prove himself on the field. Each play became an essential measure of his value to the club. Without the pedigree of a major football school, his NFL career could be cut short. Lost chances were squandered opportunities. When the pass was intercepted that day in Denver, Clark missed his chance to score in his first game. In frustration, he lashed out at Hackbart.

THE COURT'S RATIONALE

Judge Matsch denied Hackbart recovery for Clark's attack, ruling that he "must have recognized and accepted the risk that he would be injured by such an act as that committed by defendant Clark." The judge was undoubtedly correct in dismissing the suit on the merits. Whether characterized as consent or assumption of risk, a player who engages in a professional football match knows he will be subject to fierce, deliberate, and harmful contact. The same intentional contact off the playing field would be an actionable battery, allowing the injured party to recover compensatory and even punitive damages in court. Yet on the field of play, deliberate collisions between participants is the essence of the game. Some of that contact, like tackling a running back, falls within the rules. Some of that contact, like blocking from the back below the waist on a kickoff, violates the rules of the game. If proscribed conduct is seen by a referee, it results in a penalty of precious yardage. Whether a foul or not, however, it is very much a foreseeable part of the game.

What then about Clark's attack on Hackbart? It was clearly a violation of the rules and would have resulted in imposition of a territorial penalty (if the referees had seen it). By playing a game where such conduct was foreseeable, even if in violation of the rules of the game, Hackbart was held to have allowed the harmful and offensive contact. Wrongful contact is part of the professional game.

What is particularly interesting about Judge Matsch's opinion, however, is that he then proceeded to explain why injuries caused to players during a football game should *never* be subject to adjudication in a court of law. America's most popular game, he reasoned, is a species of warfare with real blood, bound only by "the morality of the battlefield" without "the restraints of civilization." Courts, Matsch explained, were ill-equipped to enter this "thicket" to adjudicate football disputes, even if serious injuries resulted. If the violence level is too high, one must turn to the state legislature or even Congress for regulation, not a court.

Matsch was certainly correct in characterizing the violence of the game. Dick Butkus, the Hall of Fame linebacker for the Chicago Bears, once said:

"When I played pro football, I never set out to hurt anybody deliberately . . . unless it was, you know, important, like a league game or something." Considering the expectations of both participants and spectators, football competition naturally leads to ill will and aggression. Clark certainly intended to cause grievous harm to Hackbart, but Hackbart placed himself in harm's way by playing the game.

In his opinion, Judge Matsch recited the testimony of John Ralston, the Denver Broncos coach at the time, about the team's pre-game psychological preparation. Ralston testified that the coach must incite his warriors to a fever pitch. His appeal should be:

> designed to generate an emotion equivalent to that which would be experienced by a father whose family had been endangered by another driver who had attempted to force the family car off the edge of a mountain road. The precise pitch of motivation for the players at the beginning of the game should be the feeling of that father when, after overtaking and stopping the offending vehicle, he is about to open the door to take revenge upon the person of the other driver.

Matsch wanted no part of such bloodthirsty bedlam.

Unlike boxing, which has been outlawed in many states, football has won full public approval. (The games, the judge noted, are often played in stadiums built with public funds, so the public must have approved of what goes on in their arenas.) Although football is a legal activity, the game is so violent and the standards of required behavior so vague that, according to Judge Matsch, the courts should abstain from hearing these disputes.

Recent studies have supported Matsch's apprehensions about providing a judicial arena for the resolution of disputes over football injuries. The game is abnormally dangerous to participants. Although death is rare, professional football players leave the game with severe physical and mental injuries. Future studies will likely show similar — if not quite as appalling — life injuries to those who played the game on the high school and college level. Would the Roman courts allow a suit for damages caused during a gladiators' bout at the Coliseum?

There is some attraction to Matsch's approach. Football can be barbaric, vulgar, and profane. The raw power of sanctioned violence can demean our humanness and degrade our society. Football even uses military metaphors to describe its play: the quarterback throws a "bomb," while avoiding the defensive "blitz." We revel in the warrior culture, the dehumanized infliction of pain that lies at the core of the game. Matsch says, in effect, take your wounded elsewhere.

Football is not the singular culprit in this regard, as violence has marred many sports. Tonya Harding's cohorts assaulted her rival, Nancy Kerrigan, before the U.S. National Figure Skating Championships in 1994. On June 28, 1997, Mike Tyson bit off a portion of Evander Holyfield's ear during a boxing match in Las Vegas. On August 21, 1965, Giants pitcher Juan Marichal attacked Dodgers catcher John Roseboro with a bat, opening a two-inch cut on his head that bled profusely. Sports outrages are not limited to North America, of course, as brawling soccer hooligans and head-butting soccer players have demonstrated around the world. Verbal aggression is commonplace. Frenchman Christophe Fauviau went a step further in evil deviousness; for four years he spiked the water bottles of the opponents of his tennis-playing children. At least one person died as a result, and Fauviau served eight years in jail.

Perhaps no premeditated incident on the field of play outranks the rugby match in 1974 between the British Lions and their South African opponents. Concerned that the local referees would not penalize the South African players, the Brits were determined to fight back. It was arranged that when their captain sounded the call of "99," the Lions would launch an all-out physical attack on every member of the South African team. The Lions had correctly assumed that the referees would not banish their entire squad from the pitch based on the simultaneous violence.

The National Football League establishment was generally pleased with the outcome of Hackbart's case. The general counsel of the defendant Cincinnati Bengals, Mike Brown, commented: "What it did was confirm what we always assumed to be the arrangement under which football has been played — that players assume the risk for injuries not just within the rules, but outside the rules. If that assumption had been changed, there would have been so many suits filed you couldn't have counted them." But wouldn't the Hackbart ruling encourage violence? Brown was sure it would not: "I think the league is going to police that kind of thing more severely than ever. We recognize it as a problem. We don't condone it, the other clubs don't condone it, the commissioner doesn't condone it and the players themselves don't."

Under Judge Matsch's analysis, sports torts would lay beyond the jurisdiction of our customary legal institutions. The judge sounded much like George Orwell, the renowned critic of sporting events: "Serious sport has nothing to do with fair play. It is bound up with hatred, jealousy, boastfulness, disregard of all rules and sadistic pleasure in witnessing violence. In other words, it is war minus the shooting."

The court's pronouncements concerning the limitations of the judiciary were not necessary in order to reach the ultimate conclusion that Hackbart should not recover damages. Hackbart chose to play a rough game where fights were known to occur and intentional torts were commonplace. By entering the field of play, Hackbart accepted a range of behaviors both within and without the rules of the game, including Clark's brutal attack. Matsch's dictum about judicial abstention, however, would bar *all* victims of sports violence from courts that were otherwise open to physically injured parties.

Matsch said that judges would be confused by the rules of the war-like game of football. He wrote:

> [The rules] are so legalistic in their statement and so difficult of application because of the speed and violence of the play that the difference between violations which could be called deliberate, reckless or outrageous and those which are "fair play" would be so small and subjective as to be incapable of articulation.

He worried that if courts heard cases involving sports injuries, they would be inundated with a mass "volume of . . . litigation" which would result in varying standards of play and different liability for participants on a state-by-state basis. The National Football League, Matsch suggested, would find this crazy-quilt of regulations quite detrimental. Thus, in order to save the NFL from itself, Matsch would lock all courthouse doors.

Matsch's ominous prediction—that allowing a judicial avenue of redress would be disastrous—was unfounded. On appeal of his decision, the U.S. Court of Appeals for the Tenth Circuit rejected Matsch's dictum: "There are no principles of law which allow a court to rule out certain tortious conduct by reason of general roughness of the game or difficulty of administering it." The circuit court quoted from an 1821 opinion by Supreme Court Chief Justice John Marshall: "We have no more right to decline the exercise of jurisdiction which is given, than to usurp that which is not given." Even more to the point was Justice Marshall's 1803 tour de force, *Marbury v. Madison*: "The very essence of civil liberty certainly consists in the right of every individual to claim the protection of the law, whenever he received an injury. One of the first duties of government is to afford that protection." The district court could not abdicate its responsibility.

The circuit court remanded the case for trial, and the dispute was quickly settled in July 1981 for $200,000. One immediate positive impact of Hackbart's injury and the resulting litigation was that the National Football League required that all stadiums be equipped with x-ray machines. The NFL Rules Committee also banned the head slap.

"Boobie" Clark continued his fine career on the gridiron. He was named the Rookie of the Year for the 1973 season during which he attacked Hackbart. The bulky fullback with the colorful nickname gained 2,978 yards in his career, the third highest total in Bengals history. He was released by the club in 1979, played sparingly with Houston, and retired after six years in the league, slightly longer than the average for running backs. Clark died tragically at age thirty-seven from a blood clot in his left lung, one of many professional football players to meet an early demise.

Dale Hackbart's case remains the only reported decision in which a court suggests that a player should never be able to recover damages for injuries incurred during a sporting event. In fact, very few cases have been brought against opponents for injuries caused in this way. Under the current standard NFL player contract, medical care is paid by the club and football income maintained through the season in which a player is injured. Future losses are normally covered by insurance policies.

For well over a century, courts have been asked to adjudicate personal injury cases arising out of playing sports. They have established a generally sound set of principles that normally result in plaintiffs leaving the court empty-handed, after having been given the respect and due process of a hearing. Injuries suffered during a game as a result of conduct that falls within the rules of the contest, while regrettable, are part of the game. A running back tackled and injured while running with the football through a hole created by his offensive line cannot recover damages against the hard-hitting safety who delivers a resounding tackle. A special team player injured when blocked in the back during a kickoff has a better case, at least on the surface. His injury was the result of a clear violation of the rules. The better-reasoned court decisions reject these claims as well. Foreseeable and normal violations of the rules of the game are also "part of the game." It is part of the risk that players accept when they step on the field.

Judge Matsch was concerned with the subjectivity of the rules of the NFL and their application. Some behaviors result in penalties; other behaviors not seen, or seen but ignored, are not penalized. Judge Matsch's concern that courts would not be able to distinguish rule violations from fair play in the sports context seems misguided. In many situations, courts are asked to master even more mysterious data than the application of the rules of a game of football. The battlefields of the gridiron and the courts can coexist.

What Judge Matsch failed to appreciate is that the rules of the game do not determine outcomes in later adjudication for injuries received. Players consent to contact both within the bounds of the rules and outside those bounds. Contact in violation of the rules results in a penalty, but such contact also is foreseeable. The focus should be on what might be called the "customs" of the sport. Hackbart's neck injury, while serious, was not outside the realm of possible injuries caused by foreseeable misconduct on the field in violation of football's rules. Clark's actions were certainly within the neighborhood of foreseeable player misconduct. Hackbart should have been able to bring his action in court, but ultimately, based on the facts of the case, he should not have been able to recover damages.

HUMAN LIFE IN MICROCOSM

We return once again to Howard Cosell, the pompous but erudite lawyer who became a transformative figure in American sports broadcasting. He said that sports were "life in miniature." Never one to mince words or trim his hyperbole, Cosell saw sports as a very limited endeavor, despite his grandiose commentary. If "The people of this country have allowed sports to get completely out of hand," as he argued, it was in no small measure due to Cosell's weekly televised outbursts. At best, he suggested, sport is just a part of life, an exhibition, a pastime that should not be confused with reality: "After all," Cosell asked, "is football a game or a religion?"

Lewis Lapham, longtime editor of *Harper's* magazine, in his brilliant dissection of the American elite, *Money and Class in America*, offered a similarly narrow view on sports:

Unlike any other business in the United States, sports must preserve an illusion of perfect innocence. The mounting of this illusion defines the purpose and accounts for the immense wealth of American sports. It is the ceremony of innocence that the fans pay to see — not the game or the match or the bout, but the ritual portrayal of a world in which time stops and all hope remains plausible, in which everybody present can recover the blameless expectations of a child, where the forces of light always triumph over the powers of darkness.

But both Cosell and Lapham misread sport. It is neither a "microcosm of life" nor "an illusion of perfect innocence." Rather, sport is more important than a mere diversion. It is one of the few places in life where we can — and do — wear our hearts on our sleeves. We can risk it all. As Benjamin Franklin wrote: "Games lubricate the body and the mind." Sports provide oxygen to our life's blood.

Most would say that there is little about America that is unaffected by our system of public laws and adjudication. We rejoice as a society in the truism that adorns the U.S. Supreme Court, that we are a "nation of laws and not of men" (or women). We entrust our present and our future to those who enact legislation and enforce our laws. Yet, despite the legal system's reputation as the glue which holds society together, there is very little in the full panoply of American life that is directly affected by it. We are much more influenced by family and social groups, customs, rituals, and religious beliefs. Law deserves recognition, but it is not, to use a sports metaphor, the 350-pound defensive lineman with 4.4 speed running through the kitchen. It is more like a field-goal kicker who breaks the tie in the last minute of play. And there are very few ties.

Most aspects of American life are the result of private, informal interactions, not public directives. That includes sports. The games we play and the games we watch operate under rules established and enforced privately, not by those clothed with official governing authority. We start sports young. Children's games are the products of imagination and grow with complexity as physical coordination evolves. Adult games challenge both our dexterity and our intelligence, although in varying degrees.

There are times when sports and the law intersect, when those who are personally involved resort to third parties for authoritative dispute resolution in the defense and perfection of private and public rights. This interface of law and society's sports presents challenging issues of appropriateness, as Judge Matsch recognized. But the instruments of decision making cannot avoid their appointed functions simply because the task would be challenging or they find the subject matter objectionable.

We have used the term "just"—as in sports justice—simply to denote the product of these authoritative bodies, primarily courts and labor arbitrators. More generally, people use "just" to describe decisions that are recognized as fair, ethical, and unbiased. At times the interaction of authoritative decision making and sports reaches conclusions that we would agree are just under this normative meaning.

We value promise keeping, at least when engaged in by parties with a rough equality of bargaining power who have the discretion to chose not to enter into the deal in the first place. Enforcing promises is just because it confirms legitimate expectations of contracting parties and allows all others to plan their lives with some confidence. Similarly, arbitration opinions that enforce contractual promises are just.

Persons who join together in communities, states, and nations establish governments to promulgate laws that benefit society as a whole, such as statutes that mandate competition among businesses rather than collusion in the marketplace. Laws legitimately enacted and uniformly enforced produce just results in the run of cases. (Here we may be returning to the concept of "just" as simply the decisions of an authoritative body. Some legislation is normatively fair, but certainly not all statutes would meet that test.) Any decision by an authoritative body outside of sports has an impact on the sport itself. Even if the playing field quickly adjusts, court involvement has affected the game.

In addition to being an important part of our lives and our commerce, sport presents complexities that challenge our minds and, at times, our sensibilities. It is a big business involving competition within and between sports entities. Each sport, association, league, or club may have its own parochial interests which motivate decisions that affect the property interests of others. Courts must stand ready to adjudicate disputes involving these interests in a manner consistent with society's laws, not just the laws of the sport. Those decisions, both internal and external to sports, are worthy of our investigation.

CHAPTER 2

SWING FOR THE GREEN, IF YOU CAN
THE RIGHTS OF DISABLED ATHLETES

It may be that all games are silly. But then, so are humans.
ROBERT LYND

In our opinion, walking is better than golf.
DRS. PAUL & PATRICIA BRAGG

• • • The game of golf can be the epitome of human frustration. Unlike bowling, our nation's most popular participation sport, no one ever shoots the equivalent of a 300 game in golf. No golfer ever pitches a perfect game, like Don Larsen for the Yankees in the 1956 World Series. Your goal in golf is to beat par by as many strokes as you can, but everyone — even Tiger Woods — misses a shot and bogeys a hole or two (or more). Intended as a tranquil and pastoral pastime, golf baffles both the duffer and the pro. Winston Churchill, a man who knew how to stay the course in the face of terrible odds, explained it best: "Golf is a game whose aim it is to hit a very small ball into an even smaller hole with weapons singularly ill-designed for the purpose."

The difficulties of the game for the casual player are multiplied for the professional, matched against skilled rivals with his or her livelihood at stake. For those who master the hazards and avoid slicing the dimpled white ball into the ubiquitous sand traps, golf can be a lucrative endeavor with multimillion-dollar payouts and endorsement deals that can escalate a player's annual earnings to eight figures or more. For others, it is nothing more than a weekend frustration or a career aspiration unfulfilled.

As a disabled youngster, Casey Martin dreamed of being a star professional on the links. He was a terrific amateur golfer growing up in Oregon. As a teenager, he fought the courses of the Northwest, sometimes wearing a splint on his right leg, but he won numerous trophies. As his reputation grew, so too did the effects of his physical disability. Martin has Klippel-Trenaunay-Weber syndrome (KTW), a very rare birth defect that was not diagnosed until he was five years old. The valves in the veins of his right leg never close. Blood drains back down his leg when he is standing and walking, pooling in his lower leg and causing swelling. Now in his mid-thirties, Martin's right tibia has become increasingly brittle. The pain is constant, his leg continues to degenerate, and there is no known cure.

By the time Martin was ready to participate in the game as a professional, he could not walk the golf course. Martin was a brilliant golfer with a serious physical impairment. His upper body rotation powered drives deep down the fairway; his approach shots to the green were superb; his

previous page
Casey Martin was a splendid professional golfer who played at the highest levels of the game until a rare and painful degenerative condition forced him to use a cart.
AP Photo / Harry Cabluck

putting, at least on a good day, made him a champion. The degenerative condition in his right leg, however, caused him such pain that, without the assistance of a golf cart, he could not walk the course and compete in the game he loved—the game that he wanted to play as a professional.

Martin vowed that he would not play a course using a golf cart unless he absolutely had to. He agreed that walking was better, until he could no longer walk. His only deficiency, he felt, was in "getting to the game" where he could make his shots. He simply could not walk the five-mile course. Martin wasn't injured. He was disabled, and his condition was degenerative.

Casey Martin may have been one of a kind: an athlete who could play all aspects of his sport with professional proficiency, but who was unable to follow the customary, but certainly not uniform, practice of walking the course. That deficiency could have been easily remedied. At many tournaments, able-bodied professional golfers use golf carts to move from tee to fairway, then on to the putting green. If Martin could be assured the use of a cart, he could be a professional golfer, at least until KTW syndrome affected his ability to swing a golf club. Eventually, Martin knew, his leg would have to be amputated.

Reluctantly, Casey Martin sought sports justice by bringing an action against the PGA Tour under federal law in the federal courts. His ultimate triumph created enormous public controversy, probably because there are thirty million golfers in America, all of whom would like some help with their games. For legions of duffers, Martin's cart became a symbol of the "unfairness" they faced because they were not championship golfers. (Of course, amateur golfers are always allowed to use golf carts, if they wish.) Martin, however, was not a crusading plaintiff, intent on championing the rights of the disadvantaged. He once told his local newspaper: "I'm at peace with myself. If for some reason I can't play anymore, it's okay with me." He was not willing to give up his dream, however, without the same amount of effort he used to play the game.

In order to win his case, Martin had to prevail in the nation's highest court, a tribunal not normally called upon to adjudicate disputes involving manicured fairways and putting greens. His victory was not well received among many of his professional brethren or the golfing public. How could the Supreme Court authorize a professional golfer to use a golf cart while everyone else had to walk the course? Those who criticized Martin, however, didn't know him or his story. Those who ridiculed his suit or the law on which it was based—like Supreme Court Justice Antonin Scalia—had never walked in his shoes.

THE MAN

Casey Martin came from an upper-middle-class family that enjoyed all the advantages of class, race, and religion. His father, King Martin, was a stockbroker with Smith, Barney. His mother, Melinda Martin, would chauffeur Casey from doctor to doctor and from golf course to golf course. A devout Christian and rock-ribbed Republican, Martin was well liked in high school, even if he wouldn't walk on the wild side and preferred playing classical music on the family's piano. He was quiet about his disability, but when asked he would respond directly: "I was born without a deep venous system."

Martin used two special stockings, running from his hip to his ankle, to keep the blood circulating in his right leg. When the blood began to pool, Martin might lay prone on the floor and place his leg up on the wall. The degenerative circulatory disorder was, at times, totally debilitating.

Except for the KTW, Martin lived a privileged life. Growing up in Eugene, Oregon, he was tall and good-looking, a model youngster, and developed the inner strength essential to play any sport. Because he was a right-handed golfer, his good left leg supported his swing. Martin won his first tournament at the age of ten and began having knee surgeries shortly thereafter. He and his older brother Cameron led their high school golf team, the South Eugene High School Axemen, to a state title. Casey won many individual titles in his adolescent years. Although offered the opportunity to use a golf cart in high school, he almost always refused. He told his local newspaper: "Golf is the one sport I can do. It forces me to forget the pain. It's given me the determination and work ethic to overcome." And he did. By the time he graduated from high school, Martin was his state's premier amateur golfer, having won seventeen championships.

At Stanford University, Martin became a leader on a collegiate golf team that won the NCAA title in 1994, the year before the team added the already famous teenage phenomenon, Tiger Woods. In Palo Alto, Martin played piano at fraternity parties, studied the Bible, and mentored underprivileged youngsters. He was named among the best golfers in the Pacific Coast Conference for three seasons. After graduating from Stanford with a degree in economics, Martin knew what all aspiring professional golfers know: the chances of making it on the pro tour are slim, even without a disability.

A CAREER IN GOLF

Professional golf is played at various levels or "tours" around the world. The highest level of play, with the largest pools of prize money, is sponsored by the Professional Golfers Association. Golfers establish their eligibility to play in a tour (known as "holding a tour card") by playing in PGA tournaments. Players often start their careers in a second- or third-tier tour, then move up to higher levels based on their performance.

Martin began the process of qualifying for the elite PGA Tour after graduating from college. Each fall, thousands of excellent golfers enter the PGA Tour's qualifying school, known as "Q-school," but only a few successfully make it through the three grueling rounds. For two years, Martin failed to qualify at Q-school. To work on his game, he played in the regional Hooters Tour and some mini-tour events in the Southeast. It cost him $1,000 to join the Hooters Tour with a $550 entry fee for each tournament. He played an abbreviated schedule, returning home periodically to rest his leg. His leg was not getting any better; in fact, he had reached the point where he could no longer play without the assistance of a cart.

The name Q-school is a relic of its earlier purpose. Started in 1965, players who participated in the event actually attended classes to learn how to teach golf. All golf pros were expected to be golf instructors as well. That aspect of the competition has fallen by the wayside, but the name remains part of the general parlance of professional sport.

Martin's third try at Q-school would provoke the litigation that made him a reluctant public figure, a subject of controversy, and a hero to every disabled person in America. He paid his $3,000 entry fee for Q-school — the fee would increase to $4,500 in 2005 — and showed up at the Dayton Valley Country Club in Dayton, Nevada, in October 1998 for the first round. In accordance with Q-school rules, he was allowed to use a golf cart in the first round and was one of twenty-three men to make it through to the second round. The next month at the Bayonet Black Horse course in Seaside, California, Martin once again used a cart, making the cut in the second stage by three shots. He then moved on to the final round, where the use of carts was prohibited.

Martin petitioned the PGA Tour for permission to use a cart in the six-day tournament, as he had in the prior two rounds, but the Tour refused—despite the fact that for many years it had allowed the use of carts in the final stage. Martin's lawyer cautioned PGA Tour Commissioner Tim Finchem that Martin's only other option would be to pursue his rights in court under the Americans with Disabilities Act (A.D.A.), which reads in part:

> No individual shall be discriminated against on the basis of disability in the full enjoyment of the goods, services, facilities, privileges, advantages, or accommodations of any place of public accommodation by any person who owns, leases (or leases to), or operates a place of public accommodation.

Counsel for the PGA Tour responded that professional sports fell outside the scope of the A.D.A. and, in any case, walking was essential to the game of golf (even though Martin had not been required to walk during the prior two rounds of Q-school). If the game required walking as well as shot making, Martin was effectively barred from competing because of his physical disability.

THE PGA TOUR

The PGA Tour has had a long exclusionary history. Before November 1961, the by-laws of the association limited tour events to "Caucasians only." The business of the sport had always been the exclusive preserve of wealthy white businessmen. At the behest of pioneer black golfer Charlie Sifford, Stanley Mosk—then attorney general of California and later a distinguished justice of the California Supreme Court—informed the PGA Tour that it would be illegal to bar professionals from the 1962 PGA Championship at the Wilshire Country Club in Los Angeles because of their race. The PGA Tour quickly moved the event to Philadelphia. Eventually, public outrage at the openly racist rule forced the tour to amend its by-laws. In Martin's case, however, the organization had drawn an exclusionary line to keep out golfers with disabilities.

It is difficult to know precisely why the PGA Tour reacted in this way to Martin's petition. It certainly did not want outsiders, including a federal judge, interfering with the game it ruled. Perhaps its position was based on a considered and principled judgment that walking is an essential part of the game, the reason it would later offer in court. Perhaps the tour thought Martin was cheating, or at least that he wanted to cheat.

But is walking an essential part of the game? Golf aficionados were quick to recall Ken Venturi's monumental victory over physical adversity at the U.S. Open in 1964, which elevated his performance to mythical status. During that tournament's thirty-six-hole playoff, held in blistering triple-digit heat at the Congressional Country Club in Washington, D.C., the wilted and dehydrated Venturi fought on to victory. (What golf historians ignore is the fact that the PGA Tour granted special permission for Venturi's doctor to feed him salt tablets and accompany him as he struggled onward. Tour officials also did not penalize Venturi for playing at a snail's pace.)

Alternatively, it is possible that the PGA Tour's position might have been based on its business judgment. Television viewers and spectators might be disturbed by watching disabled golfers playing in the same tournament as able-bodied golfers. As Frank Hannigan wrote in *Golf Digest*, golf is "an aesthetic experience." "Golf carts," he suggested, "are ugly." Image control is a critical part of marketing any sports business. Handsome, fair-haired professional golfers with handsome, blond wives are a marketer's delight. The sport of golf might be able to countenance one John Daly, the tour's lovable slob and resident rogue, with a drinking problem that periodically got him into trouble with the law. Perhaps the PGA Tour thought it could not promote a sport played by "cripples" riding in golf carts.

There is one final, and perhaps compelling, reason why the Tour might have turned down Casey Martin's request. The Q-school experience is a unique entrance barrier into a professional sport, a rite of passage for almost all professional golfers. (A few, like Tiger Woods, are not required to conquer Q-school because they demonstrate excellence in tour events to which they are invited by sponsors.) It is not unusual for the winner of a PGA tournament to find himself, a few years later, back in Q-school, playing against a horde of talented youngsters in order to fight his way back to the tour, the headlines, and the significant cash prizes. There is no job security for professional golfers except in making long drives and steady putts. Only the top 125 golfers on the tour retain full privileges for the coming year, a very small number compared with the 450 NBA basketball players, 750 Major League baseball players, and the almost 1,700 NFL football players.

During the three stages of Q-school — held each year in October, November and December — golfers can be eliminated by reason of a single stroke, a mistake of a few inches. If, as is currently the case, only nineteen golfers (plus ties) at each of the fourteen sites of Q-school's first stage progress to the second stage, then dozens of splendid golfers — "bombers" off the tee — will never make it beyond the first week of play. Q-school is the paradigmatic zero-sum game. If Jones qualifies, Smith does not. Unlike baseball players — who can have a bad at-bat, a bad game, or even a bad week with little consequence to their professional status — golfers who suffer through a bad hole may be exiled to mini-tours where entrance fees and expenses are typically higher than their potential earnings. The odds of making it out of the first stage of Q-school are 100:1. The heartbreak of missing the qualifying score by one stroke — one bad swing during a five-hour turn on the course — can explain why some might be unwilling to give another golfer an edge, even if he is disabled. Q-school is grinding enough without such "unfair" competition.

The pressures of Q-school might make any advantage seem unfair. While his fellow golfers liked Casey Martin as a person, allowing him to use a cart in the final round might have given him someone else's spot on the tour. The PGA Tour, it could be argued, was just trying to maintain a level playing field for all golfers — all except Casey Martin.

THE LITIGATION

Martin was not easily deterred by what he saw as the tour's discrimination. His attorney William Wiswall, a family friend, brought suit in federal court in Eugene, Oregon, claiming that the PGA's denial of Martin's request violated the Americans with Disabilities Act. Congress had passed the A.D.A. in 1990 to encourage the participation of all persons — able-bodied and disabled — in the activities of society. It prohibited discrimination based on disability in places of "public accommodation." The statute listed some of the private businesses that would be considered covered by the statute: "a gymnasium, health spa, bowling alley, golf course, or other place of exercise or recreation."

The statute required an employer or a covered business to make a "reasonable accommodation" which would allow persons with disabilities to participate in everyday activities and pursue their chosen professions. The A.D.A., the greatest legislative triumph of the George H. W. Bush Administration, was designed to dismantle the barriers that kept persons with disabilities from entering the mainstream of American life. But would it protect Martin's right to contest for a job?

In response to Martin's suit, the PGA Tour filed a motion for summary judgment, claiming the tour was a "private entity" not covered by the provisions of the Americans with Disabilities Act. (The statute exempts "private clubs or establishments.") Foreshadowing arguments it would eventually make before the court of appeals and the Supreme Court, the defendant argued that "while plaintiff's golf skills and accomplishments may be notable, and perhaps even inspirational, Congress never intended the A.D.A. to require a private organization such as the PGA Tour to change the rules of its tournaments to accommodate a would-be participant." Martin was not an "employee" of the Tour. He was an independent contractor who received prize money only if he prevailed in tournaments.

U.S. Magistrate Tom Coffin in Eugene, Oregon, denied the PGA's motion to dismiss Martin's suit, ruling that the PGA Tour was a covered entity — anyone with the entrance fee could participate in Q-school — which must provide a reasonable accommodation for someone with a permanent disability. Golf courses, he wrote, are among the "places of public accommodation" mentioned by the statute. Coffin asked: "What is the PGA Tour? It is an organization formed to provide and operate tournaments for the economic benefit of its members. It is part of the entertainment industry, just as all professional sports are." In other words, it is a business covered by the federal statute.

At the same hearing, Coffin addressed Casey Martin's motion for a temporary restraining order, which would have allowed him to use a golf cart to compete in the third round. The PGA Tour's attorney, Michael Francis, claimed the cart would give Martin an unfair advantage. Not walking, he argued, would fundamentally alter the nature of the game of golf. Magistrate Coffin disagreed, and in November 1997 he issued the preliminary injunction that Martin requested. He scheduled a full hearing on the plaintiff's request for a permanent injunction for February 2, 1998.

Martin returned to Q-school in an effort to win his tour card. Again using a cart, he faced a six-day, 108-hole playoff at Grenelefe Resort in Haines City, Florida. The PGA Tour also received a request from a diabetic golfer to use a cart, which it immediately granted. Then, demonstrating the arrogance that has characterized the organization for decades, it offered all 166

Q-school finalists the option of using a cart. Only a handful accepted the offer, proving empirically that golfers find walking the course to be a therapeutic advantage. Even with his cart, Martin had to walk about a hundred yards on each hole, each step taken in pain. Martin did not qualify for the PGA Tour that year — due in part perhaps to the accumulated stresses of the litigation. He did, however, win his card to play on the Nike Tour, the circuit right below the PGA Tour.

Despite the pressures of the case and the resulting media coverage, Martin won the first event on the 1998 Nike Tour, held at the Grasslands Golf and Country Club in Lakeland, Florida. He later explained what was going through his mind when he limped to the first tee, before a bigger-than-normal crowd: "Don't top it. Don't shank it. Don't shoot 90 with all these people watching." Although people would be watching Martin's progress for years to come, Lakeland would prove to be Martin's only major tour victory.

THE TRIAL

To help with the trial before Magistrate Coffin, Martin's attorney William Wiswall brought in Martha Walters, an experienced civil rights and employment lawyer (and a future justice of the Oregon Supreme Court). She began the plaintiff's case with a video of Martin's leg, a dramatic presentation that proved without question the gruesome and debilitating nature of his physical disability. His orthopedic surgeon, Donald Jones, testified that the tibia in Martin's right leg was "beginning to resorb and lose bone stock." Martin's circulatory disorder was eroding the bones in his leg. There was no cure for his condition, and blood clots stemming from Martin's atrophied leg were a constant risk. Ultimately, Dr. Jones opined, Martin's leg might fracture or he would have to have his leg amputated.

Casey Martin testified about his severe and constant pain: "My condition has been steadily worsening for about the last four years, I'd say. . . . When I walk on uneven terrain, my shin just — it screams out, basically, is how I like to explain it." On cross-examination, Martin explained that the essence of the game of golf was shot making: "that's where the game is played, with your clubs." Martin maintained, as he did both inside and outside of court, that he would "much rather be walking."

The case, as far as the PGA Tour was concerned, turned on the essential role of walking in the game of golf, although it did not explain why walking was not required during the first two rounds of Q-school. Walking, the defendant said, injected fatigue into the sport. The plaintiff's expert, Dr. Gary Klug of the University of Oregon, responded that walking a golf course normally does not create fatigue: "Because of the low level of activity in golf, it is not especially taxing. It's not a particularly lot of exertion, especially because it's spread out over four or five hours." What about the PGA Tour's claim that fatigue is built up over eighteen holes? Klug responded that this does not occur with "an activity that is as low in energy consumption as golf." Klug estimated that a round of golf would expend about five hundred calories. Nutritionally, that would be "less than a Big Mac."

The game's legends lined up behind the PGA Tour's position. Arnold Palmer, perhaps the greatest golfer in the pre-Tiger Woods era, said in his deposition: "I think part of the game of golf, and the tradition and integrity of the game, is being able to walk and compete." He also thought that the PGA Tour should be able to make its own rules without judicial interference. Jack Nicklaus, who offered to take a deposition for the PGA Tour, agreed with Palmer: "I have a lot of sympathy for Casey. Unfortunately, I am going to have to go the other way." Neither Palmer nor Nicklaus objected on the grounds of "tradition" to the development and use on the PGA Tour of metal woods, graphite shafts, and titanium drivers.

Eric Johnson, who played on the Nike Tour with Martin, testified for the plaintiff that he didn't find walking difficult: "I never give it a thought. We've all done things more physical than golf." Although they were not called to testify, two of golf's greats, Greg Norman and Tom Watson, publicly agreed that shot making was the essence of golf and the tour would not be harmed if Martin prevailed.

The PGA Tour nonetheless insisted throughout the trial that walking was an inviolable rule. The defendant, however, was unable to address the inconvenient fact that carts were allowed during the first two rounds of Q-school, in some professional golf tournaments, and on some tours. Martin's attorney Wiswall hammered away at the PGA Tour's multiple exceptions to the "walk-only" rule. What about the Senior Tour (now called the Champions Tour) where the greats of the game are eligible to play after they reach the age of fifty and carts are always allowed? The defendant denigrated that tour as simply a "nostalgic" exhibition, and not a real game of golf "at the highest level," the term it invented to describe some other PGA-sanctioned tournaments. Former golfer Ken Venturi testified that the

Senior Tour was "just an outing." (As might be imagined, fellow senior golfers, informed of Venturi's characterization, were livid.)

Throughout the trial, representatives of the PGA Tour expressed their sympathy for Martin's condition, but emphasized that his disability was beside the point. Tour Commissioner Finchem, a lawyer by training, emphasized the difference that one stroke per round could make and that Martin's cart might just give him that single-stroke advantage. One stroke could be the difference between a champion and a chump. (Off the stand, Finchem complained to the press about the entire judicial proceeding, contending that a federal judge was making a golf decision, and the judge had no background in golf.)

The public, however, was moved by Martin's tenacity. Almost 80 percent of those polled favored the young golfer with the debilitating condition, who showed enormous fortitude and determination. The California legislature passed a resolution supporting the Stanford graduate, and the San Francisco Board of Supervisors praised Martin's "courage and honor in tackling an issue of interest to all Americans." Some marketing experts thought the PGA Tour had missed a golden opportunity to support inclusiveness when it decided to oppose Martin's request for equity and access. Instead, the establishment chose to fight the young man who many saw as a hero.

In her closing argument, Martha Walters explained the case in the simplest terms. No one contested the fact that Casey Martin was an "excellent player." What that term meant was that Martin could make the necessary shots. No golfer is ever evaluated based on the quality of his walking, and no one has won a tournament because of his walking ability. The PGA Tour rules, as they were applied to various tournaments, showed they were sufficiently flexible to allow for a reasonable accommodation and that accommodation would allow Martin to demonstrate his excellence: "Mr. Martin just needs a ride to the starting line." Moreover, Walters argued, federal law required that the legal rights of disabled persons be determined on an individualized basis. If the PGA Tour was concerned about making sure a golfer "suffers" from fatigue, it had nothing to worry about. Because of his proven disability, Casey Martin suffered more fatigue (and pain) even while using a golf cart than any able-bodied golfer who had to walk the course.

Counsel for the PGA Tour, William Maledon, argued in response that Casey Martin simply did not have the ability to play the game: "You don't try to compensate for those differences in ability." The game is based on the fatigue of walking eighteen holes each day. Changing that requirement for one golfer undermines the level playing field that is essential for all sports. Contrary to the plaintiff's plea, the A.D.A. does not require an individualized determination that would exempt a disabled competitor "from a substantive rule of competition applicable to all."

PGA Tour Commissioner Finchem had good reason to be concerned about the outcome of the judicial proceeding. Magistrate Coffin ruled from the bench the day after the conclusion of testimony that under federal law Martin had the right to demand a "reasonable accommodation" for his disability, in this case through the use of a golf cart. The PGA Tour was not exempt from the A.D.A. as a "private club," because the evidence proved it was a commercial enterprise offering athletic events to the public at a fee. Nothing in the rules of golf required walking, and the defendant had not demonstrated that allowing Martin to use a cart would fundamentally alter the nature of the competition. The PGA Tour immediately announced it would appeal.

While the case was pending on appeal, Martin was able to use a cart. But the PGA Tour created a set of rules for his cart that it scrupulously enforced. The cart could not carry his clubs. (That was for his caddie.) He could not give his caddie a ride. His cart could not have a covering or a windshield. It was the kind of pettiness not uncommon with a case still in litigation.

In the meantime, Martin continued to demonstrate that he was proficient on the course — once he got to the ball. In the 1998 U.S. Open, he hit the longest drive off the tee — 373 yards — at the San Francisco's Olympic Club's sixth hole. He finished twenty-third in that tournament, during what would be his best year of golf. By 1999, when his case proceeded to the appellate court, he had begun to falter on the greens.

ON APPEAL

The U.S. Court of Appeals for the Ninth Circuit sits at the James R. Browning Courthouse on Seventh Street in San Francisco. It hears appeals from lower federal courts across the entire West Coast region, including some adjoining states and Hawaii and Alaska. A panel of three judges from the circuit heard the PGA Tour's appeal on May 4, 1999, but did not issue its opinion until ten months later on March 6, 2000.

Writing for a unanimous panel, Judge William Cameron Canby, Jr., affirmed Magistrate Coffin's rulings. Golf courses, Judge Canby concluded, were "places of public accommodation" covered by the A.D.A. On the days of its tournaments, the PGA Tour leased the courses and thus became the "operator" of the golf courses under the A.D.A. Permitting a golfer to use a cart would not fundamentally alter the nature of the services provided by the PGA Tour: "All that the cart does is permit Martin access to a type of competition in which he otherwise could not engage because of his disability. That is precisely the purpose of the A.D.A." In effect, the cart was an equalizer—a reasonable accommodation for a disabled golfer—and not an unfair advantage.

The PGA Tour vowed to bring the Martin case to the nation's highest court. The Supreme Court was well stocked with conservative Republican appointees who would be more inclined to read the A.D.A. narrowly, accept the PGA Tour's argument, and be less likely to second-guess its business judgment. Tim Finchem said publicly: "We all root for Casey, but it's not about him." Martin responded that it was about him: "No one else is riding in that cart."

TO THE SUPREME COURT

The U.S. Supreme Court is inundated with appeals of decisions of the federal circuit courts and the highest courts of the fifty states. In general, the court exercises discretion in determining which cases it will hear. Normally, a case such as Martin's—involving unique facts under a federal statute—would not draw the justices' attention. The court decided to hear the case not because the justices were golfers (a number of them were), but rather because the Seventh Circuit Court of Appeals in Chicago had issued a directly contrary reading of the Americans with Disabilities Act. That case involved a golfer, Ford Olinger, who had a degenerative hip condition. The Seventh Circuit denied his claim under the A.D.A., ruling that the use of a cart provided him with a competitive advantage over a golfer who was required to walk the course. The Supreme Court took Martin's case to resolve this split in the circuit courts' approach to reading the national statute.

The Supreme Court heard oral argument in Casey Martin's case on January 16, 2001. H. Bartow Farr III argued for the appellant PGA Tour. Professional sports, he said, were "simply tests of excellence . . . on a set of physical tasks . . . defined by the rules of the game." Those rules are set by the entity that presents the sport. Martin's request to use a cart, an advantage not allowed under those rules, therefore, would "fundamentally alter the nature of the competition." Martin's lawyer, Roy L. Reardon, responded that "the game is hitting the ball." The purpose of the A.D.A. in this context was "to give people like Casey Martin a chance to get to the game."

Justice Souter asked Martin's attorney a provocative question: "If the people who make the rules . . . say we want to make this particular game tougher than regular golf games . . . why shouldn't we respect that?" Reardon responded that walking was not fundamental to golf. Justice Scalia sneered that all this case proved was that golf can be played under different rules. He then stepped into judicial quicksand by commenting: "All sports rules are silly rules, aren't they? If some justices seemed to know as little about baseball as they did about golf . . . the former would be a greater sin." Justice Sandra Day O'Connor, an avid golfer, interjected: "Wait a minute!" (By coincidence, she had hit a hole-in-one a month earlier.) Justice John Paul Stevens looked over at Scalia and said: "In dissent again!" Justice Thomas asked no questions, as is his custom, and he was reported to have fallen asleep during the oral argument.

The Court's majority opinion in Casey Martin's case, written by Justice Stevens, wrestled with two major issues: (1) Does the Americans with Disabilities Act apply to PGA tournaments? (2) Does the statute require waiving the walking rule in Casey Martin's case?

The PGA Tour and many conservative commentators wanted the Court to rule, in effect, that any business retained the right to decide whether federal law applied to its activities. By making walking a required element of the enterprise, a golf tour could prevent disabled golfers from participating. The Court's majority, however, was not about to allow a business regulated by a federal statute to opt out of its constraints. Congress had intended that the Court would decide the coverage and applicability of the statute.

Title III of the A.D.A. prohibited discrimination based on disability by any "place of public accommodation." This phrase had been used by Congress in earlier civil rights legislation. It was intended to have broad coverage of places open for business to the public. The PGA Tour's events take place on golf courses and, in fact, Congress listed a "golf course" in the statute as an example of the kinds of places that must accommodate the disabled. The PGA Tour leases golf courses for its Q-school and operates the leased golf courses for those business purposes. Casey Martin and his fellow Q-school participants were "customers" of the PGA Tour since they paid

$3,000 for the privilege of participating in the contest and, if they prevailed, for the opportunity to play on the tour itself.

The more interesting issue addressed by the Court involved its examination of the nature of the sport of golf and the role played by walking in the sport. The PGA Tour wanted to be master of its own domain, retaining the unrestricted right to set its own rules of play. The Court rejected that approach. It defined golf as "shot making," not walking. The PGA Tour could not enforce an ancillary rule not at the core of the game that would disadvantage a person protected by federal law against discrimination based on disability. In any case, the Court majority said, the PGA Tour had to make an "individualized determination" of Martin's condition in order to determine if, because of his disability, he suffered extreme fatigue equal to that of an able-bodied golfer walking the course.

May a reasonable modification of the rules be made to accommodate the disabled golfer? Allowing Casey Martin to use a cart would not be an unreasonable accommodation of his disability, the Court said. Carts are used throughout professional golf, and the PGA Tour did not show that use of a cart would "fundamentally alter the nature" of its activity, the golf competition. Use of a cart would not give Martin a competitive advantage since he walks a quarter of the course in any case — and in excruciating pain.

In a caustic dissent, Justice Antonin Scalia demonstrated his disdain both for the federal law and for the Court's reading of that law. In a mean-spirited opinion joined only by Justice Clarence Thomas, Scalia explained, as he did in oral argument, that all sporting rules are arbitrary and silly, and that golf is a mere game, an amusement. He ignored the fact that, for Casey Martin, it was also a job. Any employer apparently can opt out of the A.D.A., according to Scalia, by carefully tailoring its operation and products, in this case to provide what Scalia termed "very special golf" which includes walking. It is not the Court's job to define golf, even though defining the activity is essential to determining the applicability of the federal statute.

Scalia bemoaned the fact that Martin would now be given an advantage every time he plays, in clear violation of the uniformity essential to a legitimate contest. While acknowledging that the majority's decision is a "decent, tolerant and progressive judgment," Scalia maintained that it was flat-out wrong, giving Martin a "game different from that offered to everyone else."

Casey Martin later characterized Scalia's opinion as "heartless." Martin acknowledged that his experience in court had taught him a lesson about hypocrisy: "What caught me off guard a little was that when the Supreme Court voted 7–2 in my favor, the two dissenters were Antonin Scalia and Clarence Thomas, who are the fellows who generally uphold things that moralists and Christians care about. I'm conservative and Christian, and I misread those guys completely."

THE NINETEENTH HOLE

Casey Martin's victory in court did not end all controversy about the participation of disabled athletes in competition. It did, however, broaden our understanding of the reach of the A.D.A.. And it gave Casey Martin a chance to play professional golf. Martin was able to compete on the Nationwide Tour using a golf cart. He even made it to the 2000 PGA Tour, but with only one top-25 finish, he ended up 179th on the money list, back in Q-school, and never returned to the PGA Tour. In 2001 the Nike company, a manufacturer of athletic equipment, began bestowing the annual Casey Martin Award to recognize disabled athletes all over the world.

Martin's victory over the PGA Tour established his place in sports law history, but it was not the beginning of a great and glorious career in professional golf. The tour gave him the necessary accommodation, but nobody could give him a new leg: "I probably have a certain number of steps left in my leg," Martin said. "It's either ride a cart or I'm done." He realized that his legacy will be based on his litigation: "I'd like to be perceived as a good golfer and a good person, but I'm afraid I'm always going to be labeled as the guy in the cart. So be it." All Martin ever wanted was to be a guy with a tour card; instead he will forever be remembered as the guy with the golf cart.

Did Martin's use of a cart give him an unfair advantage? If so, it certainly was not a lasting one. Mark Twain's well-known quip that golf is "a good walk spoiled" never did apply to the brave golfer from Oregon. Martin did not have a good walk to spoil. Each week he drained blood from his right knee.Within a few years, the degenerative condition in his leg made it impossible for him to continue to play competitively, even with a cart.

Casey Martin's case is a perfect introduction to the role that law can play in the business of sports. Did he obtain sports justice? Although the use of a cart allowed him to "get to the game," he continued to suffer after his arrival. Years later, Martin shared the difficulties he had in using the cart:

> The biggest stress of 2000 wasn't in the courtroom, or talking to the media, feeling the occasional bad vibe from people, worrying about my leg, or trying to keep my game together. It was dealing with the cart. Inching my way through crowds, looking for a place to get out and duck under the ropes, driving ahead and waiting for the other players to catch up—that was stressful. I found the logistics of riding in that environment to be very difficult, especially when there were 20,000 people out there. I never did find the knack for concentrating or getting into a rhythm, and I'm not sure it was even possible. Walking is the best way to play this game.

Justice Scalia's dissent suggests that courts should not be interested in sports at all, but for different reasons than those offered by Judge Matsch in the Hackbart case. Judge Matsch saw professional football as a species of warfare, and cautioned that the court should not get involved in the dirty business of a violent game with highly subjective rules. On the other hand, Justice Scalia saw golf as a mere amusement with artificial rules that were fundamentally silly. Neither jurist carried the day—Matsch because he was reversed on appeal and Scalia because he was outvoted 7–2 on the Supreme Court.

After giving Q-school one last try in 2005, Martin retired in 2006 at age thirty-three. His career earnings on the PGA Tour totaled $206,874, with two top-25 finishes. In May of 2006 he returned to Eugene to coach the University of Oregon's golf team: "It had become obvious to me," he told the press, "that it was time to do something else." He reflected on his successful judicial battle: "It was one of those experiences in life that I'm glad I went through, but I never would want to go through it again." Martin's experience with the judicial system converted him from a Republican to a Democrat, but throughout he stayed close to his religion. He told *Golf Digest*: "When we go to heaven, we will all be whole. We'll all have perfect bodies, physical ones. I don't know if there will be golf—the Bible sort of hints against it—but no way will there be golf carts." In any case, heavenly golf will be beyond the jurisdiction of both the PGA Tour and the U.S. Supreme Court.

As his attorney, Roy Reardon, told the Supreme Court, Martin's case is unique. In all likelihood there may never be another Casey Martin, disabled beyond question but still good enough to play golf at the highest level with the reasonable accommodation the law provided. But that situation only lasted for a brief period of time: "Let's face it," Martin concluded, "I wasn't quite good enough. Not at that level. It was time to move on."

CHAPTER 3

GENDER IDENTITY IN A CHANGING WORLD

TENNIS ANYONE?

*Tennis belongs to the individualistic past — a hero, or at most
a pair of friends or lovers, against the world.*

JACQUES BARZUN

• • • Richard Raskind was a very good male tennis player, captain of the Yale University men's team in 1955, and a journeyman professional athlete. Renee Richards was a very good female tennis player. Mr. Raskind became Ms. Richards after hormone treatment, extensive psychological counseling, and, ultimately, sex reassignment surgery. As a result, the U.S. Open, one of the four major international tennis tournaments and America's premier event, barred her from participating in the women's bracket. Playing at Forest Hills (where the tournament was then held) was an important symbol to Ms. Richards. Participating in the highly gendered world of tennis in one of its premier tournaments, she said, would constitute "an acceptance of my right to be a woman." Winning the right to participate would not be an easy contest, however. She knew the U.S. Tennis Association was discriminating against her based on her change of gender, but could she compel them to allow her to play?

Sports entities, like members of society themselves, are just beginning to recognize the concerns and interests of the transgender population. Once considered outcasts and curiosities, transgender persons are now approaching mainstream acceptance—at least in some portions of the country. If anything, the world of sports has been more accommodating to transgender athletes than the public, which may lag in its appreciation of gender identity issues. In fact, sports may be leading the way toward societal change, in a manner reminiscent of Jackie Robinson's role in the dismantling of apartheid in professional baseball. If so, Renee Richards deserves much of the credit.

TENNIS ANYONE?

Tennis finds its roots in the game of "paume" (French for "palm"), a form of handball played as early as the twelfth century by European monks who wore leather gloves while engaging in their exercise. The paume ball was an amalgam of wool, hair, and cork wrapped in cloth. The athletic pastime spread, and wooden rackets strung with catgut were added to increase the speed of the ball. The game grew popular among the French nobility

previous page
Renee Richards, a transgender tennis player, sought to play in the U.S. Open as a woman.
AP Photo / Dave Pickoff

and, not to be outdone, the English king Henry VIII built an indoor court in 1530. He no doubt played between wives.

In 1850, Charles Goodyear developed the rubber vulcanization process that allowed for the fabrication of what we now know as tennis balls. In 1872, the *New York Times* explained that tennis, considered an indoor sport, was a variation of handball and required "substantial buildings specially erected for that purpose." At that time, tennis was played with "cat gut bats" driving a ball against a wall above a defined line, a variation of modern-day squash. In 1874, Major Walter C. Wingfield obtained the British patent for the outside game of "lawn tennis." He also patented the equipment needed to participate in the sport.

Within three years the All-England Croquet and Lawn Tennis Club hosted its first men's championship at Wimbledon. In 1884, the Ladies' Singles Championship was added to the annual event. The first winner, Maud Watson, received as her prize a silver afternoon tea service. (In 2009, the women's champion received well over a million dollars.) Although later joined by three other major championships — in Australia, France, and the United States — to this day the annual Wimbledon festivities are referred to simply as "The Championships."

SEXUAL ORIENTATION AND GENDER IN THE GAME

Throughout much of the twentieth century, the sexual orientation of tennis professionals was not much of an issue. Bill Tilden, the finest tennis player of his time (he won his first Wimbledon championship in 1920), was an openly gay male. Billie Jean King and Martina Navratilova are lesbians who starred on the court for decades before making their sexual orientations public. However, there had been no known transgender tennis professionals until Renee Richards. In fact, there were few known transsexuals pursuing any careers in the public eye.

Gender identity issues have been addressed in sports before, though not always solved in a just way. Olympic medalist Mildred "Babe" Didrikson, one of the greatest women athletes of modern times, set world records in the 1930s in the women's 80-meter hurdles and javelin throw and competed in track, basketball, baseball, football, and even boxing. Sports reporters routinely wondered about her masculine appearance. Didrikson ended the controversy when she married, started wearing dresses, and turned to golf, a more acceptable feminine pastime.

Tennis had traditionally allowed men and women to play on the same court at the same time. Mixed doubles have been played at the U.S. Open since 1892, when Americans Mabel E. Cahill and Clarence Hobart teamed to win the championship, and at Wimbledon since 1913, when J. Hope Crisp and C.O. Tuckey of Great Britain won the title. In September 1973, the world witnessed the spectacle of a match between Billie Jean King and the formerly top-ranked Bobby Riggs, which King won decisively. Women everywhere saw the victory as a great triumph for the female gender, even though Riggs was an over-the-hill blowhard.

EXCLUDING RICHARDS

It is easy to understand why the U.S. Open would have problems with the prospect of Richards' participation in its tournament. At the core of every athletic competition lies an established set of rules applied equally to all who would participate in the game. There must be a "level playing field." Unfair or fraudulent competition would undermine the essential sports paradigm. We enjoy fair competition because the outcome is uncertain. If one side or one player always prevailed over the others, the event would be transformed into little more than an exhibition.

The world had witnessed Eastern European women performing in Olympic weight events with "man-like" proficiency and physiques. From the 1960s until the 1980s, many of these athletes were administered drugs that enhanced both their performance and also their male secondary characteristics. Was Renee Richards just the reverse—a man who took female hormones in order to compete unfairly against women tennis players?

The Open was concerned about the integrity of the competition it sponsored. After all, most women have different physical characteristics from most men. That, in turn, can correlate directly to how well they play tennis. Of course, there have been many great women champions of slight stature, while others have possessed strength and muscularity exceeding most men. Any categorization based only on gender is overbroad—all men are not physically superior to all women. The level of play attained by a highly skilled female tennis player is out of reach of many male tennis players.

The tennis establishment also voiced concerns about what would happen if any man could, by changing gender, compete against women. This "floodgate" theory was, of course, patently absurd. Richards' response was graphic and true: "How hungry for tennis success must you be to have your penis chopped off in pursuit of it?"

As with the PGA Tour's response to Casey Martin's request of a golf cart, the U.S. Open might also have been concerned about image. What sort of spectacle would be created when a transgender athlete participated in the nation's premier tennis tournament? Would she appear as some sort of freak or pervert? By this reasoning, it would not matter if she won or lost. What would matter was that she was there at all.

TRANSGENDER

Life in a hetero-normative world was simpler to understand. There were men. There were women. Men and women married and had children who were either boys or girls. Sexual orientation and gender identity were not topics for open conversation. That did not mean, of course, that they were not issues for some members of society. Gender variance only reached public discourse in the second half of the twentieth century, long after society recognized (but did not entirely accept) the fact that androsexual men are attracted to men and gynosexual women are attracted to women. Even as law and society evolve in the twenty-first century in recognizing the rights of homosexual men and lesbians, transgender identity remains on the boundaries, even though transsexual people have existed in all societies.

Under the *Diagnostic and Statistical Manual of Mental Disorders* (2000), persons with a "strong and persistent cross-gender identification" are diagnosed as having "Gender Identity Disorder." The transgender community understandably frowns upon any notion that they should be considered "sick" and labeled as mentally ill. Even without such a diagnosis, the transgender population is socially marginalized.

While most persons are born with a typical chromosome combination — XY (male) or XX (female) — modern medical research has revealed that chromosomes also combine in a variety of other "intersex" patterns. Body shapes and secondary sex characteristics vary widely. Modern writers on these issues use the term "sex" to refer to biological combinations at birth and "gender" as the subjective sense of fit within a culture, which can change over time. People are assigned a gender at birth. Some small fraction of persons cross over the boundaries of that gender. All of these terms have both political overtones and legal implications.

Richard Raskind's chromosomes combined before birth to make his sex and assigned gender male at birth. As a child, he began to experience gender confusion and discomfort. Eventually, he moved away from his initially assigned gender to become a "transwoman" at a time when that category did not enjoy a positive representation in American society.

The U.S. Open may have opposed Richards' petition out of fear of the unknown. In a society where being different can be dangerous, a transgender person has good reason to be afraid for his or her own safety. Some "normal" people have difficulty empathizing with or even understanding the transgender norm. For many, a transgender person is to be scorned, abused, and reviled.

Before Renee Richards became a news story, most Americans had only heard of one other transgender woman, Christine Jorgensen, although thousands had undergone sex reassignment surgery in Europe by the time Jorgensen became an international celebrity in the 1950s. Her case was the first one described in the popular media. Born in the Bronx in 1926, George Jorgensen began taking the female hormone ethinyl estradiol on his own after he returned from service in the Army. In Denmark, he engaged in a course of treatment of hormone replacement therapy. After sex reassignment surgery—it is thought she leaked the story of her own "transformation"—Christine Jorgensen became a celebrity. On December 1, 1952, a headline in the *New York Daily News* blared: "Ex-G.I. Becomes Blond Beauty: Operations Transform Bronx Youth."

The 1970s were a time of change in society's perceptions of its constituent members. Women's liberation attacked the shackles of gender bias. While gay men and lesbians were not fully accepted by the establishment, they were at least recognized as a part of an increasingly confusing societal mélange. The same cannot be said of the transgender population. Conventional assumptions about gender might countenance women's liberation and might even encompass gay men and women as a recognized sexual minority, but the transgender phenomenon was still beyond general acceptance. *Sports Illustrated* called Renee Richards an "extraordinary spectacle" and characterized reactions to her as "veering from astonishment to suspicion, sympathy, resentment and, more often than not, utter confusion."

INSIDE RICHARD RASKIND

For Renee Richards, affirmation by her sport paled in comparison to her personal battle with gender identity. Richards vividly described this internal conflict in *Second Serve*, her autobiography. Richard Raskind grew up as an all-American boy in a prosperous New York City family, the son of two doctors, with their home in Forest Hills, Queens. In high school, he played wide receiver on the football team, swam the backstroke on the swimming team, and was a pitcher on the baseball team.

Richards writes that an oppressive family environment in her formative years contributed to her gender confusion. Although she criticized her domineering psychiatrist mother, her passive doctor father, and even her tomboy older sister (whom her parents named Michael), Richards ultimately recognized that she was born a transsexual and had to wage the internal battle of gender identity until finally accepting her feminine personae.

Richard Raskind began to cross-dress in adolescence, as his alter ego "Renee" emerged to contest for his psyche and public appearance. Richard excelled at school, captained Yale's tennis team, grew to over six feet tall, 180 pounds, and then proceeded to the University of Rochester Medical School, choosing a specialty in ophthalmology. (Richards chose ophthalmology because, as a third-year medical student, she had watched a doctor restore sight to an injured eye. "Wow!" she remembers saying to herself: "That's for me."). After medical school, Raskind served two years of internship at Lenox Hill Hospital in New York, two years of residency at Manhattan Eye and Ear Hospital, and two more years as the chief eye surgeon at St. Albans Hospital.

At the same time Raskind was succeeding in the male-dominated field of medicine, he played competitive tennis and was ranked sixth nationally in the thirty-five-and-over category. Renee, his other self, constantly battled for control of both his personality and his physical body. At a time when cross-dressing was an illegal perversion and transsexualism was classified as a form of lunacy, Richard/Renee walked a tightrope, faced with sexual confusion, depression, and suicidal tendencies. Tennis was the only safe refuge. Richard would prevail in the daytime — at work and on the court — but only in the short run.

Hormone treatments and painful electrolysis changed Raskind's body, and a decade of psychoanalysis addressed his psychic pain, but only sexual reassignment surgery would make the change from Richard to Renee permanent. Only then could she accept herself. After his service as a doctor in the Navy, an outwardly normal heterosexual marriage and the birth of a son, the dominant Renee Richards finally emerged. After experiencing what she considered "a lifetime of freakish behavior, forever vacillating between masculinity and femininity," she had sex reassignment surgery in 1975 at a private hospital in Queens, New York. At age forty-one, she was a post-operative male-to-female transsexual. No one could really doubt that Renee Richards had become a woman — no one except the U.S. Tennis Association.

Renee left the east coast to start a new life as an ophthalmologist in Southern California. However, it was tennis that brought her into the public spotlight. Playing in regional competitions for her local club — the John Wayne Tennis Club — under the pseudonym of Renee Clarke, Richards was identified by a San Diego reporter as the former Richard Raskind. It is possible that she might have returned to a relatively anonymous existence, but her old friend Gene Scott invited her to play in his professional tennis tournament, the Tennis Week Open, in South Orange, New Jersey. When she accepted, Richards became a reluctant standard bearer for all groups who are disadvantaged by the norms and prejudices of society: "I heard from blacks, convicts, Chicanos, hippies, homosexuals, people with physical handicaps and, of course, transsexuals. My god, the whole world seemed to be looking for me to be their Joan of Arc." All she had wanted to do was to play tennis. The U.S. Tennis Association and the Women's Tennis Association quickly withdrew their sanction for the South Orange tournament.

Tournament play began in late August 1976, in ninety-five-degree temperatures combined with high humidity. Richards' match with Kathy Beene attracted national attention, and both players were nervous. (Who wouldn't be, with Howard Cosell providing commentary during the match for Wide World of Sports?) Richards prevailed 6–0, 6–2. The Women's Tennis Association had put pressure on women players to pull out of the South Orange tournament — of the thirty-two professionals originally scheduled to participate, twenty-five withdrew — and it quickly organized a rival event in Westchester County in the New York City suburbs. Richards beat Caroline Stoll and Kathy Harter on the way to the South Orange semifinals, where she lost to seventeen-year-old Lea Antonoplis in straight sets.

THE RIGHT TO PLAY

A few days later, Richards applied to play in the 1976 U.S. Open, then held only blocks from Richards' former home in Forest Hills. Both the U.S. Tennis Association and the Women's Tennis Association quickly refused to sanction her participation. The associations told Richards that she had to pass a gender verification test. Based on her chromosomes, she would be classified as either a man or a woman. Because sex reassignment surgery did not change her chromosomes from male to female, the result was foreseeable. She would be barred from playing as a woman. Some women tennis players were outspoken about competing against Richards. Rosie Casals, a prominent female tennis player, said: "Richards is still physically a man, and that gives her a tremendous and unfair advantage. [She] has to be stopped." Richards vowed, nonetheless, to pursue her right to play in future tournaments. The U.S. Tennis Association replied: "Just try it."

The U.S. Tennis Association had not adopted the gender verification test until after Richards had applied to play in women's singles, the first time in the ninety-five-year history of the Open that such a test would be used. Richards did not contest her 1976 exclusion, but she did prepare to use the legal process to gain access to the 1977 Open.

With the help of Roy Cohn's law partner, Mike Rosen, Richards brought suit in New York state courts claiming that her treatment by the tennis associations was discriminatory, that requiring the sex verification test would be "insufficient, grossly unfair, inaccurate, faulty and inequitable." The case was heard by Judge Alfred M. Ascione, sitting in the First District in Manhattan. Judge Ascione was a journeyman judge, born in New York, and educated at City College with a law degree from St. John's. He served on the municipal and civil courts in New York before being elected in 1966 to the Supreme Court, the name New York uses for its trial court of general jurisdiction. He would rule on Richards' petition, and it would become his most famous case. In doing so, he avoided passing moral judgment on Richards' need to change her birth-assigned gender. Instead, he focused on the law of New York — which barred discrimination based on gender.

Richards' suit claimed that after her sex reassignment surgery in 1975, "for all intents and purposes, I became a female, psychologically, socially and physically, as has been attested to by my doctors." Not allowing her to participate as a woman, therefore, discriminated against her in violation of the New York State Human Rights Law. The U.S. Tennis Association, Richards claimed, had purposefully instituted the Barr body or sex-chromatin test to exclude Richards, knowing she would have a Y chromosome.

Sex verification was first conducted at the European Track and Field Championships in Budapest in 1966. All women athletes were required to parade nude in front of a panel of doctors, who verified their genitalia. The Barr test—the one the U.S. Open insisted that Richards pass—was designed to avoid this embarrassing display of naked athletes. It was first adopted by the International Olympic Committee for the 1968 Olympics in Mexico. Using a buccal smear from inside a competitor's mouth, the analysis determined the presence of a stainable chromatin mass (the Barr body), which is found only in females. Women who proved they had the correct combination of chromosomes were issued a "femininity card" that could be presented at future competitions.

The parties presented the case to Judge Ascione based on affidavits from medical experts, the principals themselves, and a few female tennis players. Richards' surgeon, Roberto Granato, explained that as a result of the sex reassignment surgery, "I would say that Dr. Richards' internal sexual structure is anatomically similar to a biological woman who underwent a total hysterectomy and ovariectomy." Not surprisingly, Dr. Granato saw no unfair advantage for Richards "when competing against other women. Her muscle development, weight, height and physique fit within the female norm." It was his "professional conclusion [that] except for reproduction, Dr. Richards should be considered a woman, classified as a female and allowed to compete as such."

Leo Wollman, Richards' doctor and co-author of the "standards of care" which remain the definitive guide for doctors treating transsexual patients, considered his patient a female based on her external genital appearance, internal organ appearance, gonadal identity, endocrinological makeup, and psychological and social development. He concluded that she would be considered a female by any reasonable test of sexuality.

The defendants' affidavits offered a very different perspective. George W. Gowen, an attorney who was vice president and general counsel of the U.S. Tennis Association, explained the defendants' worry about Richards' competitive advantage and the potential for massive fraud:

We have reason to believe that there are as many as 10,000 transsexuals in the United States and many more female impersonators or imposters. The total number of such persons throughout the world is not known. Because of the millions of dollars of prize money available to competitors, because of nationalistic desires to excel in athletics, and because of world-wide experiments, especially in the iron curtain countries, to produce athletic stars by means undreamed of a few years ago, the USTA has been especially sensitive to its obligation to assure fairness of competition among the athletes competing in the U.S. Open, the leading international tennis tournament in the United States. The USTA believes that the Olympic type sex determination procedures are a reasonable way to assure fairness and equality of competition when dealing with numerous competitors from around the world. The USTA believes the question at issue transcends the factual background or medical history of one applicant.

Three female tennis players, Francoise Durr, Janet Newberry and Kristien K. Shaw, each submitted affidavits stating the obvious: based on their experience "the taller a player is the greater advantage the player has. . . . Similarly, the stronger a player is, the greater advantage the player has, assuming like ability." None of them had ever played against Ms. Richards, and their affidavits spoke only to height and strength, not gender. Plaintiff, in turn, submitted the affidavit of Billie Jean King, among the greatest modern female tennis players. King and Richards were doubles partners in one tournament, and King participated in two tournaments in which Richards played. It was her judgment that Richards "does not enjoy physical superiority or strength so as to have an advantage over women competitors in the sport of tennis." (In fact, compared with some later women tennis players, Renee Richards would have been at a distinct physical disadvantage. She is two inches shorter than Lindsey Davenport, one inch shorter than Maria Sharapova, and the same height as Venus Williams without her muscle tone and physical development.)

Renee Richards took the Barr test on June 27 and July 1, 1977, at the Institute of Sports Medicine and Athletic Trauma at Lenox Hill Hospital in New York, the facility selected by the U.S. Tennis Association. The results were "ambiguous." Richards refused to take a retest. Thus, she was barred from the tournament. Judge Ascione would have to determine whether this was gender discrimination in violation of the law of New York.

There are many problems with the Barr test. It assumes only two possible combinations of chromosomes—xx and xy, with a conclusion that results in an irrebuttable presumption of sexual identity. If Richards' test showed she had the xy chromosome pair, she would be classified as a man. John Money, a psychologist on the faculty at Johns Hopkins Medical School, explained to the court that using that one test as the sole criterion of sex determination is both "unfair and misguided." Chromosomal abnormalities are common. Some females are born with only one x chromosome; others have three or more x chromosomes. Males born with genotype xxy have Klinefelter's Syndrome, which inhibits the development of the male reproductive system, and results in a generally androgynous appearance and gynecomastia. Some males are born with the genotype xyy and experience few symptoms.

Despite being inundated with medical and social data, Judge Ascione understood the basic nature of the dispute. He wrote in his opinion:

> What is a transsexual? A transsexual is an individual anatomically of one sex who firmly believes he belongs to the other sex. This belief is so strong that the transsexual is obsessed with the desire to have his body, appearance and social status altered to conform to that of his "rightful" gender. They are not homosexual. They consider themselves to be members of the opposite sex cursed with the wrong sexual apparatus. They desire the removal of this apparatus and further surgical assistance in order that they may enter into normal heterosexual relationships. On the contrary, a homosexual enjoys and uses his genitalia with members of his own anatomical sex. Medical science has not found any organic cause or cure (other than sex reassignment surgery and hormone therapy) for transsexualism, nor has psychotherapy been successful in altering the transsexual's identification with the other sex or his desire for surgical change.

In a prescient ruling for the mid-1970s, Judge Ascione reasoned that gender identity was the product of a complex series of factors; using the chromosome test as the single determining factor was "grossly unfair, discriminatory and inequitable." The experts had convinced the court that Ms. Richards, the post-operative plaintiff, was physically and psychologically a female. The judge concluded the U.S. Tennis Association intentionally discriminated against the plaintiff:

It seems clear that defendants knowingly instituted this test for the sole purpose of preventing plaintiff from participating in the tournament. The only justification for using a sex determination test in athletic competition is to prevent fraud—in other words, men masquerading as women, competing against women.

He saw little risk that male tennis players would go through the physical and emotional trauma of sex reassignment surgery, hormone treatments, and psychological counseling in order to commit a fraud on the public in a tennis match:

> When an individual such as plaintiff, a successful physician, a husband and father, finds it necessary for his own mental sanity to undergo a sex reassignment, the unfounded fears and misconceptions of defendants must give way to the overwhelming medical evidence that this person is now female.

On August 16, 1977, finding that "this person is now female," the court granted Richards an injunction against the U.S. Tennis Association and the U.S. Open which allowed her to play in the 1977 Open as a woman. Renee Richards would finish her tennis career participating in tournaments as the woman she had become. The defendants did not seem too worried about the outcome. Richards, they concluded, had passed her prime.

POST-LITIGATION

Under the court's order, Renee Richards was entitled to play in the U.S. Open as a woman. She had become one of the most famous (or perhaps notorious) people in the world, but that was certainly not her intention or desire. She lost to Virginia Wade in the first round at Forest Hills before a sympathetic crowd. Because of her age—she was forty-three years old—Richards did not have an extended career ahead of her as a female tennis player. However, she was ranked as high as number 20 in the world and was twice a semifinalist in mixed doubles (with Ilie Nastase) at the U.S. Open: "I want to play professional tennis, which brings me into the public eye, but I don't want to be in the public eye. I've had my fill of being ogled and exploited and used." After four years of the "zoo-like atmosphere" on the tour, she returned to her medical practice: "I had to admit that I was a better doctor than I was an athlete." She did stay close to the sport, however, coaching Martina Navratilova and introducing her when she was inducted into the Tennis Hall of Fame in 2000.

Richards moved her ophthalmology practice from the West Coast to Park Avenue in New York. She returned to the city as the professional woman she had always wanted to be. Well respected in her field, she became the surgeon director of ophthalmology and head of the eye-muscle clinic at Manhattan Eye, Ear, and Throat Hospital and served on the editorial board of the *Journal of Pediatric Ophthalmology and Strabismus*. In 2001, she received the Helen Keller Services Award for the Blind for her work in ophthalmology. More recently, Richards moved her practice upstate to Carmel, New York, where she writes books and papers, stays current reading ophthalmology journals, and is focused on her practice. She has good friends and is a struggling golfer.

Long after Richards' victory for fairness and human rights in court, public attitudes concerning the transgender population have slowly begun to catch up with the law. Only a small portion of the population — estimated at from 0.1 to 0.2 percent of persons nationwide — are transgender. Employers have found that being receptive to inclusion and diversity attracts better workers — and that includes persons with different gender identities. The *New York Times* reported in 2008 that 125 of the Fortune 500 companies included "gender identity" in their corporate non-discrimination policies. These companies also actively recruited transgender employees; many offered benefits directed at attracting this population, including medical treatments, psychological counseling, and gender reassignment surgery. Twenty states and about one hundred cities now ban discrimination against the transgender population. There are approximately 1,200 sexual reassignment surgeries each year, and there are many more transgender people who choose not to have the surgery. Most transgender persons, often with the support of hormone treatment and psychotherapy, live as members of the gender that is discordant with their anatomic sex.

The Richards case, and the resulting development in public understanding of gender identity issues, have created a significant improvement in the rights of transgender athletes. For example, Michelle Dumaresq — one of the top Canadian mountain bikers (and a former male steelworker from Vancouver) — now rides in the female professional biking circuit after undergoing eight years of hormone treatment and sex reassignment surgery. In 1999, before the Sydney Olympics, the International Olympic Committee discontinued mandatory sex testing; by the 2004 Athens Olympics it had announced a new policy. To be eligible to compete in their gender, transsexual athletes must have undergone hormone therapy and sex reassignment surgery. If that surgery was post-puberty, transitioners must wait two years before competing.

Renee Richards did not choose her gender. She was born into the wrong body, not unlike others in society. When she chose to alter her sex identity, she was compelled to use the judicial process to be allowed to participate in the sport she loved as the woman she had become. Opposition to Richards, however, cannot simply be written off as know-nothingism. She posed a legitimate threat to the established order that makes life's imponderables and uncertainties tolerable for most people. Our sexual and gender identities are submerged within socially assigned roles. As with Casey Martin, it is not likely that there will be many others like Renee Richards, who could both test societal norms in court and then participate in professional sports at the highest level. Nonetheless, the precedent she set will pave the way for others caught in our bimodal sex/gender world.

CHAPTER 4

THE IDEAL OF AMATEURISM

NCAA REGULATION OF THE
COLLEGE CARTEL

Can't anything be done about calling these guys "student athletes"?
That's like referring to Attila the Hun's cavalry as "weekend warriors."
RUSSELL BAKER

• • • The academic performance of America's colleges and universities is a matter of great national pride. The smartest and most ambitious of the world's youth long for the opportunity to further their education and their employment prospects by obtaining degrees at American institutions of higher learning. Faculty members at those institutions produce the scientific research and scholarly work that serve as the engines of global business and intellectual ferment. And, as a result of a quirk of history, those same non-profit, tax-exempt institutions provide the public with entertainment through sporting exhibitions, primarily by presenting football contests and basketball games fought between men in their late teens and early twenties. That is certainly an unusual business for academia, and it is uniquely an American phenomenon.

Although college sports in the aggregate are the source of millions of dollars of annual gross revenue for colleges and universities, student athletes — the performers in these entertainments — do not receive a salary for their participation. As Professor Andrew Zimbalist noted in *Unpaid Professionals*, "No other industry in the United States manages not to pay its principal producers a wage or salary." Although gross receipts from football and men's basketball at many schools are substantial, these sports produce little net revenue because the surplus funds coaches' salaries and the costs of non-revenue-producing sports. In fact, considered as a whole, college sports normally constitute a drain on an institution's academic resources, even with the economic exploitation of the athletes. While many, if not most, college football and basketball players aspire to continue their careers at the professional level after their college apprenticeships, very few ever do so. And many athletes do not leave school with their college degrees. Some, like Dexter Manley of the Washington Redskins, complete college without learning how to read or write.

Outside of the revenue-producing sports of football and men's basketball, most athletes do not receive sufficient scholarship aid from their schools to cover their tuition. Nonetheless, they are limited under the rules of the National Collegiate Athletic Association in their ability to earn income. This tragic combination of no compensation for services performed,

previous page
In order to play for the University of Colorado Buffaloes, Jeremy Bloom was forced to give up the endorsement income he earned as a professional skier.
AP Photo / David Zalubowski

little prospect for professional accomplishment, and inadequate, if any, real educational value is the great shame of America's colleges, all administered under the watchful eye of the National Collegiate Athletic Association.

How can we justify the hypocritical reality of college sports and the treatment of college athletes? Here is one convenient, albeit fictional, explanation. Colleges and their agent, the NCAA, decided that student-athletes should be considered "amateurs," a Victorian concept first developed to apply to nineteenth-century, upper-class lads of means. Because there were few paid professional athletes at the time outside of baseball, the definition fit. In order to preserve the spirit of pure competition, colleges decided that athletes should be strictly forbidden from receiving compensation. These athletes would then remain amateurs because they received no compensation. This prevailing tautology of purity has never been justified by demonstrating that it produced some social good, although when college sports were simply expanded intramural exhibitions, it did little harm. But how can we possibly explain the necessity of the norm of amateurism after revenue-producing college sports became highly commercialized, national entertainment products?

Colleges have no difficulty filling the ranks of their revenue-producing sports teams—football and men's basketball—even without offering a salary to the participants. High school boys willingly accept the norms of amateurism while they dream of professional riches. More to the point, by playing for universities such as Notre Dame or USC, a football player can become the object of something approaching public adoration. Each new generation of athletes joins a long lineage of footballers, inheriting past glories and inspiring reverence in those who will follow. If they are injured or defeated, others will suffer with them. It is not just a game. It is a hallowed tradition.

IN THE BEGINNING

North American college-based sports entertainment was the result of historical coincidence rather than premeditated design. The first colleges were established along the Eastern seaboard during the colonial period. They normally had some church affiliation. Harvard, Yale, Princeton, and their contemporaries educated men of a certain social class. Part of the obligation of these schools was to inculcate the upper-class values that graduates would need to lead American society, business, government, and religious organizations. The students engaged in competitive recreation—horseback riding or rudimentary forms of bat-and-ball games that would later develop into baseball—but their pastimes never approached that of organized team sports.

Today's big-time college sports derived from nineteenth-century, student-run social and athletic clubs. The first intercollegiate athletic contest was a crew competition between two student clubs—the Oneida Boat Club of Harvard and the Undine Boat Club of Yale—held on New Hampshire's Lake Winnipesaukee on August 3, 1852. Even at its inception, collegiate sport was closely aligned with business interests. The race was sponsored by the Boston, Concord, and Montreal Railroad, which owned the lake's resort and used the event to promote both its rail service and its hotel. In exchange, the company offered the rowers "lavish prizes" and "unlimited alcohol"—quite an attraction for college boys. Today, these rewards would constitute compensation banned under NCAA rules.

Harvard's Oneida Boat Club had trained for the encounter by eating fewer pastries, which proved sufficient to best the men from Yale. The winner's trophy was a set of black walnut oars, which was kept in the club's Charles River boathouse for decades. The two institutions raced again three years later, on the Connecticut River in Springfield, Massachusetts. This time Harvard used Alexander Agassiz, a graduate, as its coxswain. (Agassiz would have been declared ineligible under current rules and, even in the mid-nineteenth century, this might have constituted a violation of the spirit of fair competition. Nonetheless, Agassiz continued to participate for another three years.) Harvard once again prevailed. Both the New Hampshire and the Springfield contests attracted spectators who came with cash to gamble on the outcome. By 1858, intercollegiate crew competitions had become a regular occurrence, although the 1897 *Encyclopedia of Sports* continued to maintain that "Rowing was a recreation, first, last and always."

Student-run sporting clubs evolved into teams that represented their universities, primarily in football. The Rutgers-Princeton match of November 6, 1869, is generally considered the first intercollegiate football game, although the rules involved simple variations of soccer and the players from each college were members of established soccer clubs. It is said that a Rutgers professor bicycled by the spectacle and commented: "You men will come to no Christian end." (He may have been quite correct.) Spectators willingly paid admission to watch the mayhem on the field. These violent and aggressive athletic performances spread to other colleges. "Princeton," its president, Woodrow Wilson, stated with disgust in 1890, "is noted in this wide world for three things: football, baseball, and collegiate instruction."

University sports teams eventually formed into leagues and conferences based on geographic proximity, and clubs hired non-student ringers to fortify their squads. Attendance blossomed: for example, the 1897 Harvard-Pennsylvania game at Franklin Field drew 24,000 people. After the turn of the century, colleges began hiring non-academic coaches to guide their teams to victory. Percy Haughton was among the first of these paid college coaches. A member of the Harvard team that held Yale to a scoreless tie in a famous football game of 1897, he coached first at Cornell in 1899, then at Harvard from 1908–16, and finally at Columbia in 1923 and 1924. Even as professional football and basketball took root in the twentieth century, college sports continued to be the public's primary focus, transforming colleges into centers of athletic development and performance.

Some professional sports, such as baseball, were already well established by the 1870s, before colleges began to provide athletic entertainment. A few college men, such as Christy Mathewson of Bucknell and Frankie Frisch of Fordham, pursued successful professional baseball careers after graduation, although most baseball professionals did not have college experience. Today about half of all Major League baseball players attend college, even if few graduate before taking their turn in the professional ranks.

THE NCAA

The National Collegiate Athletic Association controls the American collegiate sports cartel as the instrument of its member schools and conferences. It regulates the activities of some 400,000 athletes and staunchly protects both the principle of amateurism and its own administrative prerogatives. Its first charter, however, had nothing to do with amateurism. The association was first formed to reduce the toll of violence on the football field.

The game of football remained predominantly a college pastime until well into the twentieth century, with squads from the Ivy League, Chicago,

Rutgers, Notre Dame, and Michigan as the principal objects of public attention. But the game proved inordinately and unacceptably dangerous. An average of twenty collegians died on the field each year. President Theodore Roosevelt, Harvard class of 1880, loved the games, "especially in their rougher forms, because they tend to develop courage." (Not all U.S. presidents were similarly devoted to athletics. Grover Cleveland, who weighed 240 pounds, loathed exercise: "Bodily movement alone . . . is among the dreary and unsatisfying things of life.") Roosevelt decided to save football from itself; he vowed to put an end to the carnage that the game had engendered.

President Roosevelt commanded that college football decrease the risk of serious injury and death. Otherwise, he vowed, he would ban the sport. He invited representatives of three Ivy League colleges — Harvard, Yale and Princeton — to the White House for lunch. The most notable attendee was Walter Camp, a founding father of the game, who represented Yale. Roosevelt was forceful in his arguments. Hundreds of young men had died playing the barbaric game between 1890 and 1905. (Roosevelt's own son, Ted Jr., broke his nose and ankle while playing on Harvard's second string.) These schools and other institutions responded to Roosevelt's threats, creating the National Intercollegiate Football Conference in 1905, a predecessor to what became the NCAA. The organization quickly codified the rules of the game of football and outlawed the flying wedge — a Harvard invention for its game against Yale in 1892 where, as Amos Alonzo Stagg explained, a "slow-moving mass of players clinging to one another moved forward in a slow lock-step run." The flying wedge had caused numerous deaths and many injuries. (Today, the NCAA bestows the annual Flying Wedge Award on an individual who exemplifies outstanding leadership. One recent recipient was Vice President Dick Cheney.)

Even though the games had been made safer — fewer deaths, but still a considerable number of serious injuries — football did not fit comfortably in a university. The awkward relationship between athletics and higher education was the subject of criticism by the Carnegie Foundation as early as 1929. Investigators had studied practices at 130 colleges in the United States and Canada. In "Bulletin 23," the foundation's president, Henry S. Pritchard, cautioned that the conflict between academics and sports entertainment created a substantial risk to the central mission of higher education. Colleges, the report concluded, were recruiting athletes who were anything but "scholars," and the prevailing practices of athletics demonstrated a "lack of intellectual challenge to the young and alert mind." However, no fundamental changes were made in college athletics as a result of the Carnegie report.

The rough-and-tumble, anti-intellectual athletes who played college football did not easily coexist with those who entered academia for its more traditional, educational role. Some schools abolished team sports that interfered with the predominant academic, research, and scholarly missions of their institutions. Robert Hutchins, the young president of the University of Chicago, then one of the country's strongest football schools, convinced his board of trustees to ban the sport in 1939: "College is not a great athletic association and social club in which provision is made, merely incidentally, for intellectual activity on the part of the physically and socially unfit." When asked by a querulous alumnus what would replace football, Hutchins responded: "Education." He said with conviction: "This is a university, not a circus." Most colleges, especially state-supported institutions, charted a very different course, toward big-time football played in huge stadiums built with state funds and booster contributions. The circus had come to town.

At its inception, the NCAA ignored many of the issues raised by the norm of amateurism in college sports. It left the question of athletic eligibility up to each institution under a "home rule" policy. For those schools, especially public institutions, that found competition on the field an easier road to distinction than excellence in academic pursuits, this noninterference was a license to recruit — and even pay — the best young athletes. For example, Paul "Bear" Bryant, the football coach who would later achieve immortality as the steward of Alabama's Crimson Tide, hired his best players when he coached at the Universities of Maryland and Kentucky in the late 1940s.

Eventually, the NCAA could no longer ignore the obvious. There was growing evidence that college football was overrun by corruption, with recruited professionals on the field of play who did not even pretend to be students. Individuals were awarded so-called "scholarships" based solely on their athletic ability. In 1946, the NCAA took an extreme position with regard to these practices. It proposed the "Principles for the Conduct of Intercollegiate Athletics," which banned all non-academic, athletic-based financial aid. The member schools adopted this "Sanity Code" in 1948 over the strong objection of southern universities, but then quickly repealed it in 1951. In its stead, the NCAA imposed detailed bureaucratic regulations on athletic eligibility that have continued to multiply over time and have proven impossible to administer in a uniform and fair manner. Over the same period, the NCAA has evolved into a sometimes arbitrary, but always self-assured, overseer of the increasingly commercialized business of college athletics. NCAA member institutions have used the organization to hold down personnel costs by limiting the money that could be paid to players while capturing the profits made by their games.

The main actor in this new regulatory regime was Executive Director Walter Byers, who served the NCAA in that capacity from 1951 until 1987. In 1953, Byers invented the term "student-athlete" to describe "amateur college players"—a designation worthy of Madison Avenue. Byers thought these athletes should be "patriots," who would be free of avarice, rather than paid "mercenaries," like employees who perform a service for hire. For most of the subsequent decades, the NCAA would place priority on the "athlete" part of the student-athlete formulation. Director Byers was not an educator; he was a former sportswriter and businessman and, at times, an autocrat. Upon completion of his tenure at the NCAA, Byers wrote a memoir, *Unsportsmanlike Conduct*, to present his side of the many controversies faced by the association. The book was also his opportunity to apologize for those few mistakes he admits he made. (Although he remained remarkably free of taint, considering the cauldron of college sports, some have claimed that Byers became wealthy by accepting interest-free loans and favors from those who did business with the NCAA.)

In full control of what Byers acknowledged was the collegiate economic "cartel," the NCAA was able to present the television networks with a package of sports programming that captured the interest of the viewing public. College sports were sold as a different product from the professional game. Here were men—until recently, few women's sports were featured—who participated only for the fun, honor, and joy of the game, while earning their college degrees in the process. It was an attractive fantasy. The networks needed programming that would appeal to a profitable demographic—men ages eighteen to forty-nine—and college sports were tailor-made. Accordingly, the NCAA would share the growing wealth it received from television contracts with all its member schools.

Walter Byers should be given much of the credit—and should bear much of the blame—for this remarkable state of affairs. While making lucrative deals and selling a thoroughly commercialized product, he successfully sought to prevent colleges from paying taxes levied against other partici-pants in the entertainment business. And he recognized the possible fi-nancial exposure that would occur if student-athletes were considered university employees. Injured employees would be entitled to workers' compensation. It would be much better for business if injured student-athletes were simply cut from their teams, under the terms of scholarships that were limited to one-year periods.

During Byers' thirty-six years at the helm of college sports, he served without much accountability for his decisions and without any real chal-lenge to his authority. The NCAA was responsible to no one but itself, and that was no easy feat. He created an enforcement mechanism designed to foster blind obedience by member schools, candidly telling *Sports Illus-trated* that violating NCAA rules was not morally wrong: "[I]t is wrong be-cause we say it's wrong." And he left a legacy of autocratic rules and proce-dures designed to protect the NCAA brand, although he himself estimated that 30 percent of the member schools were cheating on those rules.

Byers' version of the college sports universe presents a different narrative from that offered by its critics. Balancing espoused idealism with hard-nosed pragmatism, Byers recalls fighting with religious fervor against what he called "college sports crime," echoing the sentiments of Captain Palmer Pierce of West Point, the first president of the NCAA, who said in 1907: "Hard, honest, honorable playing of any game, win or lose, is what this As-sociation desires." He admits that college sports was operated by an old-boys' network of drinking "friends," and addresses rivalries and conflicts that developed "within the family." According to Byers, college athletics could be a swamp filled with evildoers — including university presidents unable to resist either the money produced by the business of sports or the demands of radical students protesting social injustice. Conference com-missioners could not even enforce their own rules against member schools. Expediency prevailed.

There was only one referee in this donnybrook: the NCAA. That was why, Byers wrote, he earned his reputation as "a puritanical dictator" who fought "the infidels," a group that variously included college coaches, university presidents, conference commissioners, and anyone else who contested the authority of the NCAA. If there was any criticism of NCAA methods, how-ever, Byers insisted it should be directed at the member schools; it was they who would not allow the association to take the high road.

Byers had harsh criticism for upstart universities seeking to use athletic bootstraps to achieve respect, like UNLV, UCLA, Michigan State, and Florida State. They were all recidivist offenders of NCAA rules: "Respect for academic quality is seldom the governing criterion for university under-graduate decision making." Faced with point-shaving scandals, competitive bidding by universities and boosters for premier recruits, and other athletics crimes, the NCAA did all it could with the limited tools and resources it had been granted by its members, while at the same time running what had become a very big business.

Very little of Byers' account of his years with the NCAA is devoted to the concerns of athletes, who are painted with a broad brush as lawless and corrupt. Athletes are "a specialized group brought to the campus for a specific purpose." It is unclear whether Byers ever met with student-athletes to ascertain their interests and needs. He does state, however, that the NCAA must provide athletes with "an honorable workplace," a remarkable admission of their status as employees. Ultimately, he recommends that athletes be freed of those NCAA regulations that only benefit the commercial interests of colleges and universities.

In order to maintain its status as a feared regulator, the NCAA would publicly target particularly recalcitrant schools for punitive sanctions, while leaving other violators alone. There were no guidelines on the exercise of prosecutorial discretion or the severity of association punishments, and the NCAA's application of rules could be sometimes capricious or simply ludicrous. Over the years, the NCAA manual of regulations morphed into an encyclopedic compendium, containing sufficient particulars under which almost any college sports program could be found to be in violation.

Although college athletes are not members of the NCAA and have no say in the development and application of its rules, they cannot play college sports unless they strictly adhere to its regulations. Many of these rules, Byers now argues, are designed to divert money from the athletes—who, through their athletic performances, created that wealth—to the colleges and the NCAA.

All those involved in the NCAA appeared to believe deeply in its mission to protect the integrity of college sports. The organization regularly depended upon the "voluntary" confessions of rule violations by member institutions, and it demanded respect from university presidents under the aegis of "the spirit of cooperation." Under this regime, presidents would contact the NCAA to confess the sins of their athletic programs, hoping for lenient treatment (which they would occasionally receive). Schools that did not come clean voluntarily would suffer from an administrative process that was often vindictive. Those few institutions that were openly critical of the association would suffer extra retaliation. The worst thing a college could do was to criticize or sue the arrogant, arbitrary NCAA.

Over the years, some of the accused complained about the absence of fair and open procedures for investigating rule violations and imposing penalties. The NCAA's all-powerful, but overworked, investigatory staff could be sloppy on occasion. Investigators would write notes, but not record conversations; or they would reconstruct conversations, writing memos long after the fact. But these investigative failures never really mattered because the staff would always prevail before the association's Committee on Infractions.

Lawyers schooled in the basic due-process requirements of judicial proceedings were appalled by the NCAA's failure to provide a fair hearing. Accused parties could not confront or cross-examine witnesses against them, and the association refused to disclose the supporting evidence for its determinations until shortly before decisions were made. The NCAA did not pretend to be an adjudicator. It was a prosecutorial body that imposed sanctions and issued threats. Even state and federal courts deferred to what they considered the "expertise" of the sole regulator of college sports.

THE BLOOM LITIGATION

Jeremy Bloom's effort to obtain sports justice presents a particularly interesting example of the NCAA's inflexible administration of college sports and the role that the courts played in facilitating the association's control. His case highlights both the NCAA's hypocrisy and the commercial exploitation of college athletes. The NCAA rule that Bloom allegedly violated made no sense, but the state court enforced it anyway.

Jeremy Bloom first hit the slopes in Loveland, Colorado, at age three. He began skiing moguls when he was ten years old, regularly winning prizes in his age group. He was the first one on the ski lift each morning, and the last to leave the mountain each night. Bloom remembered: "If it was snowing, we skied. If it was cold, we skied. This was not about sipping hot chocolate and waiting for apres-ski. It was great family time. And I loved going fast." By age fifteen, Bloom was competing on the national team and participating in World Cup competition. He won the 2002 World Cup Championship in mogul skiing, becoming the youngest champion in history.

Mogul skiing should not be confused with a Saturday afternoon run down the bunny slope. Moguls jar the most proficient downhill athletes, who are baffled by the bumps. Techniques that work well on groomed trails do not work at all in moguls. Half of a skier's score in moguls is based on the technical quality of his turns and skiing, a quarter is based on his jumps, and the remaining quarter on elapsed time. Mogul skiers, who call themselves "bumpers," are a special breed. You need confidence to make a run, and Bloom had plenty of that.

In addition to his proficiency in moguls, Bloom was a premier freestyle skier. This aspect of the sport is equal parts skiing, gymnastics, and hot-dogging. To do his 720 Iron Cross, for example, Bloom rotates 720 degrees in the air off an upright launch with his skis crossed. His D-Spin 720 Iron Cross requires a single inverted backflip and two spins with his skis crossed. It is not for the faint of heart.

Bloom possessed an unusually diverse array of talents. He earned a black belt in karate at age 12. He was an aspiring actor and model who was an advertiser's dream, handsome and muscular. That was fortunate because travel and training costs for professional skiers at Bloom's level of competition can reach $100,000 a year. Bloom was Tommy Hilfiger's featured model for fall 2002 and other endorsements and advertisements followed soon thereafter.

Bloom's real dream, however, did not reside on the slopes. Although he was only five foot nine inches tall and weighed 170 pounds, he wanted to play football for the University of Colorado (known in the Centennial State as CU rather than UC, for no known reason). In high school in Loveland, Bloom was the star receiver on a state championship football team — he had 1,116 receiving yards in his senior year. (He also ran the forty-yard dash in 4.3 seconds.) Despite his enormous success in skiing, Bloom had his heart set on football at CU. Ultimately, he hoped to play that sport professionally.

Playing end for the University of Colorado, Bloom would be an amateur under NCAA rules, like all college football players. As a skier, Bloom was a professional, winning prizes and gathering endorsements. Under NCAA regulations, an athlete may maintain his amateur eligibility in one sport while working as a professional in another. In fact, there is one specific

NCAA bylaw authorizing the two-sport rule and another specifically allowing Olympic athletes to maintain their amateur status, even though such athletes can receive a $25,000 reward for winning a gold medal and other non-monetary benefits, including clothing and equipment. Most commonly, the NCAA two-sport rule has been applied to college basketball players who played professional minor league baseball during the summer months, as Danny Ainge did in the 1970s. (Ainge made it to the majors with the Toronto Blue Jays while still playing basketball in college.)

Professional skiers, however, are not members of organized teams or clubs; they receive most of their income from sponsors (through endorsements), rather than as salaried employees. Bloom's endorsement income allowed him to continue to participate in international skiing competitions, but it would keep him from playing college football.

The NCAA flatly prohibited this two-sport athlete from accepting endorsement income while maintaining his amateur status. The University of Colorado, on behalf of Bloom, requested a waiver of this rule, which would have allowed Bloom to continue to compete for the Buffaloes on the football field. It stated in its NCAA appeal:

> Jeremy Bloom is the top-rated mogul skier on the World Cup tour this year. He currently has a handful of endorsement deals, but receives no salary and very little help with training expenses. Competitive skiing is an expensive sport, which is not entirely supported financially by the [United States Olympic Committee]. Endorsements received by a skier are the athlete's salary. Jeremy's living, training, and day-to-day expenses are paid by the money he receives from these endorsements. . . . To lose his skiing endorsement revenue would severely cripple Jeremy's attempts to remain competitive in mogul skiing.

The NCAA denied the requested waiver. Bloom's endorsements would bar him from playing as an amateur for the University of Colorado. The association's reasoning was quite doctrinaire. Accepting *any* endorsement money, as opposed to straight pay, would result in the "commercial exploitation" of the student athlete.

The Bloom appeal came to the NCAA long after Walter Byers had retired as executive director. In his book, however, Byers states that in 1985 he suggested to the NCAA Council and Executive Committee that it abolish this rule and allow student-athletes to endorse products. Their income would be placed in a trust fund until the student graduated or completed his eligibility. Byers argued that "the athletes deserved the same access to the free market as the coaches enjoyed." The NCAA's rule was an "artificial restraint on individual rights" that simply maximized the commercial opportunities of the colleges and exploited the athlete. Athletes should be entitled "to use their name and reputation for financial gain." Byers concluded that the rule "protecting young people from commercial evils [was] a transparent excuse for monopoly operations that benefit others." The association did not accept Byers' recommendation.

The University of Colorado, of course, could sell tickets to the public who would come to watch Bloom play. Boosted by Bloom's performance, CU could commercially endorse athletic equipment. CU could employ pictures of Bloom using that equipment in its commercial promotions. The NCAA itself could use Bloom's picture to promote a NCAA championship. Bloom's football uniform could be adorned by the Nike "swoosh" as part of the university's one-million-dollar-a-year contract with the equipment manufacturer. None of this violated NCAA rules nor, apparently, did it "commercially exploit" the amateur athlete.

All Bloom had to do in order to play CU football for no salary was to give up his skiing endorsements, his work as a model, and his real potential as a professionally paid actor. As Walter Byers writes: "This is not about amateurism. This has to do with who controls the negotiations and gets the money." Years later, in 2009, the NCAA would open an on-line photo store, selling images of college athletes. Under the NCAA regime, colleges and the association are in control, and they cut the pie for themselves.

Although Jeremy Bloom stated publicly that he didn't want the NCAA to be "mad" at him, he sued the NCAA in the Colorado state courts, seeking an injunction against its absurd rule. That made the NCAA mad at him.

In his petition to the court, Bloom sought a declaration that the NCAA's denial of his university's request for a waiver interfered with his "pre-NCAA" professions. His endorsements had preceded his matriculation at the Boulder school, and they had nothing to do with his amateur football participation at CU. Bloom argued that the contractual membership relationship between the University of Colorado and the NCAA was designed to benefit student-athletes such as himself, and thus he claimed to be a "third-party" beneficiary of that membership contract. The suit claimed that the NCAA's arbitrary and capricious rule, instead of producing a benefit for the athlete, denied Bloom a right that all non-student-athletes possess: the right to endorse commercial products.

The NCAA responded that its rules were not intended to benefit athletes, but rather were designed "to create a system of fairness and accountability among member institutions." It remarked quite candidly that Bloom and other athletes were not the "intended beneficiary" of those rules. Ignoring the reality of the collegiate sports business, the NCAA explained that education, rather than commerce, was its primary goal and athletics were simply a "recreational pursuit." If Bloom could object to any particular NCAA bylaws, the association argued, this would "usurp" the NCAA's authority, and "the organization would be fraught with frustration at every turn and would flounder in the waters of impotence and debility." If Bloom wanted to play college football, he would have to stop making paid appearances and endorsing products, and defer his dreams of television stardom until after his college career was over.

In a brief in support of Bloom's request for a preliminary injunction, his counsel laid out the basic irrationality of the NCAA's rules:

> The appearance, name, picture and filmed performances of amateur student athletes in their amateur sport and on coaches shows directly related to their amateur sport can be used for pay and to endorse, advertise, recommend and promote products, including products generated by the NCAA. Jeremy's performance of these activities *outside of college football* and unrelated to college football, cannot possibly provide a reason to cancel his amateur status *in football*.

In a deposition taken July 31, 2002, by the NCAA, Bloom said: "I don't understand why the NCAA is doing this." His football coach at CU had been fully supportive of his efforts to continue skiing while playing Division I-A football, and promised that the team would "work around" his skiing schedule. Bloom had turned down an offer to host a national cable television show so he could train for the upcoming football season. He gave motivational speeches to youngsters telling them to dream big: "Follow your dreams and don't let anyone get in your way, because there's going to be tons of roadblocks ahead. [Believe] in yourself." Bloom had managed to heed his own advice — until he ran head-first into the NCAA.

After a two-day hearing on Bloom's petition, Boulder County District Judge Daniel Hale denied Bloom's request for a preliminary injunction against the NCAA on August 15, 2002. The association had argued that its regulations were necessary "in order to assure proper emphasis on educational objectives." The court, the NCAA urged, "cannot rewrite the regulations of a voluntary organization." The court agreed, ruling that the NCAA was justly enforcing its by-laws when it denied Bloom permission to play college football and that those rules are "rationally related" to the NCAA's mission of protecting amateurism. The association was simply "implementing" the terms of the membership contract between the NCAA and the University of Colorado. Bloom appealed to the Colorado Court of Appeals.

The Colorado Court of Appeals sits in a modern building at the end of the Sixteenth Street pedestrian walkway in Denver. The court has seven judges and hears appeals in panels of three judges, assigned at random. Judge John Daniel Dailey, writing for a unanimous panel, would ultimately deny Bloom's claim. But a close examination of his reasoning reveals some interesting contradictions.

First, the panel had to address the issue of whether Bloom could actually sue the NCAA, what is called "standing" in the law. He was not a member of the NCAA — only schools and conferences can be members — and he had no contractual relationship with it. But his university was a member, and Bloom claimed to be a "third-party beneficiary" of that relationship. The court stated the prevailing rule:

> A person not a party to an express contract may bring an action on the contract if the parties to the agreement intended to benefit the nonparty, provided that the benefit claimed is a direct and not merely incidental benefit of the contract. While the intent to benefit the nonparty need not be expressly recited in the contract, the intent must be apparent from the terms of the agreement, the surrounding circumstances, or both.

The court found that the NCAA constitution, by-laws, and regulations were clearly intended to benefit student-athletes. In this case, therefore, the NCAA could be held to its stated purpose, even though by its actions it might not, in fact, have benefited student-athletes. Bloom could sue, seeking an injunction against the association and claiming that the application of its eligibility rules was arbitrary and capricious. Prevailing on this important but preliminary issue would turn out to be a pyrrhic victory for Bloom, but the decision might prove helpful to other college athletes who claim to have been treated unfairly by the association.

Bloom argued that NCAA Bylaw 12.1.2 allows an athlete to "get paid" in one professional sport and maintain his amateur eligibility in another sport. What he sought was the right to earn the "customary income" of his professional sport: skiing. Professional skiers, like professional golfers and tennis players, are normally and customarily compensated by endorsement income. To prohibit this income — or penalize its recipients by banning athletes from NCAA eligibility in another collegiate sport — draws a bizarre and unreasonable distinction between sports. Could the NCAA really have meant to allow a college basketball player to play professional baseball, but not to engage in professional skiing?

The NCAA, however, did not ban Bloom from college football because he earned income from engaging in a professional sport. That is expressly allowed under Bylaw 12.1.2, which states that "[a] professional athlete in one sport may represent a member institution in a different sport." NCAA Bylaw 12.5.2.1, on the other hand, clearly bans "any remuneration . . . to advertise, recommend or promote directly the sale or use of a commercial product or service of any kind." Endorsements were prohibited, unless "the individual became involved in such activities for reasons independent of athletics ability." (Bloom was approached about the endorsements because of his ability in athletics.) But why would the NCAA ban such pay, especially because that is the way that professional skiers are customarily paid? The court of appeals did not inquire.

The court explained that the NCAA rule was simple and straightforward: if a college athlete does endorsements of any kind, he or she cannot be an amateur athlete eligible under NCAA regulations. The court said that it examined whether the NCAA's bylaws were "rationally related" to the purpose sought to be obtained — maintaining amateurism and "educating the whole person." Repeating the NCAA's argument, the court stated that the association sought to avoid the "commercial exploitation" of college athletes. To achieve that goal, the court reasoned, the NCAA needed a blanket rule to cover *all* situations, as opposed to a rule precisely tailored to a skier's circumstances. The NCAA had similar restrictions regarding paid internships and externships. While amateur athletes were allowed to take unpaid internships, paid activities — other than direct pay from playing another sport—were strictly prohibited. The NCAA's purpose was to demarcate a clear and enforceable line between professional and amateur athletes. Judge Dailey emphasized that courts normally give great deference to the decisions of voluntary private associations, such as the NCAA, taken here pursuant to its goal to protect amateurism. The court clearly was not prepared to set aside the NCAA's ruling.

In a case like Jeremy Bloom's, the NCAA's approach to commercial activities is based on the assumption that athletes will be exploited by others because of their athletic prowess. The University of Colorado could commercially exploit Bloom for his athletic prowess by selling T-shirts with his likeness and videotapes of his football exploits. Bloom, however, could not make paid appearances for Tommy Hilfiger, nor could he endorse skiing equipment. What is the difference between receiving pay directly for success in skiing competition or indirectly, from the positive image that is created by success in skiing competition? No satisfactory explanation was ever offered in court, but none apparently was required.

The Colorado Court of Appeals showed great deference to the NCAA in denying Bloom's request for relief, much as most courts would in reviewing decisions of voluntary private associations, especially those of the stature of the association. As Walter Byers appreciated, if there was to be any relief for athletes like Jeremy Bloom, it would have to come through changes in the way that the NCAA regulated two-sport athletes, a prospect that seems unlikely.

The no-endorsements rule is a perfect example of the cartel at work. The value of the commercial exploitation of players by member schools would be substantially reduced if student-athletes could market themselves. Many college football and basketball players could command substantial payments in the free market in exchange for their product endorsements. The only way to effectively protect their member schools' exclusive option on endorsements is to prohibit the players' freedom across the board. It is irrational to expect that colleges and universities would voluntarily abolish a rule designed to protect them from competition from their own student-athletes. As the NCAA "Principle of Amateurism" states:

> Student-athletes shall be amateurs in an intercollegiate sport, and their participation should be motivated primarily by education and by the physical, mental and social benefits to be derived. Student participa-

tion in intercollegiate athletics is an avocation, and student-athletes should be protected from exploitation by professional and commercial enterprises.

This is just the kind of American myth that courts adore.

THE NEXT RACE

In order to fulfill his lifelong dream to play college football (and while his appeal was pending in the Colorado courts), Jeremy Bloom gave up his endorsement deals. In his first game against Colorado State, he returned a punt seventy-five yards for a touchdown. He set a school record with a ninety-four-yard touchdown reception against Kansas State. In total, he scored five touchdowns on plays of seventy-five yards or more. Eight days after Bloom returned a punt for a score against Oklahoma in the December 7, 2002, Big 12 title game, he flew to Ruka, Finland, to ski in his first World Cup moguls competition of the season—and without endorsement income. His family covered the cost of his travel and participation. He returned to the States in time to participate in Colorado's contest against Wisconsin in the Alamo Bowl. (Colorado lost in overtime 31–28.)

In an op-ed column in the *New York Times* on August 1, 2003, Bloom explained how the NCAA "limits the opportunities of the . . . student-athletes it purports to serve." He laid out his case against the association and proposed a "Student-Athlete's Bill of Rights." The NCAA was not moved to reform, however. Bloom's effort went nowhere. As he told the *Times* in January 2005: "Chasing dreams can be complicated, but worth it."

After two seasons playing college football, Bloom returned full time to international mogul skiing (with his endorsements) and prevailed once again in the World Cup mogul championship, winning a remarkable six events in a row. He also appeared on the cover of the Abercrombie & Fitch Christmas catalogue. Bloom missed college football, but reasoned that "I will always have those memories. Now I just have to make some new ones." He painted his skiing helmet Colorado gold, with the Buffaloes emblem and his number 15. He told *Sports Illustrated*: "Football, for me, is unfinished business. It was taken away from me."

Within days after competing, but not medaling, in the 2006 Turin Olympics (one mistake cost him a gold), Bloom participated in the National Football League scouting combine, demonstrating his speed and skills for the assembled representatives of the NFL clubs. Although he had not played football in twenty-seven months, Bloom was drafted in the fifth round, number 147 overall, by the Philadelphia Eagles. Once again he prepared to pursue his gridiron dream, this time without the NCAA hanging over his head. He injured a hamstring in summer practice, however, and the Eagles placed him on injured reserve when he missed most of camp. After his release by the Eagles in the following season, the Pittsburgh Steelers signed Bloom in January 2008 to their practice squad. By the end of that year Bloom had returned to skiing, joining the 2009 U.S. freestyle team.

Jeremy Bloom's case established the precedent that athletes can sue the NCAA as third-party beneficiaries of the contract between their institutions and the national organization. This is an important first step into court, where fundamental rights and basic fairness might find protection, even if not in the Colorado Court of Appeals.

CHAPTER 5

SPORTS ARBITRATION AND
ENFORCING PROMISES

I'm tired of hearing about money, money, money, money, money.
I just want to play the game, drink Pepsi, and wear Reeboks.

SHAQUILLE O'NEAL

* * * Some sports commentators say that professional basketball players are the world's finest athletes. Only a few men make it to the pinnacle of the sport, the National Basketball Association, although many more play in professional leagues around the world. For them the game can be quite lucrative, even without adding in their endorsement income. These tall, agile, and fleet-footed denizens of the court play a game of modest origins. Basketball was invented in the winter of 1891 at a school for Presbyterian missionaries held at the YMCA in Springfield, Massachusetts. The creative Canadian-born instructor, Dr. James Naismith, was instructed to develop an athletic "distraction" that would amuse the physical education students during the dreary months of a New England winter. The activity was to offer the opportunity for vigorous exercise, for men bored with exercises, without indulging in violent contact. From such humble (and perhaps naïve) beginnings, the game grew nationally and internationally. The first game was played on January 20, 1892; by that fall it had spread across the country, played by men and women alike. (Naismith married Maude Sherman of Springfield, the first woman to play the game.) Within a year YMCA missionaries had spread the game worldwide. Basketball is now the world's second most popular sport (after soccer) and is played in virtually every country in the world.

The game has evolved into an improvisational masterpiece, with set plays on offense and defense combined with impromptu variations spurred by individual athletic excellence. Like football, it is a team sport with pre-established arrangements of play, but basketball's development in the latter half of the twentieth century has allowed for the intricate collaborations of jazz. Players adjust to the circumstances, harmonize their playing styles, and perform balletic spectacles with elegance and ease.

Basketball has become an inner-city playground pastime and a suburban gymnasium passion for millions of boys and girls. For a few entrepreneurs, basketball has also become a prosperous business. It is the favorite participation sport of many adult males, including President Barack Obama, who has a basketball court at the White House. As might be expected, the money generated by the business of basketball has often fostered dis-

previous page
After Brian Shaw's contractual obligations to the Boston Celtics were enforced in labor arbitration, the club traded Shaw to the Miami Heat.
AP Photo / Jeffrey Boan

putes between players and clubs. Although courts have been used on occasion, many of those disputes are resolved using the procedures of labor arbitration.

The professional game prospered when it produced player and club rivalries that captured the public's attention. In the 1960s, the face-off between two big men — Bill Russell and Wilt Chamberlain — became its own show within the overall drama of the game. And an entire generation of fans watched the Boston Celtics and the Los Angeles Lakers battle for NBA supremacy. In the 1990s, Michael Jordan's Chicago Bulls bested all comers. None could reach Jordan's level of excellence, even the Lakers' Ervin "Magic" Johnson and the Celtics' Larry Bird. Some of the conflicts in basketball's boardrooms were equally contested, and examining one of those disputes will demonstrate how participants in the business of basketball turned to neutral outsiders to resolve their differences.

THE PROTAGONIST: BRIAN SHAW

Brian Shaw was one of the fortunate few athletes who were able to graduate from the schoolyard game to the highest professional ranks. He grew up in blue-collar Oakland, California, the first of a series of all-star professional basketball players groomed on the east side of San Francisco Bay, including Antonio Davis, Jason Kidd, and Gary Payton. From an early age, Shaw showed unique talent on the basketball court. As a student at Bishop O'Dowd High School, Shaw excelled in class as well. Because he was not recruited by the Division I college basketball powerhouses, Shaw spent his freshman and sophomore years at St. Mary's College in Moraga, California, fifteen miles east of Oakland. He then transferred to the University of California in Santa Barbara for his junior and senior years. While playing for the Gauchos, Shaw received the press coverage that would bring him to the attention of professional scouts. During his senior year, he was named the 1988 Pacific Coast Athletic Association player of the year. Shaw would play fourteen seasons in the National Basketball Association and, after his playing days were over, would continue in the game as an assistant coach for the Los Angeles Lakers.

The Boston Celtics selected Brian Shaw in the first round of the 1988 NBA draft with the twenty-fourth overall pick. During the preseason, the Celtics traveled to Europe to play in a tournament, and the players were allowed to bring one guest. Others brought wives or girlfriends, but Shaw brought his mother, a touch that endeared him to Celtics' patriarch Red Auerbach. The six foot six inch tall rookie guard immediately showed leadership on the court, feeding the ball to his more famous teammates: Dennis Johnson, Danny Ainge, Kevin McHale, Larry Bird, and Robert Parish. Shaw played in all eighty-two games of the 1988–89 season, the only member of the squad to do so, and averaged 8.6 points and 5.8 assists a game. He earned a modest NBA minimum salary of $75,000. The Celtics finished third in the division and were eliminated by the Detroit Pistons in the first round of the playoffs. Shaw's individual performance was recognized when he was named to the NBA's all-rookie second team.

The Celtics offered Shaw $550,000 to play the 1989–90 season in Boston. However, Shaw's Los Angeles–based agent, Leonard Armato, had other ideas. While Shaw was bound by the league's reserve system to play for the Celtics if he stayed in the NBA, Armato steered his client toward a more lucrative contract in the Italian Basketball League. The Celtics were not prepared to participate in an international bidding war for the young star. General manager Jan Volk said with disdain: "Brian better brush up on his Italian." It was a significant blunder to underestimate Shaw's threat to head to the Continent to play ball.

On August 10, 1989, Shaw signed a two-year contract with Rome's new Il Messaggero club, for what was reported to be a million dollars a season. The Celtics' Volk was quoted as saying: "In Shaw's case, we have no regrets about the offer we made. If the numbers being reported are correct, we couldn't compete against them."

In the same year, the Rome club also signed Duke University's glamorous forward Danny Ferry—for two million dollars a season. The Italian league, Lega Basket Serie A, was founded in 1920 and had long reigned as Europe's premier association of clubs. Over-the-hill veterans like Bob Mc-Adoo, Tom McMillan, Darryl Dawkins, and Micheal Ray Richardson had found new life on the Italian courts. The Shaw and Ferry signings, however, were the first time that the league had attracted talented young American players, although Bill Bradley played a season with the Milan club while studying at Oxford in the 1960s.

Shaw tried to make a graceful exit from Boston: "I feel that the Celtics organization is a great organization. I would like to remain in Boston. I love the fans, and I love all the people I met and have been associated with. There's no need for me to be embarrassed. I'm doing what I have to do." It was reported that Celtics president Red Auerbach was "steamed." He could not countenance anyone turning his back on him or the Celtics' Green, even for almost double the salary. He knew that the Celtics prevailed on the court because they played the game as a team: how could Shaw abandon the family?

THE LEGEND: RED AUERBACH

Arnold Jacob "Red" Auerbach was the NBA's greatest coach. When he joined the wretched Boston Celtics franchise in 1950, the club had never had a winning season. Auerbach retired as Celtics coach in 1966. During his seventeen years at the helm, the Celtics never had a losing season.

Born in the Williamsburg section of Brooklyn to Jewish immigrant parents, Red was drawn to athletics, although he lacked the playing skills of his charges in Boston. (Under Auerbach's tutelage, Ed Macauley, Bill Russell, Bob Cousy, John Havlicek, Tommy Heinsohn, Bill Sharman, Frank Ramsay, Sam Jones, and K. C. Jones all became Hall of Fame players.) Auerbach did play some college ball at George Washington University, where he had trained to become a teacher and a coach. On the parquet floor of the Boston Garden, he would use those skills to perfection.

During World War II, Auerbach was assigned to handle all recreational activities at the Navy base in Norfolk, Virginia. It was there that he refined his basketball coaching techniques. He also helped Washington Redskins football players stay in shape during the off-season by playing basketball. Through his Washington connections, Auerbach befriended Mike Uline, one of the founders of the Basketball Association of America, later renamed the National Basketball Association. Uline hired Auerbach to assemble and coach the Washington Caps, one of the eight original clubs in the association. After a detour coaching the Tri-Cities Blackhawks in western Illinois, Auerbach was hired by the owner of the Boston Celtics, Walter Brown, to turn around the Hub's dreadful basketball franchise.

During Red's tenure, the Celtics prospered on the scoreboard and in the standings, but the club was never rich. Lack of resources was always an issue. A child of the Depression, Auerbach spent the club's money carefully. Boston's hockey team, the Bruins, owned the Boston Garden, with the Celtics as their tenants. The Celtics never shared in the income from concessions and parking. Even during the glory years, Celtics attendance was modest—until 1989, when Larry Bird became the mainstay of the club.

Auerbach's innovations, both on and off the court, changed the game. He created the famous "sixth man" strategy that would bring a fresh star off the bench, like John Havlicek, Paul Silas or Kevin McHale, just when opponents were getting tired. He emphasized the psychological facets of the game. As his protégé Bill Russell said: "The idea is not to block every shot. The idea is to make your opponent believe that you might block every shot."

Auerbach's arrogance also was legendary. In the fourth quarter of home games, when the Celtics were safely ahead, he would light a trademark cigar. This "victory cigar" was obnoxious to all but the Celtics faithful. Beginning in 1959, the team won eight straight NBA titles. Exhausted by the pressures of the job, Auerbach finally gave up coaching prior to the 1966 season. He made Bill Russell the Celtic's player-manager, the first African-American to coach a team in a major American professional sport. Auerbach assumed the general manager's position and later served as Celtics president.

For Red Auerbach, being a Celtic was a matter of great pride and intense loyalty. He simply could not understand why Brian Shaw would voluntarily give up that opportunity after one year. This was not supposed to happen with a Celtic.

A PLANNED RETURN ABORTED

Brian Shaw arrived in Rome to great acclaim. He explained: "Being here will make me more rounded as a person. I'll be more worldly as a whole. It's a different culture, and that's the biggest education you can get." Raul Gardini, known as Il Contadino (the peasant farmer), was the money man behind the Ferruzzi Group, which owned the basketball club as well as both of Rome's leading newspapers. He invited Shaw to his Venice palazzo overlooking the Grand Canal. Shaw was duly impressed. He used some of his earnings to buy a BMW and braved the Roman traffic, which he found even more chaotic than Boston's: "All the traffic signals are just suggestions," he told the *New York Times*. Shaw quickly acquired the nickname of Signor Quattro Formaggi for the four cheeses he ordered on every dish.

Within a few months of his arrival in Europe, however, Shaw had second thoughts about his move. Although his level of play on the basketball court did not suffer, Shaw was homesick. In November 1989, Shaw asked Leonard Armato to contact the Celtics about a return to the NBA for the following season. (The Celtics retained exclusive NBA rights to contract with Shaw, under the provisions of the collective bargaining agreement between the NBA and the National Basketball Players Association.) Shaw then took over the negotiations, speaking by telephone with Alan Cohen, a Celtics co-owner and vice chairman and treasurer of the club. Cohen agreed to Shaw's demands for salary and a signing bonus. General Manager Volk called Shaw in Rome to confirm the terms. The Celtics would pay him a $400,000 signing bonus and a salary of $1.1 million for the 1990–91 season; $1.2 million for the 1991–92 season; $1.3 million for the 1992–93 season; and $1.4 million for the 1993–94 season. Volk also suggested that, although the Celtics had loaned Shaw $50,000 during his rookie season, the note should be treated as paid in full and, at the same time, his signing bonus should be increased to $450,000. Volk flew to Rome to have Shaw sign the contract, and Shaw met him at the airport.

On January 26, 1990, Brian Shaw signed that four-year deal with the Boston franchise. He executed the agreement in the presence of the U.S. Consul in Rome and before a notary public. Three weeks later, Shaw received his signing bonus of $450,000. As part of the arrangement, he promised to cancel the second year of his contract with Il Messaggero, which was allowed under the Rome contract in the event of his return to the NBA. Finally, in a provision that would turn out to have critical importance, Shaw agreed that the Celtics could seek to enforce its contract rights by arbitration. NBA Commissioner David Stern approved the Celtics' contract with Shaw. Shaw, it seemed, would once again don the fabled green uniform.

Shaw played out the 1989–90 season with Il Messaggero. He led the team in scoring, rebounding, and assists and was selected for the Italian All-Star Game. He even had time to play a game of H-O-R-S-E with an eleven-year-old kid whose American father, Joe "Jellybean" Bryant, also played professional basketball in Italy. (For years, a young Kobe Bryant claimed that he had beaten Shaw.) In his final game for Rome, Brian Shaw scored forty-six points as the club lost in the playoff quarterfinals. Meanwhile, the Celtics were once again eliminated in the first round of the NBA playoffs.

Sometime after Shaw signed the agreement to return to the NBA, his new agent, W. Jerome Stanley, advised that if he waited an additional season, then the Celtics would no longer hold the exclusive NBA option to sign him. He would become a free agent. As a seasoned player — albeit with Italian seasonings — Shaw would then have the opportunity to substantially increase his salary by seeking competing offers from other NBA clubs. On June 6, 1990, Shaw's counsel informed the Celtics that Shaw would not cancel the second year of his Italian contract. He would not be returning to Boston.

ARBITRAL JUSTICE

Red Auerbach and the Celtics knew that Shaw had agreed in a written contract to return to the team. Shortly after executing the agreement, he had even accepted the signing bonus. Now, as the 1990–91 season approached, he had reneged on his promise. The Celtics wanted the point guard to suit up, but litigating the issue in court would take too much time. In this situation, speed was of the essence. The Celtics wanted Shaw on the basketball court, not in a court of law.

The collective bargaining agreement between the NBA and the National Basketball Players Association sets forth the terms and conditions under which NBA players are to perform their employment. It incorporates a uniform player contract that all players sign and establishes an expedited arbitration procedure to resolve conflicts between clubs and players. The Celtics immediately filed a grievance under that procedure. The matter was quickly set for hearing before Professor Daniel G. Collins, the impartial arbitrator who had been jointly appointed by basketball management and the union to hear these types of matters.

Dan Collins was a highly regarded labor arbitrator. Born in Brooklyn in 1930 and raised in Queens, he received his bachelor's degree in English literature from Hofstra University (which might explain why his arbitration opinions were always so well written). He studied law at New York University Law School, where he served as an editor of the *Law Review*. Collins practiced law with the blue-ribbon firm of Cravath Swaine & Moore before returning to NYU in 1961 as a faculty member. As a neutral arbitrator, he was well respected by both management and labor for his knowledge and fairness.

Although the National Basketball Association and its players association had named Collins their permanent arbitrator for all grievance disputes, his arbitration experience was not limited to the business of sports. For years, he had resolved grievance disputes in the aerospace and auto industries, municipal transit, and the postal service. Collins also handled highly visible disputes involving the Broadway theaters and Actors Equity, which represented actors, dancers, and singers. Collins conducted the arbitration hearing in Brian Shaw's case at the NBA's offices in New York on June 13 and 14, 1990, within days after the Celtics filed their grievance. Shaw did not attend the hearing (he was home in California), although he was informed of his opportunity to appear. His interests were represented by his counsel, Jerome Stanley, but Stanley presented no evidence to rebut the Celtics' case. Attorney John J. McGovern was allowed to attend the hearing to represent the interests of Il Messaggero, Shaw's erstwhile, and perhaps future, employer.

In his opinion resolving the dispute, Collins had to determine whether Shaw was in breach of the contract he had signed with the Celtics in January. Collins explained how the contract had been formed and detailed the mutual promises it contained, including the clause which stated that Shaw had the right to rescind his Il Messaggero contract and "agrees to exercise such right of rescission in the manner and at the time called for by the Il Messaggero Contract." (The Il Messaggero contract allowed him to void his commitment to play a second year in Rome "if the player returns to the United States to play with the NBA.")

Collins quoted at length from a June 6, 1990, letter that Jerome Stanley had written to the Celtics' Alan Cohen. Stanley stated his client was going to remain in Rome "notwithstanding any putative agreement between [Shaw] and the Celtics to the contrary." Stanley attacked the fairness of the process used in reaching that agreement with the ballplayer. Shaw's decision to return to the Celtics, Stanley wrote:

> was made in an atmosphere clearly ill-suited for thoughtful decision making on his part. He was at the time only 23 years old, impressionable, legally unsophisticated, living in a foreign country, and isolated from his family and friends. He was frustrated and overly sensitive to the adverse, misplaced and undeserved Italian press he was receiving. . . . Most importantly, his decision was made without the benefit of counsel or other representatives.

Stanley argued that the Celtics were at fault in not requiring that Shaw have counsel present when the contract was signed. Ultimately, Stanley wrote, Shaw decided to stay in Italy "as an indication of the gratitude he feels for the affection, generosity, confidence and trust displayed towards him by [Il Messaggero] over this past season."

Contrary to Stanley's assertions, the Celtics' witnesses testified that Shaw had access to the services of an agent and a legal advisor in Italy and the contract was signed before the U.S. Consul in Rome, who specifically asked Shaw whether he understood the terms of the contract and was executing it freely. Shaw had indicated that he did understand those terms, and he was executing the contract of his own free will.

Following his analysis of the facts, Collins ruled that the Celtics-Shaw agreement was enforceable. Shaw had promised to play exclusively for the Celtics. By way of remedy, Collins ordered Shaw to comply with his contractual promise, not to play for any club other than the Celtics during the term of his contract, and to exercise his right to cancel the second year of the Rome contract.

Shaw's counsel informed the Celtics that his client would not voluntarily comply with the arbitrator's decision. The next day the Celtics filed suit in Federal District Court in Boston seeking expedited judicial enforcement of the Collins award. Shaw's attorney moved to dismiss the action. Shaw's union, the Players Association, no longer supported the player's position and did not formally participate in the court litigation. In fact, the Players Association advised Shaw to comply with the arbitrator's award.

At a federal court hearing on June 26, 1990, District Court Judge A. David Mazzone ruled from the bench that Collins had the power to decide the Shaw dispute under the terms of the collective bargaining agreement, that the arbitrator's interpretation of Shaw's contract with the Celtics was a plausible, reasonable reading of the contract, and therefore his ultimate award was "valid, enforceable and binding" on Shaw. Mazzone issued an injunction ordering Shaw to terminate his contract with Il Messaggero. Otherwise, the judge stated, the Boston club would be "irreparably harmed." The next day, Shaw's counsel appealed.

The U.S. Court of Appeals for the First Circuit in Boston affirmed the district court's judgment and enforced the arbitrator's award. As Judge (later Supreme Court Justice) Stephen Breyer wrote for the First Circuit, "federal labor law gives arbitrators, not judges, the power to interpret such contracts." Citing from the controlling Supreme Court cases, Breyer emphasized the very limited role courts play in reviewing arbitration awards. Arbitration is an autonomous system established by parties to a collective bargaining agreement, and the courts are not to interfere with the results of that system except in very limited situations.

A NOTABLE NBA CAREER

Brian Shaw played for the Celtics during the 1990–91 season, his best in the NBA. He led the club in assists and averaged almost fourteen points per game. Obviously, his experiences in Italy or in arbitration did not hurt his performance. The Celtics — led by Larry Bird, Kevin McHale, and Robert Parrish — were a much better team than the one Shaw had left, in large measure because of the return of their prodigal point guard. The club made it to the second round of the playoffs before bowing to the Pistons in six games.

The Boston faithful, however, never let Shaw forget that they considered him a traitor and, despite his stellar play, boos rained down from the Garden's upper deck whenever he touched the ball. Apparently, the Celtics brass did not forget their difficulties with Shaw either. Midway through the following season, after playing only seventeen games because of an injured right hamstring, Shaw was traded to the Miami Heat in exchange for disgruntled guard Sherman Douglas. (Coach Chris Ford informed Shaw by leaving a message on his home answering machine.) Celtics Vice President Dave Gavitt commented to the press: "Both clubs feel that a change of scenery is needed for both players, and I think you'll see major contributions from both Brian and Sherman with their new teams. They are quality players and two quality individuals." Without Shaw, the Celtics again made it to the second round of the playoffs, where the club lost to the Cleveland Cavaliers in seven games.

After three seasons in Miami, Shaw signed as a free agent with the Orlando Magic, then moved on to the Golden State Warriors, the Philadelphia 76ers, the Portland Trail Blazers, and finally the Los Angeles Lakers. He won three championship rings with the Lakers in 2000, 2001, and 2002. Shaw retired as an active player following the 2002–2003 season and was appointed an assistant coach with the Lakers in 2004. His fourteen-year career earnings as a player in the NBA totaled over $28 million. In the end, Shaw did not suffer much from being required to fulfill his contractual promises.

ARBITRATION AND SPORTS JUSTICE

As Brian Shaw's case demonstrates, labor arbitration plays a vital role in the private arena of sports justice. Neutral and experienced adjudicators, like arbitrator Daniel Collins (who died of cancer in 2002 at age seventy-one), enforce promises reached by management and labor. The cases they resolve often make headlines because of the fame or notoriety of the disputants. Much like some less visible cases throughout the unionized entertainment industry, all sports disputes involve differences about the application and interpretation of the terms of collective bargaining agreements and individual employment contracts negotiated pursuant to those terms. As we have seen with Brian Shaw's case, under prevailing federal labor law, the authoritative decisions of these arbitrators are not subject to review on the merits in court except in rare circumstances.

Justice for the Celtics resulted from expedited labor arbitration and the quick judicial enforcement of an arbitrator's award. The process reaffirmed the value of promise keeping. All commerce depends upon the sanctity of promises. Contracting parties may not enjoy equal bargaining power; Shaw's rookie contract for $75,000 was the product of the NBA's monopsony, in which a single club—in this case the Celtics—holds the exclusive rights to negotiate with a player it has selected in the draft. Nonetheless, that buyers' cartel is the product of collective bargaining and therefore is exempt from antitrust laws. Players who prove themselves in the game, however, do well financially under the established system of salary determination and free agency.

The business of sports is a collection of contracts, of promises made by parties who seek to benefit from the enterprise. We value those promises, without which business activity would grind to a halt, by offering our society's court system as an available mechanism for enforcing agreements. In many instances, however, the judicial system would not move quickly enough to meet the needs of the parties. In other cases, the knowledge and skills of private neutrals may facilitate the resolution of a particular dispute consistent with the expectations of the parties. Here is where arbitration has proven so valuable in the business of sports.

There is the ever-present risk in the sports business that agents, owners, or clubs will take advantage of players whose athletic skills often far outweigh their business acumen. The Shaw case, however, matched experienced attorneys on both sides of the table. Shaw sought to avoid his promise to the Celtics because it would likely cost him money in the short run. There was no evidence that the Celtics took advantage of him, however. If anything, the Boston club had been punished in the prior season because the great Red Auerbach had misplayed the Celtics' hand, failing to correctly gauge the effect of a new international market for basketball talent and low-balling an offer to Shaw.

When Leonard Armato exercised Shaw's opportunity to play in Europe, he skillfully outmaneuvered Auerbach, who held Shaw's exclusive rights only within the National Basketball Association. It was rare for anyone to beat Red Auerbach. Shaw benefited financially and, in the process, retained the option to negate a second year's employment with Rome — if it served his purposes. Shaw did everything right until, a few months into his European adventure, he signed the agreement to return to the Celtics. Only later was he advised that he had made a bad deal. Had he waited another year, he would have been a free agent and could have negotiated with the many NBA teams that would have competed for his services.

It is not surprising that Brian Shaw only played one more full season with the Celtics. While Auerbach valued quality ballplayers and Shaw certainly fit in that category, it was typical of Red to trade someone who had failed to demonstrate loyalty to the Green. Red had a long memory.

Sports justice does not always bring riches to players or to club owners. It establishes a system of rights and responsibilities that are defined and ascertainable. The Shaw case is a useful example because it demonstrates the role played by a private arbitration mechanism under a collective bargaining agreement. While only courts can ultimately determine and apply constitutional principles and statutory proscriptions, labor arbitrators are better able to read, interpret, and apply the terms of private contracts and their decisions are final and binding.

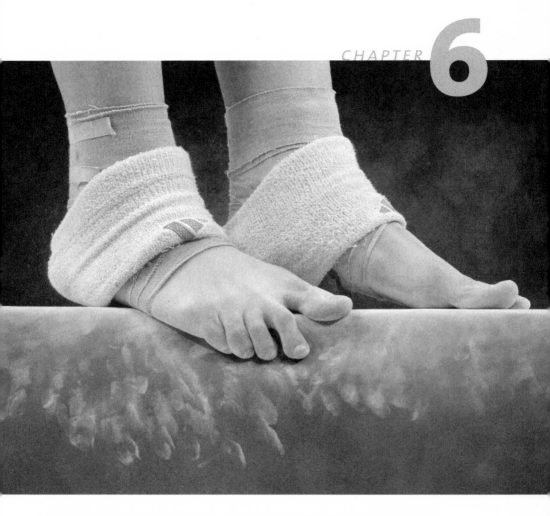

CHAPTER 6

GENDER EQUITY ON THE PARALLEL BARS

TITLE IX AND THE CHANGING VISION
OF AMERICAN SPORTS

The Olympic Games must be reserved for men.
BARON PIERRE DE COUBERTIN, 1912

• • • The emergence of women's collegiate sports at the varsity level has been a significant social phenomenon in the United States. The number of women participating in college sports has increased five-fold since the 1970s. This dramatic increase was the direct consequence of the enactment of Title IX of the Education Amendments of 1972. Under that statute, colleges were required to increase the number of opportunities that women had to participate in varsity sports. Under what economists refer to as "Say's Law," Title IX increased the supply of athletic opportunities which, in turn, created its own demand. In this instance, when colleges offered participation opportunities to women, women chose to participate. As a result, life changed on all college campuses.

In Title IX, Congress sought to outlaw discrimination against women by all educational institutions that receive federal funds. Virtually all colleges and universities are covered by the statute. Although the legislative process that produced the Education Amendments of 1972 had not focused on sports, women's athletics have received the greatest payoff from the legislation. In the years following enactment, the gender equity provisions of the administrative regulations promulgated under Title IX have generated great success, but also great controversy. Sensing that resources for college athletics were a zero-sum game, male college athletes felt shortchanged when women college athletes were promised simple fairness and equity.

Women have been historically marginalized in sports, both professional and amateur. Traditionally, relatively few young girls engaged in sports, and gender stereotypes prevailed in athletics as they did elsewhere in society. With a few notable exceptions, such as Mildred "Babe" Didrikson Zaharias, Hazel Hotchkiss Wightman, Glenna Collett-Vare, and Wilma Rudolph, sportswomen were virtually invisible until the passage of Title IX. In the absence of role models, and as a result of the unwillingness of schools and colleges to provide equal athletic opportunities, American women stayed on the sidelines. As late as 1972, only 30,000 college women participated in athletics. In 2009, there were more than 150,000 college women athletes, and studies report that young girls see women athletes as role models.

previous page
Gymnastic training is known to be difficult, but it can become
even more frustrating when your university abolishes the team.
AP Photo

Brown University, one of the nation's great institutions of higher learning, provoked the most significant challenge to the mandate of Title IX when it announced in 1991 that it was going to abolish its varsity women's gymnastics team. But the members of that team would not accept second-class status. They were furious when the university explained that it would abolish both their team and the women's volleyball team to save $64,000 annually, then about the cost of tuition for four students in a total enrollment of more than 7,000. The demise of these sports was part of a school-wide effort to address a million-dollar operating deficit but, unlike decreases in support services and maintenance, this cost-cutting measure violated the law. It was also an insult.

Instead of accepting the university's edict, the young gymnasts from Brown fought back, clearing the path toward sports justice for all women athletes. They did not accept the insult quietly, and decided to use the legal system to retain their fair share of athletic opportunities — a share guaranteed to them under Title IX. In the process, they gave content to a statutory promise, helping young women everywhere. Seeking gender equity, Amy Cohen, the team's captain, brought suit in federal court.

Gymnastics had always been part of Cohen's life. She had begun training when she was only eight years old, practicing three hours a day, five days a week. In her first year at Brown, her team won the Ivy League championship. The litigation she and her teammates initiated in federal court would be time consuming and expensive. It would last for almost a decade, long after she had graduated and become a public school teacher in New York City.

A SPORT FOR YOUNG GIRLS

Most of our major professional sports are played by men and women in their twenties and thirties. Some sports, like golf, include competitive participants in their forties. College athletes who play football or basketball might star on the national stage when as young as seventeen or eighteen. But by that age, women gymnasts are over the hill. Nearly all gymnasts, like Amy Cohen, begin serious training as children. Those who aspire to achieve international glory know their potential and their limitations by the time they are ten or eleven. Unless they show promise during that short window of time, their opportunities for Olympic glory pass by.

Gymnastics training for young girls is not a story of the healthy pursuit of athletic excellence. While we extol dedication and courage, gymnastic training also can be debilitating for children. Consider *Chalked Up*, the autobiography of Jennifer Sey, the 1986 national champion who left international competition to attend Stanford University. After years of almost day-long training, she put aside the grueling, often self-destructive regime necessary to make the 1988 Olympic team. While athletic ability and commitment were critical to her success, the overriding theme of Sey's story is the constant battle against those who would mold her body in accordance with their vision of excellence. That conflict was symbolized by an obsession with weight. When she passed the hundred-pound mark, her continued participation in the sport depended on the abuse of laxatives. Tears accompanied every failure, and there were many along the way (not to mention broken bones).

Many gymnasts reach the apex of their careers in their early teens. Romanian Nadia Comaneci was only fourteen when she achieved Olympic gold and lasting fame with her 10.0 scores. Early on, gymnasts learn how to win praise from their coaches rather than face their violent wrath. Driven, afraid, ambitious, competitive, stressed, disciplined, graceful, vain, self-centered, self-loathing, and hyper-critical, young gymnasts are weeded out through a system of clubs and gyms, falling by the wayside as they grow up, with only a few making it to the elite level. By fourth grade, gymnasts typically train four hours a day, five or six days a week. As they progress, they spend even more time in the gym, demonstrating their ability, their determination, and their willingness to accept pain and criticism—which is often harshly administered. A sport that begins as fun for a young girl becomes a humorless obsession that can destroy families and leave bodies and minds scarred for life. Fear becomes the motivating factor, fear of a despotic coach's reaction, what Jennifer Sey called a "dark tunnel." The psyche and the body can only take so much abuse, much of it self-administered. Even the best gymnasts who compete on the international level normally retire by age eighteen. But that is not the case with college gymnasts, who either went through the training regimen and fell short or chose not to give up their teenage years in exchange for glory.

Gymnastics—or, more precisely, artistic gymnastics—traces its origin back to ancient Greece, China, and India. It was introduced in American schools in the nineteenth century, exclusively as a male sport. The first modern Olympics in 1896 featured men's horizontal bar, parallel bars, pommel horse, rings, and vault. Women's events were added in 1928. Although young men continue to train in the sport, it has become substantially more popular for young women, with over four million American girls participating annually on the vault, the uneven bars, the balance beam, and the floor exercise. When done well, gymnasts fly through double backflips on the floor, demonstrate daring release moves on the uneven bars, and complete full-twisting Tsukaharas on the vault.

The women on the Brown gymnastics team were not elite gymnasts, although they were great college athletes. At some point in their youth, they dropped out of (or were excluded from) the race for Olympic gold. They had not lost their love for the sport, however. Each came to Brown, at least in part, to participate in the healthy challenge of artistic gymnastics, until the university pulled the mat from under them.

THE HISTORY OF WOMEN'S SPORTS

The mass industrialization of America in the nineteenth century created a modest amount of leisure time for working men, and they pursued athletic exercise as a way to stay fit. But the prevailing cultural norm in favor of exercise did not extend to women. God, it was thought, had made women's bodies too fragile to withstand the rigors of athletics. Therefore, organized athletic games were almost exclusively a male preserve.

Few men or women agreed with the radical ideas of Mabel Lee, a pioneering advocate of physical fitness for women from the 1920s until her death at age ninety-nine in 1985. Trained at the Boston Normal School of Gymnastics, now part of Wellesley College, Lee promoted universal exercise for women. Women's health was a critical element in "worthy citizenship," she said in a speech in 1929. But the Victorian ideal of sheltered and home-bound women, a leftover from the nineteenth century, kept athletics a male prerogative through much of the twentieth century.

When organized sports first developed on college campuses, few women attended institutions of higher learning, with notable exceptions such as Oberlin and all-women colleges such as Mount Holyoke and Elmira College. As mentioned in previous chapters, team sports began as contests between student clubs; at institutions that were exclusively male, sporting clubs also were exclusively male. Teddy Roosevelt, the self-styled model of the strenuous life, promoted sports as an arena to demonstrate "manliness." Women, on the other hand, were to be protected lest their daintiness be soiled by perspiration. In the nineteenth century, sports were perceived as a threat to women's health and femininity.

Women's colleges did offer their students opportunities for modest exercise. These activities were held well out of the sight of men. With informal "play days" and "sports days," these colleges developed a model for intramural and intercollegiate exercise that emphasized participation and rejected the increasingly commercialized and competitive model of male sports. For collegiate women, exercise and good health were the primary objectives, rather than the triumph over rival institutions that motivated their male counterparts. Such exercise, however, would only be done in moderation. Bulging muscles were characteristic of lower-class, working women. College students would exercise just enough to stay fit. There was also the prevailing myth that too much exercise would cause a woman's uterus to detach.

THE HISTORY OF TITLE IX

In the 1960s and 1970s, Congress was presented with the opportunity to determine whether discrimination based on race, national origin, age, and gender was consistent with American values. Since the founding of the country, we had relegated almost three-quarters of the population to diminished legal status. American mythology contained many praiseworthy archetypes — the Pilgrims who braved the seas in a small ship seeking religious freedom, the courageous frontiersmen and young families in wagon trains heading west, and the freedom fighters called to rescue Europeans from tyranny. America was also built on a portfolio of false and degrading stereotypes: persons with dark skins stolen from their African homelands were capable only of serving as slaves; women were fit only to serve their men; immigrants (at least after the first wave of white, Anglo-Saxon Protestant settlers) were dangerous and strange additions to the landscape. America was the land of the free and the home of the brave, but only for those white males who owned property and could afford to be brave.

During a single decade of transformative civil rights legislation, Congress finally decided to fulfill America's promise to all of its inhabitants. Discrimination as a national policy was foolish, odious, and un-American. It now would also be illegal.

In Title IX of the Education Amendments of 1972, Congress banned gender discrimination in educational programs receiving federal funds. The statute had but thirty-seven words: "No person in the United States shall, on the basis of sex, be excluded from participation in, be denied the benefits of, or be subjected to discrimination under any education program or activity receiving Federal financial assistance." Although not the central concern of the legislators, student athletic programs would prove to be the battleground for the college gender wars.

The legislation was sponsored by Congresswoman Edith Green of Oregon and Senator Birch Bayh of Indiana. The broad language used in the statute was designed primarily to eliminate employment discrimination against women at educational institutions. Adopting the strategy used in the other civil rights legislation, the non-discrimination precept of Title IX was tied to an institution's receipt of federal money. Based on the statute's legislative history, it is apparent that Congress did not focus on athletic opportunities. In fact, sports were mentioned only twice in the legislative proceedings. Nonetheless, the National Collegiate Athletic Association immediately saw the danger lurking in the legislation. It was more than a matter of money, although that was significant. It constituted a challenge to male dominance of college sports, an alarming threat to male pride and power. As Walter Byers, longtime executive director of the NCAA, writes in *Unsportsmanlike Conduct*, Title IX was payback legislation and "women sports leaders decided to get their share."

The threat of gender equity was felt throughout the educational system. After the Indiana Supreme Court ruled that high school girls had the right to participate in previously all-male, non-contact sports such as tennis, golf, swimming, and track, Charles Maas of the Indiana State Coaches Association bemoaned the alarming impact: "There is the possibility that a boy would be beaten by a girl and as a result be ashamed to face his family and friends. I wonder if anybody has stopped to think what that could do to a young boy." Many athletic administrators were openly hostile toward any law that could so change the natural order of things. More generally, traditionalists were concerned that changes in the athletic system could lead to changes in society as well.

Not all men saw Title IX as Armageddon. David Auxter, an academic, former collegiate football player, and coach, stated the opposing view:

In America we use athletics extensively to teach . . . attitudes. Above all, we value athletics because they are competitive. That is, they teach that achievement and success are desirable, that they are worth disciplining one's self for. By keeping girls out of sports, we have denied them this educational experience. Our male-dominated society prefers females to be physically and psychologically dependent. Denying them athletic opportunities has been a good way of molding girls into the kind of humans we want them to be. Better athletic programs will develop more aggressive females, women with confidence who value personal achievement and have a strong sense of identity. I think that would be a good thing for us all.

Women appreciated the revolutionary nature of Congress's action. University of Wisconsin Professor Kathryn Clarenbach, a founder of modern feminism and the first chairperson of the National Organization for Women, stated it plainly:

The overemphasis on protecting girls from strain or injury, and underemphasis on developing skills and experiencing teamwork, fits neatly into the pattern of the second sex. Girls are the spectators and the cheerleaders. They organize the pep clubs, sell pompons, make cute, abbreviated costumes, strut a bit between halves and idolize the current football hero. This is perfect preparation for the adult role of women — to stand decoratively on the sidelines of history and cheer on the men who make the decisions. Women who have had the regular experience of performing before others, of learning to win and to lose, of cooperating in team efforts, will be far less fearful of running for office, better able to take public positions on issues in the face of public opposition. By working toward some balance in the realm of physical activity, we may indeed begin to achieve a more wholesome, democratic balance in all phases of our life.

THE REGULATORY PROCESS

Congress charged the Department of Health, Education, and Welfare with drafting regulations that would guide covered institutions toward voluntary compliance with the new statute. As athletic directors around the country panicked at the thought of parity, the NCAA heavily lobbied the agency to avoid the "financial lunacy" of gender equity: "The men and the NCAA itself didn't discriminate against women. Women's athletics leaders discriminated against themselves through the years by refusing to accept competitive athletics as a proper pursuit for teenage women." The NCAA understood that in the absence of manna from heaven, the money for women's athletics would come out of the men's athletic budgets.

Although the association did not prevail in its effort to gut Title IX in the legislative and regulatory process, it was able to modify the regulations to avoid nurturing the preexisting norm in women's collegiate athletics — of participatory, non-competitive, and healthy exercise. If women were going to play, it would be by the men's rules. Under Title IX, women's sports would be steered toward adopting the prevailing men's commercial and competitive model, including rewarding athletes with scholarships. Any thought that women's sports could follow a model that emphasized healthy participation rather than competition was lost in the process of achieving gender equity.

The NCAA did not easily accept any legislative intrusion into its domain. Throughout the early years of Title IX, the association fought gender equity using all the tools at its disposal, showing genuine contempt for women's sports in the process. Byers spoke of the "impending doom" in intercollegiate athletics if revenue-producing sports were not exempt from Title IX. He was openly belligerent and stubbornly unyielding. He sought out allies in Congress and found prominent spokesmen for his point of view. Senator John Tower of Texas, for example, sought to protect the unique status of football and men's basketball by proposing an amendment to Title IX that would have exempted "revenue-producing sports" from the reach of the provision. Perhaps Tower was concerned that Coach Darrell Royal of the University of Texas would otherwise have to share his football profits with the Longhorn women, who had a total budget allocation in 1973 of $9,000. Ultimately, Tower's proposed proviso failed in conference committee. Instead, Congress advised the agency applying Title IX to include in its regulations only "reasonable provisions concerning the nature of particular sports."

Having lost the battle against congressional and administrative regulation, Byers returned to his theme of the catastrophe that lay ahead: "Impending doom is around the corner if these regulations are implemented." In order to prevent gender equity, the NCAA fought the implementation of Title IX in the courts. That strategy also proved unavailing. The association next turned to controlling the field of women's amateur sports. If there were going to be big-time women's sports, the NCAA would run them. It undermined an established rival organization, the Association for Inter-collegiate Athletics for Women, which the NCAA thought had the audacity to want women to control women's sports in order to avoid the "unsavory practices" of men's sports. Byers ridiculed the efforts of the AIAW to value the "social benefits to be gained from sports." And others in the NCAA made no secret of its intentions. Then secretary-treasurer James Frank said, "I don't think there's any question it would be favorable for an individual in-stitution to have a single organization governing men's and women's athlet-ics to deal with." That "single organization" would, of course, be the NCAA.

The AIAW sponsored women's championships in basketball, golf, gym-nastics, swimming, track, and volleyball. To the great distress of the AIAW, the NCAA began scheduling women's events in direct competition with AIAW events in 1981, and paid traveling expenses for women from AIAW schools to attend the NCAA championships. Using its abundant financial resources, monopoly power, and television contacts, the NCAA achieved total control of the college sports market. The AIAW sued the NCAA, claim-ing an antitrust violation, but lost. When a few leading women sports administrators defected to the NCAA, and women were guaranteed repre-sentation on NCAA committees, the die was cast. The NCAA swallowed the Association for Intercollegiate Athletics for Women, and imposed the male commercial model on women's collegiate sports.

Accepting the reality that women had equal rights, at least with regard to college sports, the NCAA made sure that the development of women's sports would follow the path it had paved for men's sports. Required to al-locate a fair share of financial resources to women's sports, colleges com-peted to attract the best athletes in an effort to assemble teams that would prevail over rival institutions. With that macho competition in women's sports came the inevitable violations of NCAA rules, in particular regarding the recruitment of women basketball players.

TWO STEPS FORWARD, ONE STEP BACKWARD ON GENDER EQUITY

Even as federal agencies were making their way through the imple-mentation process, Title IX had an immediate and dramatic impact on women's sports participation. Many colleges voluntarily reviewed their sports programs and upgraded opportunities for women students. In 1973–74, the University of Washington spent $18,000 (or 0.7 percent of its $2.6 million athletic budget) on women's varsity athletics. Its 1974–75 women's budget increased to $200,000. And the University of Washington was not alone: UCLA, the University of New Mexico, and Penn State, among others, dramatically increased resources for women's sports. There was a similar change in attitude and resource allocation at the high school level throughout the country. Maybe the time had come for voluntary acceptance and programmatic change.

The number of female college athletes doubled during the first five years under Title IX, before the federal bureaucracy had time to fully implement Congress's intent. Public opinion (as opposed to the opinion of male athletic directors) favored this increase in athletic opportunities for women. In 1975 the Department of Health, Education, and Welfare issued interim regulations that addressed various issues involving single-sex sports and offered a definition of "equal opportunity" based on expenditures. Difficult questions remained, however, about how precisely an institution would "effectively accommodate the interests and abilities of members of both sex," as the regulations provided.

The early litigation under Title IX had established the right of individual students to sue their schools claiming discrimination based on gender. This was a critical step, because federal authorities were unlikely to have the time or the resources to initiate the litigation necessary to effect compliance. Private litigation involving blatant violations of equity — gross gender disparity in scholarship awards, for example — easily succeeded in court.

In 1979, seven years after the passage of the statute, the agency's Office of Civil Rights (OCR) issued its "Policy Interpretation," the Carter Administration document that would become the definitive statement on the application of Title IX. OCR offered a three-part approach to meeting the statutory directive. Institutions would be in full compliance with the law if they "have substantially the same proportion of female athletes on varsity teams as the proportion of female students in the undergraduate population." In other words, if half the students were women and half the athletic participation opportunities were in women's sports, the school fulfilled its statutory obligations. The problem with the proportionality test was that the size of the men's football team made proportionality virtually impossible — even for institutions that wanted to comply with Title IX.

The 1979 Policy Interpretation offered a second alternative for covered schools. If institutions could demonstrate a "history and continuing practice" of expanding programs for women, they would be in presumptive compliance. This strategy was proposed without any timetables. Presumably, institutions acting in good faith could gradually increase participation opportunities for women and avoid violating Title IX. Few schools, however, took advantage of this approach. For most schools, as a result of financial exigencies, the years of program expansion had long past.

Finally, an institution could meet its statutory obligations by showing that the interests and abilities of women students were "fully and effectively" accommodated. If the institution could show that the women at a college had no interest in additional opportunities to participate in athletics, there would be no statutory violation.

The reaction was immediate. Walter Byers' assistant at the NCAA, Tom Hansen, offered his gloss: "When you start understanding them [the guidelines] is when you really get scared." Delegates to the NCAA's annual convention in January 1980 called the Policy Interpretation an "illegal power grab" by the agency, and William Davis, the president of the University of New Mexico, predicted that "a crisis of unprecedented magnitude is coming." The convention overwhelmingly passed a resolution calling the guidelines "unrealistic and unworkable." They vowed to seek judicial nullification of the guidelines because collegiate sports teams did not receive federal aid and the agency "does not have regulatory authority over intercollegiate sports programs which are not federally assisted."

Spurred on by the NCAA resolution, opponents of Title IX sought to establish that the statutory and regulatory prohibitions applied only to the programs that actually received federal funds. Since athletic programs did not receive federal funds, Title IX would be rendered a nullity. Those who sought to reestablish the *status quo ante* found allies in the Reagan White House. Gender stereotypes and epithets flourished in that conservative, misogynistic environment. Terrel Bell, Reagan's second secretary of education, wrote in his memoir, *The Thirteenth Man*, that White House staffers referred to Title IX as the "lesbian's bill of rights."

A majority of the Supreme Court agreed with the Reagan Administration's constrained view of the reach of civil rights legislation tied to receipt of federal funding in the *Grove City College* case. The statutory prohibitions could apply only to those institutional programs that actually received federal funds, thus exempting all sports programs. Despite the consistent opposition of the Republican White House, Congress immediately began to undo the damage inflicted by the Court, led by the Senate's Republican leader Bob Dole. The legislative history of his effort to correct the Court's misadventure specifically discussed the impact of Title IX on women's athletics and the value of these developments. Although President Reagan vetoed the resulting Civil Rights Restoration Act of 1988, within a week both houses of Congress overrode his veto. Although it seemed to some that gender equity in collegiate athletics was inevitable, that misread the tenacity of those who would stand in the gymnasium doorway and block women from entering.

Colleges and universities, faced as always with limited financial resources, saw in the open opposition of President Reagan and many conservative spokesmen an excuse to stall the growth in women's athletic opportunities. With athletic budgets ballooning to pay higher salaries for men's coaches, some colleges closed down women's sports, secure in the knowledge that the federal government would not penalize them. That stalling strategy worked until Brown University's young women gymnasts brought their suit.

Sometimes in the fight for civil rights, economic realities conquer prejudice, as happened with the 1955–56 Montgomery, Alabama, bus boycott. When black patrons of the city's buses refused to ride for a year, the financially crippled system's resistance to integration crumbled. Colleges, however, saw little financial incentive to build their women's programs. There was no pot of gold to be made by voluntary compliance. Despite the steady growth in women's college athletics since the passage of Title IX, there had been only a few examples of commercial success in women's sports. The women's basketball team at the University of Tennessee turned a profit of a half million dollars a year. The women's soccer club at the University of North Carolina was another notable profit center. Most college sports—men's or women's—did not produce excess revenue. Economics would not drive change this time; it would take the enforcement of the law in court to bring about gender equity. Real fairness between the sexes in college sports would be years away, and it would require courage, resources, and an enlightened judiciary to get there.

Gender equity was a difficult concept for many people to understand. Some commentators, in fact, suggested that there were really three sexes: male, female, and football. College football remained an untouchable sport, even though it was not a cash cow at most colleges. Only one out of five Division I-A football programs broke even. Nonetheless, each major football school offered full scholarships to eighty-five players. Football squads could include as many as 130 members, all counting as participation opportunities for purposes of Title IX. In the mid-1990s, Speaker of the House Dennis Hastert, a former wrestling coach who thought that women armed with Title IX were killing his sport, led an effort in Congress to legislate football out of the statute. It was the fifth time Congress had addressed the issue, and it failed again.

Although Congress had forcefully rejected the Supreme Court's and the Reagan Administration's backhand slaps at civil rights laws, it remained a difficult time for proponents of change, including in women's sports. Without governmental enforcement, there was backsliding instead of progress. Based on costs and revenue, schools covered by Title IX continued to make decisions that undercut the goal of gender equity. In 1990, the University of Oklahoma announced it would abolish the women's basketball team because it drew an average of only 200 fans a game. Oklahoma Governor Henry Bellmon could not understand the uproar that followed that announcement: "They'll still have intramural basketball, won't they? We have never had total equality in women's athletics, and I don't know that we ever will have. . . . There is no women's baseball or women's wrestling. I have heard of women's mud wrestling." The University of Oklahoma reinstated the program eight days later, after attorney Arthur Bryant of the Trial Lawyers for Public Justice agreed to represent the women. Bryant would also play a pivotal role in the Brown University litigation.

Money revealed the DNA of college sports. On male-run campuses, budgets demonstrated a broad resistance to Title IX. An NCAA study released in March 1992 showed that the average Division I school spent twice as much on men's scholarships as it spent on women's and three times as much on men's operating expenses. Men's coaches were paid an average salary of $71,511; women's coaches received $39,177. Although the NCAA's new executive director, Dick Schultz, said that "gender equity is a moral issue," it would take judicial intervention to convert good intentions into favorable results.

THE BROWN UNIVERSITY
PLAINTIFFS BRING SUIT

Test-case civil rights litigation is usually brought by a class of affected persons who claim discrimination. The women on Brown University's gymnastic team were anything but satisfied with the opportunities they were offered when the college administration announced that their program would be shut down. The university had skillfully joined the elimination of gymnastics and women's volleyball with the elimination of two men's programs, likely considering that closing down two programs for each gender would seem fair. The template against which these actions would be examined, however, was the three-part test of Title IX Policy Interpretation. And although the case involved a single, comparatively small Ivy League school, the litigation would ultimately affect all other institutions covered by Title IX.

When people think about the practice of law, they normally focus on large corporate law firms. In fact, most of the more than 1.1 million lawyers in the United States practice in firms of five or fewer, and a plurality of attorneys are solo practitioners. Some specialize in criminal work, others in civil trial work, still others in real estate, divorce, or wills and trusts. Most become experts in a variety of fields, equipped to handle the needs of the next client who comes through the door.

The Trial Lawyers for Public Justice (TLPJ) was a different kind of law firm. Formed in 1982 with a commitment to the public interest, TLPJ has been involved in a broad range of progressive causes in court, not the least of which involved representing women athletes in Title IX cases. (In January 2007, TLPJ changed its name to Public Justice, but did not change its mission to fight for "consumers' rights, workers' rights, civil rights and civil liberties, environmental protection, public health and safety, and access to the courts.") When approached by the Brown gymnasts, Arthur Bryant of TPLJ contacted affiliated local counsel in Providence, Lynette Labinger, about handling the matter with the support of the national organization.

Labinger is a noted civil rights lawyer in a two-person law firm with John Roney. She graduated magna cum laude from Mt. Holyoke College in 1971 and earned her J.D. cum laude from New York University Law School, where she received the University Prize for the highest cumulative grade point average. After graduation, she clerked for Federal Judge Raymond Pettine in Providence. Years later she would appear before Judge Pettine on behalf of members of the Brown University women's gymnastics team.

In the context of higher education, students will come and go, while attorneys may stay with a case long after the named plaintiffs have graduated. The lawyers are the continuous thread in the litigation. As the case dragged on for years, Lynette Labinger and Arthur Bryant would continue to represent Amy Cohen and the class of current and future female athletes at Brown. Labinger deserves much of the credit for the success of the suit.

THE *COHEN* LITIGATION

When plaintiffs brought their legal action protesting the decision of Brown University, there had not been any court precedents on the meaning and application of the three-part test for meeting Title IX's requirements as set forth by the Office of Civil Rights in its Policy Interpretation. The *Cohen* case was heard in the federal district court in Providence, a few blocks from Brown. Longtime federal judge Raymond Pettine presided at the trial without a jury. Judge Pettine had a well-deserved reputation as a staunch defender of Constitutional rights and liberties. Would he recognize the statutory rights of gymnasts as equivalent to the rights of free speech and assembly?

The defendant was founded in 1764 as the College of Rhode Island, the third oldest college in New England. It changed its name to Brown University in 1804, in recognition of a gift from the Brown family, merchants involved in the slave trade. In 1891, a women's component of the institution was established, later named Pembroke, and ultimately merged into the university in 1971. At the time of the merger, the women's athletic program was funded by bake sales and had a reserve account of $2,000. Within a short period of time, the university poured resources into women's athletics, although it never reached parity with the already century-old men's program. In 1990, for example, Brown replaced its entire football coaching staff after a dreadful year on the gridiron, incurring an expense of $250,000.

In April 1991, Brown announced that it was going to eliminate four athletic teams—men's golf and water polo and women's gymnastics and volleyball—claiming that this would save the institution more than $75,000 a year. It offered the affected athletes the opportunity to continue their programs as varsity sports if they could raise replacement funds— $16,000 annually for the two men's teams and $62,000 for the two women's teams. No one explained how the athletes were to accomplish this while enrolled as full-time students at an Ivy League school. No one explained that teams with unfunded varsity status would not have assured access to Brown's athletic facilities or equal access to its weight rooms, trainers, or locker rooms.

After this announcement, the members of the women's gymnastics team considered filing a complaint under Title IX with the Office of Civil Rights, an approach that would likely have bogged down in the federal bureaucracy. Then they learned about Arthur Bryant, executive director of the Trial Lawyers for Public Justice, who had pursued successful gender equity litigation against Temple University. TLPJ agreed to underwrite the gymnasts' suit and provide the local counsel.

Lynette Labinger did not immediately run to the courtroom. She knew that litigation would be lengthy and expensive. She contacted counsel for Brown and explained how the matter could and should be resolved based on the Office of Civil Rights Policy Interpretation. University counsel was not impressed with OCR's interpretation of Title IX and, in any case, he told Labinger that she did not have the correct data upon which to base a claim. Hearing nothing further from Brown, plaintiffs filed a class action suit in federal court in April 1992.

Brown's vice president for public affairs, Robert A. Reichley, quickly responded to the filing of the plaintiffs' suit. Brown University, he noted for the press, offered women more sports than 291 of the 292 Division I institutions in the country. Thirty-nine percent of Brown's varsity athletes were women, compared with only 31 percent of Division I athletes nationwide. (Reichley did not report that 49 percent of Brown's undergraduates were women, or that women's sports received less than 30 percent of the school's athletic budget.) Finally, Reichley explained, when Brown cut the two men's teams, 37 male athletes were affected. Cuts to the two women's sports affected only 23 female athletes. But Reichley and Brown University would learn that none of these defenses could excuse a Title IX violation that eliminated women's sports when there were women students whose interests in playing sports were not met.

In response to the suit, Brown filed a motion to dismiss the litigation. Julius Michaelson, counsel for Brown, told the court that judicial interference would result in a "loss of control of the budgeting process of Brown University." This argument paralleled that made by most businesses accused of racial discrimination, that a court hearing a claim would affect their business discretion. That, of course, is the purpose of the law—to interfere with a business's discriminatory decision making. Michaelson also offered an argument that would be reiterated by the defendant's various attorneys for many years, that the plaintiffs were seeking an illegal quota and that "[e]qual opportunity does not require proportional representation." The plaintiffs were not seeking proportional representation, but that apparently was beside the point. Finally, harping back to age-old stereotypes, Michaelson said that fewer women were interested in sports. Brown had never tried to find out whether that was true on the Providence campus. Judge Pettine denied Brown's motion to dismiss the suit and certified plaintiffs' suit as a class action representing all women athletes at Brown.

Like many who had benefited from the status quo, Brown's distinguished president, Vartan Gregorian, believed that Title IX was a subterfuge. It was simply a quota statute, an "assault on common sense." He questioned why the federal government would be so concerned about sports, which he considered far from central to the intellectual life of the elite Providence campus. Born in Iran, Gregorian held a dual Ph.D. in history and humanities from Stanford. He saw Title IX as a personal affront. He was furious that anyone, including the federal court, the federal government, or the Congress, could tell him how to run his university.

In the fall of 1992, the district court heard plaintiffs' motion for a preliminary injunction to hold matters in place while the suit was pending. Brown had agreed to allow the cancelled sports to continue only for the 1992–93 academic year. Plaintiffs explained to Judge Pettine how colleges like Brown recruited athletes to fill "participation opportunities" on its established sports teams. Although Ivy League schools did not grant athletic scholarships, recruited athletes received additional consideration in the admission's process and received need-based financial assistance. In order to protect the quality of the programs, it was essential that recruits know gymnastics and volleyball would be available in the coming years.

After three weeks of trial, Judge Pettine granted the plaintiffs a preliminary injunction in December 1992, based on the three tests of the 1979 OCR Policy Interpretation: "Brown," Judge Pettine wrote, "is cutting off varsity opportunities where there is great interest and talent, and where Brown still has an imbalance between men and women." Brown's assumption that women were not interested or able to play sports was rebutted by the facts of this case. The gymnasts were ready, willing, and able to participate. Pettine also granted plaintiffs' request that the injunction extend to all women's teams out of concern that, having lost the first stage in this case, Brown would simply cut participation opportunities for other women. The university immediately vowed to appeal.

The *Cohen* case was heard on an expedited basis by a panel of the U.S. Court of Appeals for the First Circuit, sitting in Boston early the following year. Judge Selya's opinion for that panel set forth the approach that would be used thereafter by all courts addressing Title IX issues of gender equity. Showing appropriate deference to the federal agency's methodology, he applied the three-part test of the Policy Interpretation. Since the university did not meet the proportionality standard — the percentage of athletic participation opportunities for women did not match the percentage of women in the student body — and Brown was not adding sports programs for women in a gradual manner as suggested by the second standard, the court turned its attention to the third standard. Brown must, the court stated, "fully" accommodate the interests and abilities of women: "If there is sufficient interest and ability among members of the statistically under-represented gender not slaked by existing programs, an institution necessarily fails this part of the test." Eventually, the court reasoned, as an institution worked to meet the "interest and ability" of female undergraduates, it will move toward fulfilling the proportionality test. The *Cohen* opinion was quickly adopted in pending gender equity Title IX cases in the Third, Sixth, Seventh and Tenth Circuits.

Although vowing to fight on, Brown funded the women's gymnastics and volleyball teams for the 1993–94 academic year. It also admitted two female gymnasts and one volleyball player who had previously been denied admission to the class that entered in the fall of 1993. However, *Cohen v. Brown University* was far from over. Brown proceeded to execute its game plan in the media, issuing press releases defending its actions, disputing the court's conclusions, and offering what it called "evidence" that Brown was meeting the women's "stated interests and abilities."

The First Circuit Court of Appeals had returned the case to the district court for a hearing on the merits. The trial began before Judge Pettine in the fall of 1994. Shortly afterward, the parties reached a settlement on matters other than the participation opportunities issues, including coaching salaries, recruiting budgets, overall expenses, and other benefits for women athletes. Brown also agreed to maintain volleyball as a varsity sport for five years, renovate the women's locker rooms, and make women's skiing a varsity sport.

Toward the conclusion of the three-month trial on the merits of plaintiffs' request for a permanent injunction, Brown's lawyer, Beverly E. Ledbetter, reiterated the university's position that women had a lower level of interest in sports participation, and that the Policy Interpretation was an invalid revision of previous agency regulations and the statute itself. It was as if the parties' prior two years of litigation had accomplished nothing. Brown wanted to retry the validity of the three-part test. The plaintiffs' response, presented through expert witnesses, was that when offered the opportunity to participate, women do participate. Furthermore, following the *Cohen* decision in the First Circuit, all courts that had addressed the issue had showed great deference to the court's ruling and the agency's Policy Interpretation.

In March 1995, Judge Pettine once again held for the plaintiffs. The Policy Interpretation was valid, and the university's surveys could not rebut the clear evidence that there were women on campus who were interested and able to participate in the sports Brown had abolished. Brown then threatened to eliminate all men's teams if the judge ordered the university to reinstate the women's teams. Judge Pettine was not cowed by the threat and ordered the university to submit a plan within sixty days, explaining how it would comply with the law. Brown did so reluctantly. Its plan was to cap the sizes of men's teams, impose minimum roster sizes on women's teams, and add "junior varsity" women's teams in a variety of sports. Pettine rejected Brown's proposal because only genuine varsity participation opportunities could be counted toward fulfilling the requirements of Title IX.

Once again, the university appealed to the First Circuit, attacking Judge Pettine's actions as "poor public policy which violates the spirit and intent of Title IX." By now, the Brown University case had become the *cause célèbre* for all institutions of higher education. Amicus briefs from colleges and universities flooded the First Circuit, all in support of Brown. In November 1996, the circuit reaffirmed its prior opinion. Brown sought review in the Supreme Court, and sixty colleges and universities filed briefs in support of its petition. In a response to the petition for certiorari, plaintiffs emphasized that there was no conflict between the circuits. All courts had agreed with the First Circuit's opinion in *Cohen*, and thus there was no reason for the Supreme Court to hear the matter. In April 1997, the Supreme Court refused to hear the case.

To determine a remedy, the litigation headed back to trial court. Counsel for Brown University, Maureen E. Mahoney, bemoaned any preferential treatment for women, as well as the willingness of the courts to require that Brown equalize participation opportunities for women even though more men than women wanted to play sports. Mahoney misstated the holding in the case by castigating non-existent "mathematical formulas."

Brown offered the trial court a woefully inadequate plan. The plaintiffs objected to Brown's proposal, which was mostly "a wish and a prayer" rather than a set of particular actions it intended to take. In June 1997, Judge Pettine retired and a new federal judge took over the litigation. Around the same time, Brown University President Gregorian left the institution to become president of the Carnegie Corporation, a position he continues to hold. On the eve of the next hearing, the parties finally reached a comprehensive settlement of all matters in the dispute, which was approved by the district court in 1998.

The Brown University case set the definitive tests for compliance with Title IX. It was a costly exercise, however. The court eventually ordered the university to pay the plaintiffs' legal fees — over one million dollars. (Brown also had to bear its own fees, which likely were substantially higher.) How many athletic opportunities for women could Brown have provided with the millions it had spent on litigation? In an effort to save a few dollars from its budget, the university violated national law and it paid for those violations.

In the wake of the *Cohen* victory, the National Women's Law Center filed twenty-five suits against colleges and universities, targeting the unequal division of scholarship aid. In all of these schools, football soaked up the plurality of scholarships. Decisions in these cases joined a growing body of equal-pay case precedent. However, coaches of women's teams continued to be shortchanged.

The Clinton Administration's Department of Education issued a policy clarification in 1996, building on the *Cohen* analysis. If a college had women who were interested in a particular sport, with the talent to sustain a team with a reasonable expectation of intercollegiate competition, Title IX required the college to act. The department required colleges to assess not only the interests of enrolled students, but also the interests of high-school students in the region where the college recruited students, as well as members of amateur athletic associations and participants in community sports leagues. Although most colleges still remained out of compliance, Title IX enforcement had reached its high-water mark.

JUSTICE FOR GYMNASTS

Justice for the gymnasts at Brown University came late. All those students immediately affected by the university's decision to shut down programs had long since graduated and their athletic careers were over. Although Amy Cohen sought immediate relief, ultimate victory was a long time coming. Test case litigation such as this one tends to be generational in nature.

The *Cohen* case stands as a monument in the fight for gender equality. Unwilling to accept disparate treatment, the women and their counsel stood strong in the face of university intransigence. In the process, they established a precedent that guided a thousand colleges and universities and many federal courts across the country.

Title IX continues to have an impact, visible not only in America but around the world. The public first saw and celebrated what Title IX had accomplished when the American women's soccer team won the 1999 World Cup. Brandi Chastain and Mia Hamm became household names, especially in those households with young girls who could now aspire to achieve athletic greatness like their role models.

The work is far from done, of course. A study by the *Chronicle of Higher Education* reported that, by the end of the 1990s, both the percentage of athletic opportunities for women and the budgets for scholarships had increased, but a wide disparity remained in recruiting budgets (31 percent spent on women), coaching salaries (34 percent), and total operating expenses (33 percent). The increase in participation rate, however, was impressive. In 1972, one in twenty-seven high school girls participated in sports. By the thirtieth anniversary of Title IX, that number had increased more than tenfold, to two in five. Colleges added 3,714 new women's teams, as well as 989 additional men's programs. Although it is true that 170 men's wrestling programs were shut down, that was not the fault of Title IX. It was simply a matter of reallocating resources among men's sports based on the interests of potential participants.

When President George W. Bush took office in 2001, some anticipated that Title IX would be substantially revised or even abolished. Even without Congressional action, the Bush Administration could have made significant changes in implementation that would have dulled the impact of the law. In order to establish a record upon which to pursue what the administration called "reform," it vowed to study Title IX.

Much to the surprise of the civil rights and gender rights communities, the committee studying the issue did not recommend trashing Title IX. Instead, it suggested only modest modifications. In the wake of these comparatively moderate recommendations, the Office of Civil Rights focused on the ways that colleges could determine whether the needs and interests of the affected minority, women in this instance, could be considered "fully accommodated."

The new methodology allowed a college to determine the interests of college women by using an email survey and included a draft of a model survey. If women did not respond to the survey, that would indicate they had no interest in participating in athletics, a troubling behavioral assumption at best. The assistant secretary of education, James F. Manning, explained that the *Cohen* tests remained in place. The survey would simply assess whether there were "unmet needs." The burden of establishing a breach of Title IX would no longer be on the covered institutions, but rather on students and government investigators.

On the other hand, the new regulations did not mandate the dismantling of existing programs. Title IX women's programs have become entrenched both in high schools and in colleges. There is little evidence that the new regulations caused much damage. By 2007–2008, the NCAA reported, there was a record 9,380 women's teams and 8,302 men's teams, for a total of 17,682 championship sport teams, an increase of 60 percent from 1981–82. A total of 412,768 students participated in intercollegiate athletics in 2007–2008, 57.4 percent of whom were male. The number of women's teams had increased exponentially, but the number of men's teams had also increased. In April 2010, the Obama Administration reversed the Bush methodology and reinstated federal support for true gender equity in sports.

The *Cohen* case remains an example of achieving sports justice using litigation based on legislation and administrative regulations. A court could not have ordered Brown University to do anything without Title IX, but without Amy Cohen's suit, nothing would have been done to reverse Brown's discrimination.

Many male critics of Title IX blame the legislation for the demise of men's sports on campus. Of course, there is nothing in the legislation or the regulations that requires a college to reduce or eliminate men's programs. Institutions find it convenient to blame their budgetary decisions to eliminate wrestling or men's gymnastics on the requirements of Title IX even if that is not the case. Men still maintain a greater share of the college sports dollar than women, and any marginal losses in the number of men's programs are the result of budgetary decisions rather than the prevailing legislation.

President Obama has established a White House Council on Women and Girls, charged with finding ways to further enhance opportunities. And he is on record as supporting the High School Sports Information Act, which requires high schools to issue annual reports on gender equity issues. It should not be forgotten that President Obama has two young daughters and sports participation remains an important part of his own life.

CHAPTER 7

STICKS ARE SWINGING, BUT IS IT A CRIME?

Ice hockey is a form of disorderly conduct in which the score is kept.
DOUG LARSON

A puck is a hard rubber disc that hockey players strike when they can't hit one another.
JIMMY CANNON

• • • Wayne Maki and Ted Green were rough, tough hockey players. They performed as the fans of the sport expected, with reckless disregard for their own bodies and their opponents' physical well-being. Green had been an all-star in the National Hockey League, having played with the Boston Bruins for almost a decade at the time of the brutal incident that almost took his life and led to two criminal trials. Maki, on the other hand, had been up and down between the minor leagues and the NHL. He was trying to catch on with the Vancouver Canucks for the 1969–70 season when he engaged in a confrontation with Green during a preseason game.

In his autobiography, *High Stick*, Green relates his version of what happened that night on the ice in Ottawa, Canada, and the truly remarkable tale of his return to the game. Green's narrative presents the Canadian version of a Horatio Alger story: a small-town boy who played hockey from age seven, progressed through multiple levels of the amateur sport, grew in strength and size until eventually he reached the professional ranks where he achieved all-star status. Green's forte was his aggressive defense work accompanied by a penchant — even an appetite — for fighting at the drop of a glove. His well-earned nickname was "Terrible Teddy." Green seemed to spend almost as many minutes in the penalty box as he did on the ice. Any offensive player entering Green's corner of the ice would be guaranteed an assault. Green played the game aggressively.

Green was not alone in his attitude toward playing the game of hockey. A pastime born on the frozen ponds of Canada, ice hockey was derived from English field hockey and the Irish game of hurling. James G. Creighton formulated the rules of modern ice hockey while studying engineering at McGill University, and in 1875 the first game was played under Creighton's rules at Victoria Skating Rink in Montreal. According to a wire dispatch from the *Kingston Daily British Whig*, the game ended in a brawl: "Shins and heads were battered, benches smashed, and the lady spectators fled in confusion." The sport became an obsession with Canadian youth, who played it as soon as they could walk. Since the 1930s, "Hockey Night in Canada" on the Canadian Broadcasting Company network has accumulated that nation's highest radio and television ratings.

previous page
The Boston Bruins dedicated their 1970 Stanley Cup victory to Teddy Green, the team's warrior on ice until he was injured by a slash from Wayne Maki's hockey stick.
AP Photo

The men of Canada are generally appreciated for their calm demeanor and their ability to survive in a sometimes harsh physical environment. A remarkable change occurs, however, when it comes to a brutal body check delivered to an opposing player who has touched the puck. Fights break out during the normal course of a hockey game, symptoms of a passionate and masculine culture of aggression that is considered part of the sport. The game is stopped while the referees allow the fisticuffs to proceed. The only saving grace is that, while skating on ice, players normally lack sufficient traction to do too much damage to an opponent. The sticks that players carry to maneuver the puck, however, can do significant injury when used as weapons, as was the case when Wayne Maki attacked Ted Green.

From its earliest days, hockey proved a crowd-pleaser because of its row-diness, and the game quickly spread south of the Canadian border to the United States. Entrepreneur Albert Spalding was the first to bring hockey equipment to the general public. His 1898 *Spalding Ice Hockey and Ice Polo Guide*, among the earliest texts on hockey, promoted the sport as having "that purely American outburst of effort known as 'boom.'" The *Guide* assured its readers that the game did not have the roughness or danger of lacrosse or polo: "[T]he time [of the game] is employed in brilliant rushes, quick checking and clever passes." Contact within bounds was always acceptable, however: "A successful hockey player must be very active on his feet, quick with his hand, keen of eye and have all his faculties alert." Spalding cautioned that extremely high-risk behavior, such as the use of the hockey stick as a weapon, would be penalized. The offending player would have to sit in the penalty box for two or five minutes, leaving his club short-handed on the ice. But the following quotation (author unknown) more accurately describes the reality of the game as it has been played for over a century: "High sticking, tripping, slashing, spearing, charging, hooking, fighting, unsportsmanlike conduct, interference, roughing . . . everything else is just figure skating."

Those who defend fighting in hockey explain that incidents on the ice are merely the spontaneous result of the speed of the game and the contact that is permitted. Aggressive behavior has long been ingrained in the sport. Yet, much of the violence seems planned to intimidate the opposition and please the crowd. Violence is one of the game's main attractions. Many fights appear scripted. As Bob Stewart, a veteran of the NHL in the 1970s, said: "Red ice sells hockey tickets."

Hockey players who fight are glorified as modern-day gladiators. Youngsters who pattern their behaviors after their NHL role models develop anti-social attitudes and values. Their hockey play and social life mirror the hostile behavior of their heroes. Instead of learning the value of physical, moral, and social excellence, young boys learn the lessons of aggression.

There is no reason why this must be the case. College, Olympic, and international hockey are played without fights. There are still hard body checks, but anyone who drops his gloves and fights is automatically ejected. A fighter also receives a game suspension, and those suspensions accumulate under college rules (fighting a second time results in a two-game suspension, a third results in a three-game suspension, and so on). That rule effectively stopped fighting in college hockey, but it has not diminished the attraction of the college sport. As a matter of machismo and marketing, however, the National Hockey League has not taken this step.

Ted Green was one of the most feared of the NHL gladiators. Superbly confident in his ability to control and pass the puck, Green made his opponents pay a physical price for entering his space on the rink. Green was never afraid on the ice and, as the team's enforcer, he often aggressively provoked fights. Although Green was a modest man off the ice, he became a fearsome terror in his team uniform. His club and his fans expected him to play that role. Green was twenty-nine at the time of the incident, at the top of his game.

Wayne Maki was at the opposite end of the career spectrum. At age twenty-four, the Sault Sainte Marie, Ontario, native had yet to make his mark in the National Hockey League. He first made it to the league for part of the 1967–68 season, playing with his brother, Ronald "Chico" Maki, an established star with the Chicago Blackhawks. For most of the next two seasons, Wayne Maki played minor league hockey. The games of the 1969 pre-season were a critical opportunity to demonstrate his hockey-playing abilities.

THE INCIDENT

Green and Maki came from similar backgrounds. Both were excellent athletes and loved hockey. They will be remembered for a single incident of extreme violence, part of the game they played with passion and without restraint. On September 21, 1969, during a typical melee in an Ottawa exhibition game between the Boston Bruins and the St. Louis Blues, Maki almost killed Green with a well-placed slash of his Sher-Wood hockey stick across Green's skull. (In 1969, players did not wear helmets. They would not be required to do so until 1979, and even then the rule was phased in over time and made applicable only to rookies.) As a result of the episode in Ottawa, Green experienced massive brain hemorrhaging. Two brain operations saved his life and a permanent plate was later inserted in his head.

The incident itself lasted only a few seconds, following a pattern of escalation common in violent outbursts. It began at the thirteen-minute mark of the first period, when left-winger Maki shot the puck over the blue line into the Bruins end. Most fights and injuries occur in the corners of the rink behind the goal line, and the incident this night would follow that model. Green played the puck with his skate while Maki headed for Green and hit him from behind. Green roughly pushed Maki down to the ice with his gloved left hand. That was sufficient for the referee, Ken Bodendistel, to raise his arm, indicating that a penalty would be called against Green as soon as a Boston player obtained control of the puck. This small, inconsequential contact then spiraled out of control.

From his knees, Maki speared Green in the genitals, perhaps the most egregious attack that can be committed on the ice and a clear violation of both the unwritten code and the written rules of hockey. As Green turned to skate toward the penalty box, he swung his stick and slashed Maki on the arm, once again knocking him to the ice. Maki's immediate response would resound throughout the sports world, focusing the public's attention on the relationship among games, violence, and criminal law.

Maki answered Green's second assault by slashing at Green's skull with his hockey stick. Green had turned his head away, thinking that the fight was over. Maki slashed with the hardest part of the stick, at the bend where the shaft joins the blade. Green fell helplessly to the ice.

The right side of his head had been crushed. Because that part of the brain controls speech, the left arm, and the left leg, the left side of Green's body was paralyzed. Pieces of skull mixed with pieces of his brain. Green lost consciousness on the way to the Ottawa hospital. When he regained awareness, he immediately asked for a priest to administer the last rites.

After neurosurgeon Michael Richard performed emergency surgery, Green's condition began to improve. By the end of the week, however, Green took a turn for the worse, something Dr. Richard had feared would occur. Suffering from further hemorrhaging and convulsions, Green was rushed back into surgery for a two-hour operation to reopen the scalp and drain blood from his brain. The second operation removed a blood clot that had formed at the skull fracture point. That likely saved his life. Green remained paralyzed on his left side from his face to his toes; his physicians feared that the condition was permanent.

Newspapers published on the day after the incident downplayed the extent of Green's injuries. They reported that he might be able to return to the ice before the end of the season. The Bruins team physician stated that Green's life was no longer in danger, although Green's doctors in Ottawa were not so sure. (The team doctor, Ashley Moncur of Massachusetts General Hospital, had not examined Green, who was hospitalized three hundred miles away.) After the second operation, the news accounts became far more pessimistic, relating that Green's paralysis would linger for months. Somewhat belatedly, on December 14, 1969, the Bruins formally filed a motion with the league's rules committee to require players to wear helmets.

Green blamed himself for the injury. He understood that Maki's attack was just part of a game he had loved since childhood. He had turned away from Maki, and therefore had not seen the blow coming, something an experienced brawler should never do.

Through months of rehabilitation near his home outside Winnipeg, Green regained the use of his left hand and arm. No one thought he could possibly recover the full use of his extremities, let alone skate or play hockey again. His Bruin teammates asked that a Catholic Mass be said for him. In one final operation months later, Green's doctor, Michael Richard, inserted an acrylic plate to cover the open skull wound.

In response to the Maki-Green mayhem, the National Hockey League's referee-in-chief, Sonny Morrison, instructed his officials to "rule with an iron hand" regarding stick swinging and to issue game misconduct penalties to violators. It was announced that Clarence Campbell, the league president, would personally review all such incidents. (The first to receive close scrutiny was Green's teammate Phil Esposito, who had been ejected from the same September 21 game for pushing the referee, minutes before the attack on Green.)

President Campbell summoned both Maki and Green to the NHL office in Ottawa for a hearing and to mete out the league's punishment to the players. He seemed unconcerned that Green had spent five weeks in the hospital and remained heavily sedated and partially paralyzed at the time of the hearing. Despite accounts and photographs to the contrary, Campbell believed that Maki's almost fatal stick attack had ricocheted off Green's raised stick. Maki denied the spearing and said little else. Green struggled to stay awake during the ordeal. Later, Campbell would fine each player three hundred dollars, suspend Maki for thirty days, and Green for thirteen days (to be served if and when Green ever returned to the ice, a possibility that seemed quite remote). The fines represented the automatic one-hundred-dollar penalty each received for a match misconduct plus an additional two-hundred-dollar fine for stick swinging.

Because of the severity of Green's injury and the notoriety of the incident, the public (or, at least, the media) pressured Canadian authorities to take action. The Ottawa police conducted an investigation. Two months after the event, on November 21, 1969, the constables swore out criminal charges against both Maki and Green for "assault occasioning bodily harm." If convicted, each defendant faced a possible sentence of up to two years in jail. This was the first time in the history of professional sports that police authorities had issued a complaint against players because of an incident that occurred during a game. NHL President Campbell, who was also an attorney, expressed surprise at the charges. He told the *New York Times*: "So long as the game of hockey is kept within the bounds proscribed by society, do you send a policeman to every game?" The league wanted to keep all matters of discipline and control of misconduct in-house.

The Blues played the Bruins at the Boston Garden on February 9, 1970, and the soon-to-be Stanley Cup champion Bostonians took their revenge on Wayne Maki as part of a 7–1 dismantling of the St. Louis club. The miscreant took a pounding, as he knew he would. The *New York Times* reported that St. Louis coach Scotty Bowen asked referee Lloyd Gilmour during the game why he wasn't calling charging penalties against the Bruins. He was said to have responded: "You started it," referring to Maki's stick attack on Green.

THE CRIMINAL CASES

The Maki and Green criminal cases were heard by two justices of the Ontario provincial court. At Maki's hearing on February 16, 1970, Crown Attorney John Cassells suggested that Maki, who was charged with assault with intent to cause injury, could have just skated away from Green or moved behind the game officials. Maki responded that he was only trying to protect himself. Had he backed off, the word would be out that he "was a scaredy cat. If you skate away from a person like that, it could drive you out of the League." Referee Ken Bodendistel testified that it was Green who had initiated the stick swinging.

On March 5, 1970, Judge Edward Carter acquitted Maki based on his finding that he had acted in self-defense. He had used only "reasonable force" to protect himself. The judge quoted the defendant's testimony: "I was trying to protect myself. . . . I didn't aim at any particular part of his body. . . . I swung in desperation to protect myself." On cross-examination, Maki repeated his claim that he was "trying to ward off Green. . . . I was not angry at Green. I was just protecting myself. . . . I expected he would still come after me if I turned away. . . . swung in desperation. . . . I didn't know I would cause him serious injury." Green, who the court concluded was the aggressor in the incident, did not testify at Maki's proceeding.

On April 7, 1970, the trial of Ted Green began. The charge against him had been reduced to common assault, a lesser crime under Canadian law than the charge against Maki. Green was tried by Provincial Judge Michael Fitzpatrick. (Judge Carter, who had acquitted Maki, died shortly after Maki's trial.) The Bruins hired an Ottawa lawyer, Edward Houston, to represent Green in the proceedings. On September 3, 1970, almost a year after the stick-swinging incident, Judge Fitzpatrick acquitted Green on the basis that Maki had consented to Green's conduct by playing in the contest: "We must remember that we are dealing with a hockey game. We are dealing with two competent hockey players at the peak of their form. We are not now dealing with the ordinary facts of life, the ordinary going and coming."

Judge Fitzpatrick concluded that simple assaults that occur during hockey games are never criminal activity. They are part of the sporting affair. Green was also quoted as saying: "I accept the skull fracture as part of the game. There aren't a lot of guys wearing panties out there, you know."

RETURN TO THE ICE

A few months after his acquittal, in a most remarkable demonstration of personal determination, Ted Green returned to play for the Bruins. He wore (and always complained about) a full black helmet. But in addition to the loss of feeling in his fingertips and some numbness in his left arm, Green had lost both his aggressive spirit and the quickness that made him "Terrible Teddy." Hockey was his profession, however, even at this reduced level of proficiency, and his teammates covered for his deficiencies as he worked his way back. In reference to Green's plate, his Bruins teammates called themselves the "Hole in the Head Gang."

Green scored his first post-operative goal during a home contest on October 25, 1970, against Philadelphia and received a standing ovation from the Boston Garden crowd. For Green himself, however, the bellwether of his recovery was a fight with Dan Maloney of the Chicago Blackhawks on December 2. He had avoided mixing it up on the ice when he first returned, but passivity was not his game. Green could tell that opposing teams favored his side of the defense because he wouldn't fight. (Opposing wingers, on the other hand, did not want to injure him further.) In that game in early December, Green went to the aid of his fellow defenseman, Don Awry, who was being punched from behind by Maloney, a twenty-year-old rookie. Green dropped his gloves and his stick and pinned Maloney's arms, pulling him away from Awry. Maloney threw a punch at Green, who ducked, avoiding contact. Green then yanked off his own black helmet and hit Maloney with four left-handed shots. Maloney headed to the dressing room for repairs and, as Green later explained in *Sports Illustrated*, "I guess I wasn't even thinking as I picked up my gloves and stick and skated over to the penalty box. But I know I felt a sudden warmth, the comfort that comes when something very good happens. I was grinning, almost laughing, as I served my time in the penalty box." Green had regained confidence in his game, apparently forgetting the two occasions on which he had received last rites. Soon the *New York Times* was again able to refer to the "fierce" Green as "one of the best in the trade," although Green freely admitted: "The spark's still not there. It'll take time, I guess."

Ted Green played for two more seasons in the NHL, including Boston's 1972 Stanley Cup win. He then jumped to the rival World Hockey Association, finishing his career in 1979. After his playing days, Green coached for various NHL clubs, including serving as head coach of the Edmonton Oilers in the early 1990s.

Green's near-death experience was not unique in the annals of the National Hockey League. Only twenty months earlier, a fellow Manitoban, Bill Masterson, was fatally injured in a game between the Minnesota North Stars and the Oakland Seals. Checked by two Seals, Masterson fell backward and hit his helmet-less head on the ice. He died two days later without regaining consciousness. Years earlier, in 1937, Howie Morenz suffered multiple fractures while playing for the Montreal Canadians at home against the Chicago Blackhawks. He died in the hospital as a result of complications, including untreated blood clots.Ted Green's recovery was miraculous. Wayne Maki's story, however, ends tragically. Claimed by the Vancouver Canucks in the 1970 expansion draft, Maki played for two more seasons until he was diagnosed with brain cancer on December 14, 1972. He retired from the game and found work as an electrician until his death at age twenty-nine on May 1, 1974. He had played only three full seasons in the National Hockey League.

PUT JUSTICE ON THE ICE

Was sports justice served in the Green-Maki criminal cases? Neither man wanted to be involved in the judicial resolution of the criminal charges. Neither sought revenge through the criminal prosecution of his opponent. Revenge, if it was to come, would be done on the ice. The malevolent chaos in Ottawa that night did not produce a public outcry to stop violence in NHL hockey.

The aftermath of the Green-Maki incident in the Canadian criminal justice system illustrates the difficulty that courts have in dealing with the often perverse nature of sports violence. All hockey players are impressed early in life with the need to demonstrate their manhood through violent acts inflicted on others. Green's comment — "There aren't a lot of guys wearing panties out there, you know" — provides compelling proof of this mind-set.

Some have suggested that the Green-Maki event was exceptional, even aberrational. ESPN, the media arbiter of all things sport, pronounced Maki's attack on Green as the "dirtiest" incident in the history of hockey. It ranks first on its listing of the ten worst incidents of hockey violence. While notable for the severity of the injury Maki caused Green, the event is better viewed as characteristic of a sport without internal boundaries designed to protect the physical well-being (or even the lives) of the participants.

Through that lens, Wayne Maki's stick just happened to cause Ted Green grievous harm. If Maki had missed his target, the event would have gone unnoticed. If we are to censure hockey, it should not be because of the injury that Green suffered, but for the encouragement to violence that the game offers. Courts have proven ineffective in policing and punishing hockey violence. The result is that such misconduct is effectively immune from criminal prosecution.

Hockey without any contact at all would be a very different game from the sport as played today. The frequent and regular collisions rarely cause grievous harm. The rules and understandings internal to the sport generally punish those who create the most extreme risk of injury and generally stem the worst of the offenses. Otherwise, ESPN would not have a list of ten worst incidents, but rather ten thousand.

As hockey fans know, the Green-Maki incident did not end mayhem on the ice. Periodically, the ordinary brutality erupts into repulsive acts of violence. Three incidents demonstrate that the prospect of criminal prosecution does not deter misconduct. On January 6, 1988, in a game played at Toronto's Maple Leaf Gardens, Dino Ciccarelli of the Minnesota North Stars attacked Toronto's rookie defenseman Luke Richardson with his stick. As a result, Ciccarelli was convicted of criminal assault, fined one thousand dollars, and sentenced to one day in jail. (Actually, the "day" was but a few hours during which Ciccarelli, a future Hall of Famer, signed autographs for fans among the guards.)

On February 21, 2000, Marty McSorley, an enforcer playing for the Boston Bruins, was sent on the ice to wreak vengeance on Vancouver Canuck tough guy Donald Brashear with only seconds left in the game. McSorley slashed him from behind. Brashear lost consciousness, fell backward, and hit his head on the ice, suffering a grade III concussion. Later that year, a jury found McSorley guilty of assault with a weapon for the attack; he was sentenced to eighteen months probation. McSorley, who was thirty-seven at the time of his conviction, never played NHL hockey again, but Brashear soon returned to the ice to continue his rough play for another decade.

On March 8, 2004, Todd Bertuzzi of the Vancouver Canucks skated behind Colorado Avalanche forward Steve Moore to retaliate for Moore's hit three weeks earlier on Canucks team captain Markus Näslund. Bertuzzi smashed Moore on the side of the head and drove him to the ice face first. Moore suffered three broken vertebrae and a severe concussion. He lay face down on the ice in a pool of blood and had to be carted off, ending his NHL career. Bertuzzi was charged with criminal assault causing bodily harm. He pleaded guilty, was placed on one year's probation and, after serving a league suspension, returned to play the game.

A COHERENT DOCTRINE

One problem with the criminal prosecution of hockey players for assaults on the ice is the absence of a coherent doctrine concerning these potential crimes. We should move toward identifying the principles that courts should follow in these circumstances, standards that would allow the game to be played well short of anarchy.

The officers of the provincial government brought criminal actions against Green and Maki to establish the supremacy of the public's interest in restraint and concord over the private commercial interest of the NHL in presenting dangerous and potentially lethal entertainment for profit. While that public intervention was commendable, it has certainly failed to stem the violence. Although many were aghast at the extent of Green's injury, there was no public boycott. Hockey fans continue to enjoy the occasional melee, and often attend games in hopes of witnessing a fight, although they likely would have found Green's demise unfortunate. With fighting confined to the rink during game time, the public sees little risk that violence on the ice will spread like a contagion throughout society. If anything, many consider that watching violence — whether in hockey, boxing, or football — acts as a public catharsis.

Anyone who plays sports as a professional appreciates the physical risk of participating. While revenge lies outside the pale, self-defense is a basic human instinct that should not, and cannot, be voided by a court. Players will act in self-defense rather than passively accept an assault. There is significant question about whether Wayne Maki actually acted in self-defense, as the criminal court found. However, the court's ultimate ruling that self-defense would negate the criminal charge was sound.

The alternative defense used by the court in the criminal case against Ted Green is more problematic. Unlike self-defense, consent is a societal construct without any inherent limitations. Self-defense, by comparison, is limited to situations where force is reasonably and apparently necessary to repel an attack and only to an extent proportionate to the threat. Consent is not similarly limited — once one concludes that the players know what they are getting into by stepping on the ice.

Consent as a defense has a commercial underpinning. Spectators will pay to watch hockey, but only if the game is played in a certain way. The players must be willing to accept the physical risks of injury in order to please the public. Those who organize and sell this entertainment to the public set the level of violence to maximize fan interest and the resulting profits to the promoters. There is no justice in a criminal law system that allows the travails of life and death to be determined by the commercial interests of profit.

It is apparent that the defenses of consent and self-defense are related. Consent is set by the design of the game and its approved (albeit penalized) misconduct. Consider a higher-risk game, like the fictional roller-ball, where participants know that one object of the contest is to kill the opponent, and thus consent to dangerous conduct where death is a possible, perhaps inevitable, outcome. The design of this game creates uninterrupted confrontations where self-defense is necessary to protect each player's life.

While proof of reasonable and proportionate acts taken in self-defense may be sufficient to acquit a player who is attacked in any game, it does not decrease the general level of violence in that game. Here positive action by public authorities may be the only option. If the public becomes distressed by the extreme violence of a sport, and criminal prosecution and civil damage actions are unable to stem the tide, then a legislature must act to regulate or even ban the activity. There is no indication, however, that NHL hockey has aroused that level of public outrage.

In the first instance, it would be more efficient and effective for the sport itself to determine an appropriate amount of violence. No sport is more inherently dangerous to its participants than professional football, for example, and the promoters of that game absolutely forbid fighting between players. By comparison, hockey club owners must believe that fighting is essential to marketing the product. They excuse fighting as a necessary safety valve. If war is a continuation of politics by other means, than fighting is a continuation of hockey by other means. It is a good thing that fans do not expect their gladiators to kill each other. As Ken Dryden, the Hall of Fame goalie, explained:

> Whether it's the motivation of the coach, the chanting of the crowd, the taunting of the crowd, the rhythm of the music inside the arena — all of those things are intended to pitch the emotions higher and higher and higher . . . and then, when something really dumb happens, we sort of step back and say, "You fool, how could you allow that to happen?" Then we shake our heads and walk away.

In June 2009, NHL general managers discussed a special rule that penalizes hits to the head. A study by the National Academy of Neuropsychology found that, in the period from 1997 to 2008, 759 NHL players sustained concussions. The Junior A Ontario Hockey League, a prime feeder of talent to the NHL, had already banned checks to the head, but NHL general managers refused to act. Bob Gainey, general manager of the Montreal Canadiens, said that such a prohibition would diminish the "robust physical play that attracts all of us to the game." Colin Campbell, vice president of the NHL for hockey operations, agreed: "We don't like when players get hurt, but it's a part of the game that fans have come to accept, and the managers didn't have any appetite to get rid of it." In March 2010, however, the league finally acted to ban blind-side hits to the head. Now it needs to enforce the new standard.

Despite the NHL's claim of the inevitability of violence, it is possible for a sport to stop the wreckage. At one time, fights were common events in the National Basketball Association. In 1977, each team had "enforcers" much like their counterparts in hockey. Yet even in that era of combat, the referees never stood back and allowed the fights to proceed, egged on by a cheering crowd, as is the case in hockey.

Everything in the NBA changed as a result of one punch. In December 1977, Kermit Washington of the Los Angeles Lakers punched Rudy Tomjanovich of the Houston Rockets when Tomjanovich tried to break up a fight between Washington and Kevin Kunnert. That blow almost killed Tomjanovich. The NBA had had enough.

The owners gave the NBA commissioner the power to fine and suspend players who fought, and commissioners have not been reluctant to use that power. While scuffles continue to occur on and off the court, the game has been tamed because that was what the lords of the league wanted. Hockey owners, however, are not of the same mind, perhaps afraid that an absence of fights will result in an absence of fans.

Even if a sport does not act to stem violence, each player retains an interest in bodily integrity. And society has a general interest in avoiding misconduct that risks loss of life. What then should the criminal courts do? Should they abstain, following the advice of Judge Matsch in the *Hackbart* case? Should they treat intentional contact on the ice in the same way it would be addressed if it had occurred in a parking lot outside the arena?

Neither approach would be appropriate. Abstention, as we have discussed, eliminates the court's traditional role in the adjudication of disputes and the enforcement of criminal law. Participants in sports anticipate intentional contact within bounds that might be censurable outside of the game, but should be countenanced within the game. Otherwise, a running back in football could not be tackled and the game would not exist. What society should not countenance is contact using excessive force intended solely or primarily to injure an opponent.

The criminal law can administer a system in which the line between liability and the absence of liability is based on proof beyond a reasonable doubt that serious injury was caused as a result of excessive force and the offender intended to injure the victim or was acting maliciously to avenge an earlier incident. Players know why they act as they do, and they can avoid liability by playing the game and not participating in gang warfare. Hockey provides sufficient room for full contact within these limits, and society has a legitimate interest in making sure that these limits are not intentionally transgressed.

Applying these guidelines to the Green-Maki incident, it seems apparent that Maki was not acting in self-defense when he struck at Green with his stick after Green had turned away, heading for the penalty box. It was revenge. Moreover, using his stick as a scythe against a helmet-less Green was excessive force. Green's glove in Maki's face, however, while warranting a two-minute penalty, was not excessive force in the hockey context.

The law, through its instrument the courts, can play a role in stemming violence in organized hockey if the owners, coaches, and commissioner's office default in their responsibility to adjust the rules and instruct the players. The law is there to pick up the reins in the name of society. As of now, criminal law has proved particularly unsuited for the task but, by applying a coherent legal standard, courts may provide a useful backstop in addressing these circumstances.

CHAPTER 8

AL DAVIS, PETE ROZELLE, AND FRANCHISE FREE AGENCY

It's praising myself, but I've done more than anyone else by all the things I've done. Yeah, I've lived my dream, but I thought I would live my dream. But you've got to go get it. You've got to fight for it, and you've got to dominate.

AL DAVIS

Squabbling in public will eventually ruin football; there's no doubt it's hurting us already.

PETE ROZELLE

• • • Maybe there is something about the water in Brooklyn. Al Davis, Walter O'Malley, and Art Modell all spent their formative years in the City of Churches. They are best known in the professional sports world as idiosyncratic entrepreneurs who moved their franchises and, in the process, broke the hearts of millions of sports fans. While fans mostly focus on player free agency — when players move from one club to another — these three owners perfected "franchise free agency" — when clubs pick up and move to a more profitable city.

O'Malley inflicted the deepest wound, abandoning the ancestral home of baseball's Dodgers for golden Southern California in 1957. (He also induced Charles Stoneham to move his New York Giants to San Francisco.) The Dodgers were not the first club to go west — the National Football League champion Rams had relocated to Los Angeles in 1946, after eight years in Cleveland. The Dodgers, however, had been an integral part of Brooklyn for almost seventy years. More than a half century later, disdain for O'Malley remains virulent in the borough.

Born in Brooklyn in 1925, Art Modell became a major figure in the business of professional football. In 1961, Modell outmaneuvered longtime head coach Paul Brown to take control of the Cleveland Browns, the team that had replaced the Rams in that northeast Ohio metropolis. Frustrated by the state of Cleveland's Municipal Stadium, a depressing facility sometimes referred to as the "mistake on the lake," Modell moved the beloved franchise to Baltimore in 1996, filling the void created when Robert Irsay departed with his Colts in 1984.

Modell was vilified in Cleveland for his "treasonous" act. (Eight years later, one blogger referred to him as a "bottom-feeding, scum-sucking, corporate whore of a fraud.") Modell acknowledged publicly that his legacy might have been "tarnished by the move." His erstwhile Browns would be renamed the Baltimore Ravens, after the National Football League ruled that Modell did not own the uniform colors or the name of the Browns. Four years after Modell's move, the NFL placed an expansion franchise in Cleveland and named them the Browns.

And then there was Al Davis, the aggressive, moody wanderer raised in Crown Heights, Brooklyn, who was always in search of the most lucrative hundred yards of dirt and grass for his football Raiders. Born on the Fourth of July, 1929, Davis valued his independence, but strove his entire life to gain the respect he felt he deserved. His Raiders became a dominating force in America's new national game, and Davis himself became a symbol of America's new personality — restless, belligerent, enterprising, and quarrelsome.

In Oakland, Davis became frustrated with the inability (or perhaps unwillingness) of Alameda County to improve the Oakland Coliseum to his liking. Meanwhile, the Los Angeles Coliseum, having lost its main tenant, the Los Angeles Rams, to a newer stadium down the freeway in suburban Anaheim, bid Davis to relocate from the East Bay for the 1980 season. It offered him a $15 million low-interest loan for stadium improvements that would pay for ninety-nine new luxury boxes, plus a personal $4 million "relocation fee" for the owner. Davis agreed, but the National Football League owners voted 22–0 against the move and refused to schedule any games against the Raiders — if those games would be held in Los Angeles. Ironically, the motion to deny Davis the right to relocate was made by Art Modell, then the consummate NFL insider and, sixteen years later, a franchise free agent himself. Faced with the economic power of the owners (who voted as much against Al Davis as a person as against his proposed relocation), Davis stayed in Oakland for another year. At the close of that season, his club won Super Bowl XV.

Al Davis presented the National Football League owners with a unique challenge. Personally abrasive, Davis did not seek (or gain) the affection of his fellow owners. He relished his role as a maverick. Davis also actively cultivated the animosity of Alvin "Pete" Rozelle, the league's commissioner, who had steered NFL football to immense profitability. Rozelle represented everything Davis was not — an urbane, smooth operator.

The ensuing legal battle between Davis and Rozelle demonstrates how the federal antitrust laws (as enforced by the federal courts) can set the out-of-bounds markers in the business of sports. The law does not care whether Davis was an offensive person, only whether his statutory rights had been violated by the collusion of his business rivals. When Davis found that the courts would be his ally, he had all the friends he needed.

AL DAVIS: RENEGADE

Al Davis saw himself as the embodiment of all-American virtue. A tough guy who played best at games with rules that he could control and manipulate, Davis charted his own course to success. He claimed to be an athlete when he was not. (He had only played stickball on the streets of Brooklyn.) He challenged those who stood in his way and manipulated all others. Davis talked himself into a series of college coaching positions, using a combination of bluster and bluff, con and arrogance. With his pompadour hairdo — a vintage artifact from his years at Brooklyn's Erasmus High School — Davis played a role he had designed for himself. Later, he added sunglasses to his outlaw costume. (Davis actually required prescription glasses, but thought they would diminish his tough-guy image. Few knew that his ever-present sunglasses had prescription lenses.)

A college graduate at age twenty-one, this English major from Syracuse University decided he would be a football coach, although he had not played a down for the Orangemen. After being rejected for a coaching position at Hofstra University, Davis talked his way onto the staff at Adelphi University, an out-of-the way program in Garden City, New York. The Adelphi athletic director initially told him there were no positions available, but Davis went to the school's president and charmed him into hiring him on the spot, as a freshman coach. The next year, Davis moved up to line coach of the varsity team. A confident salesman, Davis sold himself through bluff or, if necessary, lies. He understood how to motivate people, and he had an insatiable and unyielding desire to win.

Davis was drafted into the Army during the Korean War and became coach of the football team at the Corps of Engineer's camp at Fort Belvoir, Virginia, an unusual post for a young private from Brooklyn. Davis recruited football players from across the armed services and created quite a squad. Many of the "graduates" of that Belvoir team went on to careers in professional football. While at Belvoir, Davis also met a young public relations man for the Los Angeles Rams, Pete Rozelle, who was scouting for prospects among the camp's football players. Davis was not impressed with the fancy fellow who would later become his chief adversary.

Davis made better use of the other connections he made at Belvoir, including that of Weeb Ewbank, then head coach of the Baltimore Colts. When his service ended, Davis dropped Ewbank's name to get his first post-Army position, as an assistant coach with the College of the Citadel in

Charleston, South Carolina. Davis' primary job was to recruit high school talent. As he scoured northern and Midwestern high schools, Davis paid little heed to the NCAA's strict rules on recruiting and promised his recruits the world. Dazed and impressed by this slick style, the recruits followed the piper to Charleston. The press book at Citadel proudly boasted of Davis' athletic prowess at Syracuse — a three-letter man, it said — and his service as "head coach" at Adelphi and as an assistant coach with the professional Colts — all pure fabrications. Ultimately, the house of cards fell in Charleston and the college fired him, but not before Davis had secured an assistant coaching position at the University of Southern California. He was a man in a hurry.

Davis' first professional coaching experience was from 1960–62, as an assistant under Sid Gilman with the then Los Angeles Chargers of the American Football League, the rival circuit that began operations in the fall of 1960. The AFL was a league of outsiders run by moneyed people who had not been allowed to buy into NFL clubs. Davis was the Chargers' primary recruiter in the heated battle against the long-established NFL for the talent coming out of colleges. His major coup was the televised signing of the University of Arkansas' Lance Alworth under the goalposts after the 1962 Sugar Bowl. In fact, Davis had contacted Alworth long before the draft — while he still had college eligibility — and signed him in violation of NCAA rules. Alworth's Hall of Fame professional career made him a San Diego legend and made Davis a marketable coaching commodity.

At age thirty-two, Davis reached his dream job as the head coach and general manager of a franchise he would eventually own, the AFL's Oakland Raiders. He was Oakland's fourth coach in four years. In fairly short order, Davis would make Oakland as famous in football circles as Gertrude Stein did in poetry. He gave residents in this blue-collar city on the east side of San Francisco Bay what they needed: an image of credibility, toughness, and pride.

The Oakland Raiders were a bedraggled bunch of losers when the franchise owners, led by Wayne Valley, took a chance on Davis. The club had been conceived in 1960, after the NFL preempted the AFL's plan to put a franchise in Minneapolis by creating the Vikings. Oakland was the AFL's last-minute substitute, and the club would not play any games in Oakland for two years. Instead, games were held across the Bay Bridge in San Francisco, at Kezar Stadium then later at Candlestick Park. Bleeding money, the

Oakland owners used resources secretly supplied by Buffalo Bills owner Ralph Wilson to keep the franchise alive.

In 1963, Davis' first season as head coach, the team came home to Oakland's muddy Frank Youell Field, built below sea level. (Fittingly, Frank Youell was an undertaker from Oakland.) It would remain the site of Raiders home games for four seasons, until the publicly funded Oakland-Alameda Coliseum was completed. Davis tried to inject the team with his personal swagger, changing the team's colors to black and silver. (Studies later confirmed that a team dressed in black appears more aggressive and sinister.) Their emblem was a pirate wearing a football helmet and a patch over one eye, with two swords that appeared to stick out of his head.

Davis came to embody the Oakland franchise. *Sports Illustrated* reported: "In Oakland everything has been beautiful since Al Davis came to town." Davis, the magazine said, was "young, vigorous and rich . . . a tall, good-looking man with powerful arms and shoulders which he keeps hard by lifting weights in his cellar. He has white, shiny teeth and blond, wavy hair which, despite constant attention, is receding on either side of the middle. Stand him on a pedestal and there he is, Mr. America."

Davis made plain from the outset that the clock was running on the Raiders franchise: "The past is now the past, and we have five years to make the Raiders economically viable. We have to be able to compete." To re-make the Raiders, Davis reached out to sign college players before their undergraduate eligibility had expired, once again patently violating NCAA rules. He traded for football apostates thought uncontrollable by other franchises and remolded them as Raiders. He traded away any player who criticized him publicly, like Fred Williamson. He used the league's draft combined with his own intuition to select future Raiders, and he scored more often than he fumbled. He wanted players who would be as aggressive and angry on the field as he was off the field. Years later his captain, left guard Gene Upshaw, would admit: "We're not a bunch of choirboys and Boy Scouts. They say we're the Halfway House of the NFL. Well, we live up to that image every chance we get."

In return for their loyalty, Davis allowed his players personal freedoms that were rare on usually conformist football clubs, but he would not countenance prejudice and racism on his squad and all his players knew that. He was especially sensitive about anti-Semitism, reflecting his Jewish heritage and the discrimination and exclusion he always thought he had suffered. He dominated, manipulated, and motivated his franchise, discrading those who proved disloyal and gradually reshaping the club.

Davis was a fierce advocate of the underdog AFL and especially successful in his battles to steal players from the rival National Football League. When AFL commissioner Joe Foss resigned, Davis moved to New York City as his successor, an unlikely choice by AFL owners considering his abrasive style, but strongly supported by Ralph Wilson, the influential owner of the AFL franchise in Buffalo. (Oakland's chief owner Wayne Valley had recommended Davis for the job as a way to free the club from Davis' control.) On his first day in New York, Davis instructed the staffer writing press releases about him to make sure to use the words "dynamic" and "genius" to describe the new commissioner. Davis continued to wage war against the NFL from the commissioner's office, even while AFL owners, on the brink of financial ruin, quietly sought peace behind his back.

Davis' plan of attack was audacious. He wanted the AFL to sign all of the NFL's quarterbacks and lined up seven for potential recruitment. That strategy was sufficient stimulus for Tex Schramm, president and general manager of the NFL's Dallas Cowboys, to approach Lamar Hunt, the owner of the Kansas City Chiefs and founding father of the AFL, about negotiating a truce and then a merger.

Over Davis' vociferous and public objection, the AFL owners accepted the NFL's offer to combine the two circuits. Three NFL clubs — the Colts, the Steelers, and the Browns — would move to the renamed American Football Conference in exchange for a $3 million payoff per team. Pete Rozelle would become the commissioner of the newly united football league. No one thought Davis would be a good choice to lead the combined enterprise. At thirty-seven, he was out of a job.

PETE ROZELLE: THE COMMISSIONER

Alvin Ray Rozelle was the polar opposite of the streetwise Al Davis. Born in South Gate, California, a suburb of Los Angeles, Rozelle attended Compton High School, spent two years in the Navy, then two years at Compton Junior College, where one of his baseball teammates was Duke Snider. He finished college at the University of San Francisco, graduating in 1950. He stayed on at USF for two years as the assistant athletic director, then left to join the Los Angeles Rams as the NFL club's publicity man. Smooth as silk, Rozelle was always the confident charmer while Davis was the insecure, abrasive anti-hero.

Rozelle rose through the ranks on the public-relations side of the Rams operation. He had been hired at the generous salary of $5,000 a year, and within five years became the general manager, a meteoric rise considering his focus was on marketing rather than player development. The club owners made him NFL commissioner at age thirty-four—a compromise choice after twenty-three ballots, but Rozelle was a man that few disliked. The *New York Times* described him as that "tall, slim young man with the Ivy League manner" who "eats, sleeps and breathes football." Rozelle would serve as commissioner for almost three decades, creating the most powerful sports business cartel in America. Art Rooney, the legendary owner of the Pittsburgh Steelers, later said that Rozelle was "a gift from the hand of Providence."

Rozelle's greatest success came when he packaged and sold the National Football League to the television networks, convincing owners that the wealth should be shared equally among the clubs. In 1956, the Green Bay Packers had received $75,000 for their television rights. In 1968, the Packers collected $1,238,735—a sixteen-fold increase. This amount would increase exponentially when ABC invented Monday Night Football, worth $3 million more for each club. At the time Rozelle became commissioner, an NFL franchise sold for about $1 million; when he retired, that average had increased to $140 million.

While Rozelle is rightfully credited with making NFL owners rich, the sports packages he sold the networks also made television commercially successful. Consumers explained to researchers that the primary reason they bought televisions was to see sports, especially football. Networks especially valued those consumers and they increased the prices they charged advertisers who appreciated the demographics of sports viewers.

SUCCESS ON THE FIELD

After Rozelle was named commissioner of the merged leagues, Davis returned to Oakland at the invitation of Wayne Valley, who offered him both the general manager's position and a share of the franchise ownership. The club would be run by a three-man triumvirate. Davis' share cost him $18,000, money he borrowed. He was given the grandiose title of Managing General Partner. Perhaps Valley felt guilty about having exiled Davis to the AFL central office, then using him as a front man while negotiations eliminated the need for his job.

Eventually, Valley would pay for this kindness. He would sue Davis in an attempt to maintain control of the club. After this and some other bitter internecine litigation, Davis would prevail. Just as Davis taught his defensive backs to play "bump and run" with receivers, the abrasive magnate played bump and run with anyone who stood in his way, including Wayne Valley, the man who had given him his first (and only) head coaching job in professional football, then offered him co-ownership of the franchise.

With John Madden and Tom Flores as his head coaches and Kenny Stabler and Jim Plunkett as his starting quarterbacks, Davis won three Super Bowls for the growing numbers of Raiders fans who filled the Oakland Coliseum. He explained: "Our only inflexible goal is to win." The Raiders compiled the best record in professional football over a period of two decades, adopting the pirate scoundrel as team paragon. Male couch potatoes around the country identified with the outlaw image of the renegade Raiders. Fans stretched the persona to the extreme, and Davis loved it all. The Oakland crowd, dressed in outrageous costumes with painted faces, crowed their joy as the club annually bested league rivals. (Opponents accused him of cheating by watering the field for home games, but it seems only fair to point out that the club played half its games on someone else's turf.) Davis finally had achieved true success, but he was not yet satisfied.

DAVIS V. ROZELLE: ROUND 1

Al Davis' first legal brawl with Pete Rozelle came as a sideshow to a suit brought by the so-called "Hitman," Raiders defensive back George Atkinson, against Steelers coach Chuck Noll. The genesis of the litigation dates from the first game of the 1976 season between the Steelers—the Super Bowl winners in 1975 and 1976—and the Raiders—who would win the Super Bowl in 1977. Lynn Swann, the Steelers' Pro Bowl receiver, ran a pattern down the right side of the field, then cut toward the middle. Pittsburgh quarterback Terry Bradshaw had to scramble, and eventually threw downfield to Franco Harris. Away from the play, Atkinson crunched Swann with a forearm to the base of Swann's helmet. No official saw the assault, and therefore no penalty was called. Swann suffered a concussion and would miss two games.

The next day at a press conference, Coach Noll, who enjoyed his public reputation as a "straight arrow," called Atkinson part of a "criminal element" that should be kicked out of the league. A week later, Commissioner Rozelle fined Noll $1,000 for his comments. (Noll had violated the league rule that prohibited criticizing another team or player.) Rozelle also fined Atkinson $1,500 for his hit on Swann and wrote to him:

> In sixteen years in this office I do not recall a more flagrant foul than your clubbing the back of Swann's head totally away from the play. . . . Our sport obviously involves intense physical contact, but it requires of all players discipline and control and remaining within the rules. Every player deserves protection from the kind of unnecessary roughness that could end his career.

Steelers' owner Dan Rooney then piled on, blaming the Raiders' coaching staff for motivating Atkinson to injure Swann. He wrote to Rozelle:

> I believe it is a cowardly act to hit someone from behind with his back turned. I also believe, because of the number of Oakland Raider players making such attacks on Lynn, the Raiders must have an opinion that Lynn is vulnerable and can be forced out of the game, which makes such acts premeditated and involves the Raiders' coaching staff as well as the players.

Atkinson sued Noll for defamation based on his "criminal element" remark. He sought $2 million in damages and claimed that Noll was part of a conspiracy with Rooney and Rozelle to put down Al Davis and the Raiders. Davis funded Atkinson's lawsuit, eagerly jumping into the scrum. This legal battle would be only the first round of the championship series between Davis and Rozelle.

At trial before Federal Judge Samuel Conti in San Francisco District Court, the case became a caterwaul of six splendid trial lawyers. Willie Brown, then a California state legislator, later speaker of the house and mayor of San Francisco, explained to the jury that the Pittsburgh Steelers were "the leading cheap-shot artists in pro football," and that the Steelers were "trying their best to destroy Mr. Atkinson's career." Commissioner Rozelle, according to Brown, had allied himself with the Rooney family and "the league office has deliberately lied on behalf of the Pittsburgh Steelers.

I think when we finally finish, the question of pro football—as we know it—continuing to be played may very well be in doubt."

The Steelers were certainly not outgunned in the litigation. James Martin MacInnis, a premier northern California defense attorney, responded in his opening statement:

> One of the morals of this case is that, in real life, Mr. Atkinson may be a charming young man. You may safely invite him to your drawing room, to your home. But you may not with equal safety encounter him past the line of scrimmage on a football field, particularly if your name is Lynn Swann and your back is turned. . . . Professional football, as outlined this afternoon, may appear as a primitive game to those who do not follow it. It may appear as gang warfare conducted in uniform, and it may be a lure to all that is violent within any one of us. But there are rules, and without those rules in football the strong would devour the weak and professional football would destroy itself within a short period of time.

The Steelers' insurance carrier had tried, but failed, to convince the club to settle the claim. Steelers owner Dan Rooney, whose father Art had been one of the NFL's early leaders, was adamant. To clean up the game, insults would have to be hurled in court.

In its case, the plaintiff showed film clips of hits on opponents made by Steelers players of the same magnitude as Atkinson's attack on Swann. The plaintiff called Coach Noll as a witness and inquired who else besides Atkinson was part of the "criminal element" in the NFL. Noll finally admitted that Mel Blount, "Mean Joe" Greene, Ernie Holmes, and Glen Edward would all be on his list. They were all Pittsburgh Steelers! (Blount later sued Noll for defamation and stated he would never play for Noll again.)

Ultimately, Commissioner Rozelle turned the tide for the defendant. He testified that Atkinson's hit on Swann, by comparison with the other inevitable contact in the sport, was "calculated to disable." His smooth demeanor, immaculate dress, and bronzed tan impressed the jury of four women and two elderly men, none of whom knew anything about football. They gasped when they saw films of the brutal violence on the gridiron, played over and over during the ten days of the ugly trial. After a mere four hours of deliberation, the jury returned a verdict for the defendant.

For Davis, the jury verdict simply meant he would have to even more vigilant in his lifelong battle for respect. He would use every opportunity to belittle and annoy the commissioner. Rozelle was equally vindictive, removing Davis from the league's important Competition Committee, which set scheduling and game rules, among other things. Nothing changed, however, regarding the reckless way the Raiders played on the field. Raider safety Jack Tatum, called "The Assassin," hit Patriots' receiver Darryl Stingley the following season, leaving Stingley a quadriplegic. Although some called them hoodlums, Davis was proud of his team. He remained unrepentant. He told *Inside Sports* magazine: "You've got to dominate to get things done."

DAVIS V. ROZELLE: ROUND 2

The litigation that brought Al Davis front and center in the history of sports justice had its origin in the following year, 1980, when another California franchise, the Los Angeles Rams, moved from the Coliseum to a better facility in Orange County's suburban Anaheim. Carroll Rosenbloom, the Rams owner, was an NFL insider. He had been the longtime owner of the Baltimore Colts, but grew tired of Baltimore's Memorial Stadium and the Baltimore media. Yearning to head west, where he had business and family connections, Rosenbloom worked a deal with Robert Irsay in July 1972 to trade Irsay's Rams for Rosenbloom's Colts, plus four million dollars in cash.

In sunny California, Rosenbloom began to explore options to the Los Angeles Coliseum. First constructed for the 1932 Olympics, the structure was showing its age. Rams attendance had declined annually even though the club continued to perform well on the field. In 1978 he announced the move south. Because Anaheim was within the club's geographic seventy-five-mile region, established under National Football League rules, the Rams could relocate without league approval. The Coliseum immediately began the search for another tenant, exploring both the possibility of an expansion team with the National Football League and the relocation of other clubs. Pete Rozelle publicly expressed his concern about any franchise relocations. Undeterred, Bill Robertson, the president of the L.A. Coliseum Commission, called Al Davis to see if he was interested in moving the Raider franchise.

The Coliseum sued the NFL for allowing the Rams to leave Los Angeles and for interfering with the stadium's ability to find another tenant. At a club owners meeting in Chicago, Rozelle prepared for the decisive legal battle he knew was coming. Rule 4.3 of the league's by-laws required a unanimous vote of the owners to approve any franchise relocation. Rozelle, advised by legal counsel, knew that a requirement of unanimity allowed a single owner to veto any move and would raise significant antitrust issues. In October 1978, the owners modified the rule to require a three-fourths majority to approve relocation. At that October meeting, Al Davis urged his league brethren to abolish Rule 4.3 altogether or to provide standards to be followed in approving relocations. They were not interested. When his fellow owners unanimously approved Rozelle's suggested modification, Davis abstained.

The L.A. Coliseum's suit against the NFL claimed that the league's interference with the facility's effort to attract a tenant violated federal antitrust laws. Davis had indicated publicly that he wanted to pursue the Los Angeles opportunity once the Raiders' lease in Oakland expired, after the 1989 season. Davis had regularly raised concerns with Alameda County about the inadequacy of the Oakland facility, in particular the absence of luxury boxes, which would produce revenue that did not have to be shared with other NFL teams. Although the Oakland Coliseum had been sold-out for eleven years, Davis explained: "I believe professional football in the '80s must have a stadium that's comfortable." He offered no evidence that any of the Oakland fans had raised any concerns about comfort at the Coliseum.

Comfort for the spectators, of course, was not Davis' primary motivation. He had outgrown Oakland and saw a move to the bright lights of Los Angeles as the vindication of his lifelong effort to achieve recognition and respect. Walter O'Malley, his fellow Brooklynite, had always been one of his role models. Moving to Los Angeles, as O'Malley had done, would reinforce Davis' self-image as a premier promoter and entrepreneur. At the same time, Los Angeles, as a huge market, certainly would increase his revenue.

The Oakland Coliseum, assured by the NFL that the Raiders could not actually move, failed to respond to Davis' demands for improvements in the stadium. Just to make sure, the Oakland city government initiated a legal action of eminent domain to "take" the Raiders franchise, just as it would a row of abandoned houses. Davis, in turn, negotiated a favorable deal with the Los Angeles Coliseum.

Davis commented to the press: "I'm not for anarchy. I love the NFL. But I'll be damned if I'm going to let those Oakland Coliseum people hold me hostage." He also had little interest in becoming just another NFL insider:

"I don't want to look like the other owners. It's establishment." Rozelle responded: "Al says he's not for anarchy, and I'm sure he wants a stable league. He just wants anarchy for himself. I don't know why he didn't seek league support when he was having trouble over his lease with the politicians in Oakland, and I know his trouble was very legitimate then. I don't know why he didn't let the other owners know what was happening." Rozelle then proceeded to explain to the press how the NFL had bludgeoned politicians in Baltimore and Minneapolis into submission. Of course, it would have done the same thing for his old pal Al.

Davis moved the team's business office to Los Angeles and set up shop at the University Hilton. Within five days, he sold 30,000 season tickets for the "Los Angeles Raiders" and leased seventy of the ninety-nine luxury boxes, which were not yet built. Although Davis was ready to take advantage of this opportunity for the 1980 season, Rozelle, on behalf of the owners, officially informed him that the league would not schedule any games against the Raiders if they were to be played in Los Angeles. Davis' fellow owners despised him. Meeting at Marriott's Rancho Las Palmas Resort in Rancho Mirage, down the freeway from Los Angeles, they had voted 22–0, with five abstentions, against authorizing the Raiders' move. Rozelle announced to the press: "Every franchise of both leagues will remain in its present location."

Al Davis then joined the L.A. Coliseum's suit against the NFL, seeking $160 million in damages and naming Rozelle as an individual defendant. This would be round 2 in his battle with Rozelle (or round 3 if you count Rozelle's triumph over Davis for commissioner of the merged AFL-NFL). Pittsburgh Steelers owner Dan Rooney recognized that the business of the professional game had come to a fork in the road: "I think [Davis will] find that we're committed to go all the way on this thing. Our constitution, our whole league is at stake."

The Raiders stayed in Oakland for the 1980 season. Davis knew he was now an official outcast. Not one owner had voted to allow a move that made good business sense to him. In an interview with the *New York Times*, Davis publicly insulted their intelligence: "Not all of them are the brightest of human beings." The owners, in turn, joined forces with Rozelle, who had made them all rich with a lucrative set of television contracts.

Forced to stay in Oakland during the pendency of the litigation, Davis suffered the scorn of the local newspapers. Attendance dropped for the first time since Davis had made the Raiders an object of local adoration. Despite a shaky start to the season—his club was picked to finish last in its division—the Raiders made the playoffs as a wild-card team and won another Super Bowl, defeating the Philadelphia Eagles 27–10. Pete Rozelle presented the Vince Lombardi Trophy to Al Davis in the locker room after the game. Rozelle used both hands, thus avoiding having to shake Davis' hand on national television. Davis mumbled: "Thanks very much, uh, thanks very much, Commissioner." Inside, he was smiling.

THE ANTITRUST PARADIGM

Any fan knows that teams in every sport compete fiercely to claim a season championship. That competition creates the spectacle that is sold to spectators and television viewers. Television, in turn, can make a sport like football a powerful and iconic force in American society. Yet in order to achieve the competition that consumers seek, sports clubs must cooperate in setting the rules of the game. Without a level playing field, the game would not be a sport. Each club must have worthy opponents in order to produce sports entertainment. There is a need, therefore, to strive to equalize talent and ensure that the outcome of each game is uncertain. On any given Sunday, as the saying goes, any NFL team should have a chance to beat any other.

The NFL has achieved these goals quite effectively. Shared television revenue almost guarantees that each club remains solvent and able to purchase the service of talented players. The annual player draft, with selections in reverse order of performance the previous season, also helps to equalize talent. The upper limit on squad size prohibits the stockpiling of players. In an effort to sell a truly national product to the television networks, the NFL spread franchises from coast to coast.

Federal antitrust laws, however, may interfere with the NFL's effort to maintain collective control over its joint enterprise. Starting with the Sherman Act in 1890 and continuing with the Clayton Act of 1914, Congress embodied in federal statutes the goal of promoting economic competition among firms in a market. The idea was to maximize consumer welfare by encouraging firms to become more efficient than their competitors and produce better products at lower prices. This goal applied to all industries, including the business of sports.

There is one exception, however. Baseball was declared exempt from these antitrust laws by a wrongheaded 1922 Supreme Court decision based on the curious finding that the National Game did not affect interstate commerce. The Court later reaffirmed its baseball-only precedent in 1953 and again in Curt Flood's case in 1972. Congress would later repair some of the damage in the Curt Flood Act of 1998, but only with regard to Major League labor relations and not to business dealings among its owners.

Congress appreciated the accuracy of Adam Smith's prediction about human behavior in *The Wealth of Nations*, first published in 1776: "People of the same trade seldom meet together, even for merriment and diversion, but the conversation ends in a conspiracy against the public, or in some contrivance to raise prices." That was why federal law prohibited "every contract, combination or conspiracy . . . in restraint of trade." As a matter of national policy and the law, Congress said that America's economy should be governed by the free market and not by business cartels or conspiracies.

The Supreme Court recognized that a blanket application of this prohibition on all contracts "in restraint of trade" would interfere with legitimate business activities that fostered consumer welfare, such as contracts to supply raw materials or to distribute finished products. Those arrangements could keep economic competitors from pursuing the same economic advantages. In a 1901 decision, the Court ruled that the Sherman Act required the application of a "Rule of Reason" in antitrust cases. An arrangement between two or more firms that had an anticompetitive effect could be immunized from antitrust liability if the defendants' business justifications were consistent with the purposes of the antitrust laws.

Deciding where to locate a business was exactly the kind of decision covered by the antitrust laws. Individual businesses in the free marketplace should make those economic decisions, not the boys in the backroom, who could divide up geographic regions to avoid competing with one another. When Al Davis wanted to relocate his franchise to Los Angeles, against the wishes of the other NFL owners, he threatened to upset the league's control over the allocation of territories. League owners wanted the stability that would foster fan loyalty and traditional geographic rivalries. They wanted to make sure that clubs did not congregate in only a few populous markets. Restrictions on relocation would certainly have an impact on business competition — competitors in the same local market, for example, might have lowered ticket prices — but the league's justifications in dispersing franchises on a national basis might outweigh the detrimental effect on competition.

THE TRIAL

The trial of Davis' suit against the NFL began in May 1981 in Los Angeles. The league had moved for a change in venue, but Judge Harry Pregerson denied the motion. The NFL bemoaned the fact that Davis now had the home-field advantage, since Angelenos would certainly want more football in Southern California rather than an empty Coliseum. They would want the "Silver and Black" in their neighborhood.

The league's principal argument at trial was that Davis had agreed to be bound by the NFL's constitution and by-laws, which included Rule 4.3 requiring approval for the relocation of franchises. Rozelle and the other owners had followed that rule to the letter. Why shouldn't a court enforce a promise that Davis freely undertook? Davis claimed that the agreement he signed violated the nation's antitrust laws. He could not be bound by the terms of an illegal contract, and the law should not enforce illegal provisions. Would the Los Angeles jury agree with him?

Davis was represented in court by Joseph Alioto, a former mayor of San Francisco and renowned courtroom performer, known especially for his expertise in antitrust law. Alioto had won the *Radovich* case in the U.S. Supreme Court in 1957, which held that football (unlike baseball) was bound by the nation's antitrust laws. Davis and the L.A. Coliseum were now using those laws to declare unconditional war on the league and its commissioner.

Both Rozelle and Davis testified at the trial, each for more than a week. Rozelle distinguished Davis' move of hundreds of miles from Carroll Rosenbloom's move of 31.4 miles to Anaheim. Rozelle was particularly worried about the impact the Raiders' move would have on fan loyalty and business reputation. Davis' pocketbook certainly had not been hurting at the Oakland Coliseum. The stadium had sold out each home game for years, and now Davis had abandoned those loyal supporters. Rozelle was rattled on cross-examination by Alioto, however, and Davis enjoyed the spectacle of the smooth operator unhinged.

During the trial, Judge Pregerson ruled on two motions that had an important impact on the litigation. He dismissed the individual defendants, including Rozelle, from the litigation. Then he denied the league's request that it should be found a "single entity." The antitrust laws required that there be a conspiracy between or among individual firms. If the NFL were considered a single economic entity, it could not be found to have conspired with itself.

The case was submitted to the Los Angeles jury, which deadlocked 8–2 in favor of Davis and the L.A. Coliseum. While awaiting a retrial, Rozelle lobbied Congress, without success, to exempt football from the antitrust laws.

The second trial commenced in March 1982. Alioto argued that the league's actions were evidence of its "monopolistic practices," designed "to shackle a competitor and to shut off the lifeline of the Los Angeles Coliseum." The San Francisco attorney was not kind to the Oakland Coliseum, referring to it as "the lousiest stadium in the league" in "an inferior city." Rozelle again testified at length about the virtues of the Rams' relocation to Anaheim and the vices of the Raiders' move to Los Angeles. He also admitted on the stand that the league wanted to keep Los Angeles available as an expansion opportunity that would benefit all the owners and not just Al Davis.

In his testimony at the second trial, Davis complained that, by moving to a better stadium, the Rams had earned five million dollars a year more than the Raiders. (He did not mention that, while still in Oakland, the Raiders' franchise had been the fifth most profitable club in the league.) The league's actions, the Raiders' move, and the interests of the stadiums were, apparently, not about loyalty or good will; the whole dispute was about money, who would receive it, and in what amounts. It was also about personalities and personal vendettas.

An all-female, six-person jury received the case on May 7, 1982, deliberated for only six hours, and reached a verdict for Al Davis and the Los Angeles Coliseum. The jury rejected the league's claims that the relocation would harm it in any foreseeable manner. Davis explained to the press that the verdict meant that Rozelle, "this one fellow with all the power, was wrong." Rozelle, in turn, predicted that if the jury's verdict was upheld on appeal, it would be the final gun for football. Nonetheless, pursuant to the court decision, the 1982 NFL schedule listed home games for the "Los Angeles Raiders."

On appeal, the Ninth Circuit Court of Appeals focused carefully on some exceedingly difficult antitrust, economic, and business issues. The trial court had dismissed the NFL's argument that it was unitary in nature. The circuit court agreed that the league was not a "single entity" as a matter of law. Expanding on the reasoning of the trial court, the circuit noted that NFL clubs are separate business entities separately owned, each with independent value. Each club establishes and follows independent management policies with regard to ticket prices, concessions, luxury box seats, and other decisions. The clubs compete to acquire players, coaches, and management personnel. This was sufficient basis, the circuit court reasoned, upon which to reject the league's "single entity" theory.

The circuit court did recognize that, while the NFL was not a single entity, club owners were not typical economic competitors. For example, while supermarkets compete within a city for customers and might succeed by driving the competition out of business, NFL clubs need each other to create the business of football competition. The clubs enjoy vertical and horizontal contractual relationships that prevent all-out economic competition. On the field, one football club may seek to shut out its opponent and score every time it touches the ball. In the boardroom, however, one football club does not seek to drive other football clubs out of business. Each needs viable and relatively equal competitors to play on Sunday afternoon. This brake on all-out competition, however, does not mean that NFL clubs are allowed under federal law to enjoy the economic rents of a classic cartel, one of the profits that result from territorial exclusivity. That was at issue in the *L.A. Coliseum* case.

There was not much doubt that the NFL's vote on Rule 4.3 "restrained competition." It had prohibited a competitor from moving to a new, and potentially more profitable, location. As a result, the suburban Rams did not have to compete against the Raiders for the L.A. football entertainment dollar. The NFL claimed that the rule as applied fostered stability within the league and avoided ruinous competition between clubs that might dilute the entertainment product. But the Sherman Act was designed to avoid what might be called "ruinous collusion." As a result of this application of Rule 4.3, the Rams could set monopoly prices for tickets, to the detriment of the consuming public. In addition, Rule 4.3 restricted competition between stadiums for tenants. As a result, the L.A. Coliseum could not lease its facility to a willing tenant.

The league explained to the court that Rule 4.3 was necessary in order to create "NFL football," and that it was merely an "ancillary restraint." Territorial divisions, the league argued, were critical in order to produce "NFL football." The problem with this blanket excuse was that some major metropolitan areas (including Los Angeles, soon to be the nation's second-largest city) could in fact afford a second franchise, much as the New York metropolitan area supports the Giants and the Jets.

In court, the NFL explained the justifications for its territorial allocations. It allowed each franchise owner to enjoy the "legitimate fruits of the contract" signed with other owners. NFL owners made a large initial investment and Rule 4.3 allowed that to be recouped. The rule also fostered financial stability, fan loyalty, traditional rivalries, attendance, and television viewing. Finally, and without much shame, the NFL argued that Rule 4.3 protected local governments that have made investments in their stadiums.

The court was willing to accept that some territorial restriction might be necessary to encourage participation in the NFL venture. At issue was the duration of those restrictions. The Rams franchise had had thirty-five years in Los Angeles to recoup its initial investment (after it fled from Cleveland). There would be no significant impact on the football television market as a result of having two NFL teams in greater Los Angeles as opposed to greater San Francisco. The court was not pleased with the NFL's self-serving concern expressed for local governments, noting that the league had used the threat of franchise relocation to obtain better deals for its member teams.

The court concluded that the National Football League had available alternatives to achieve its expressed goals without imposing such a detrimental effect on competition. Standards could be incorporated into Rule 4.3 to prevent unwise relocations. There were no durational limits in Rule 4.3 explaining how long a team must stay in a particular market. If the NFL wanted to foster team rivalries and fan loyalty, those factors should be noted in the rule. Congress, however, wanted the marketplace and not a group of seven owners (one-fourth of those entitled to vote) to determine where other clubs could do business. And those poor municipalities the NFL claimed it wanted to protect? They could protect themselves through longer leases with the clubs.

The NFL failed to prove to the court's satisfaction that the relocation of the Raiders to Los Angeles would cause the NFL any economic harm, although the application of Rule 4.3 certainly injured Davis. Although the NFL stated quite correctly that the antitrust laws were designed primarily to protect competition between brands (NFL v. MLB, for example), not within a brand, there was still the issue of the extent and duration of the restraint. A more tailored solution would be necessary to pass muster under the antitrust law. Factors such as population, quality of facilities, re-

gional balance, fan loyalty, and location continuity were relevant consider-
ations that should be made part of the internal decision-making process.

AL DAVIS AND THE BUMP-AND-RUN

Davis had gone one-on-one with the NFL establishment in a court of
law and prevailed, freeing individual franchise owners to follow the marketplace as they saw fit. No longer could cities ignore threats by clubs to
leave. The impact of Davis' victory on franchise relocation was immediate.
The NFL had been both shocked and enfeebled by the court decision. Robert Irsay's Colts migrated to Indianapolis, and Bill Bidwell's Cardinals left
St. Louis for Phoenix. Other relocations would soon follow.

Davis' litigation did not eviscerate Raider football, however, and the
Brooklyn maverick did not lose his focus. The Los Angeles Raiders began
play in the fall of 1982. On January 22, 1984, Davis and Rozelle would meet
again — after the Raiders trounced the Washington Redskins in Super Bowl
XVIII. Once again, Rozelle handed Davis the Lombardi Trophy. Five years
later, the NFL and Davis settled for a payout of $18 million to the Raiders
owner. In the same year, Rozelle would retire as perhaps the greatest commissioner in the history of professional sports.

MOVING AGAIN?

Al Davis was never comfortable in Los Angeles. He soon claimed that
the L.A. Coliseum Commission had failed to fulfill its promises to him.
Politics, combined with reduced fan interest, sent Davis shopping for a
new place to play. He had grown to hate the crumbling Los Angeles facility.
Although the stadium had 67,800 seats, it averaged only 52,290 in attendance for Raider games. The Los Angeles crowd never seemed to generate
the frenzy of the East Bay denizens. Davis estimated (without explaining his
method of calculation) that the apathetic fans cost the team four to six
points a game.

In 1987, while the L.A. Coliseum sued to enforce its contract with him,
Davis began to explore other Southern California options for his franchise.
Davis spoke with officials in Carson, twelve miles south of Los Angeles, and
at the Rose Bowl in Pasadena. The city of Irwindale, twenty-two miles east
of the Coliseum, offered Davis an abandoned quarry as the site for a new
stadium. To preserve its exclusive option, the town of 1,161 residents gave

Davis a nonrefundable deposit of $10 million. However, the deal for a promised "state of the art" stadium fell through. Davis kept the check.

In the meantime, the Oakland-Alameda County Coliseum was ready to lure the Raiders home. It promised sellouts for a decade. In 1990, Davis announced publicly that he intended to return the club to its rightful place in Oakland. After five more years of litigation, politics, and negotiations, Davis finally moved his Raiders back to the East Bay.

Before the return, Davis was sued by the NFL, which sought to recover three to four million dollars in revenue sharing from the personal seat licenses and club seats that the Raiders had sold at the renovated Oakland Coliseum. Davis and the city of Oakland responded with a $200 million countersuit, based on a variety of wrongdoings, both real and imagined. Davis also claimed that he still owned the league's expansion rights to Los Angeles — even though he had since moved eight hours north.

Litigation had become Davis' primary pastime. He spent March and April 2001 in a courtroom, wearing his silver tie and black jacket. He filed two other lawsuits, one against Oakland's Coliseum, claiming that the stadium authority had not lived up to its guarantee that home games would be sellouts. Davis also sued the NFL for damages suffered when the league allowed other teams to incorporate black into their uniforms and, in particular, for approving the logo of the Tampa Bay Buccaneers which looks a little like the Raiders' pirate.

As he roamed the practice field wearing a white warm-up suit (he would sometimes change to an all-black version), Davis was both master of his domain and a contradictory mixture of idiosyncrasies: vindictive and gracious, caring and officious, paranoid and arrogant. His one constant was the insistence that his club play "Raider football," the combination of a nasty, powerful running attack with a vertical game, and a ferocious defense with a target on the quarterback's chest. "We don't take what they give us," Davis would say about opponents: "We make them take what we give them."

Approaching the twilight of his long career, Davis had found one ally he could rely on, much as Tony Soprano could rely on Paulie Walnuts. He had found the law. The Associated Press reported that, from 1997 to 2001, he incurred $33.5 million in legal fees. As he passed his eightieth birthday in 2009, a frail Al Davis had tamed his swagger, but not his defiant spirit.

Justice for Al Davis offered him the respect he had long sought. But Davis' victory, of course, accrued to the detriment of others. The National

Football League lost unrestricted control over its brand. The NFL became gun-shy after the Davis affair, allowing clubs to move at will. The Rams, who had started the game of musical chairs by moving from Cleveland to Los Angeles to Anaheim, fled east to St. Louis in 1995. The NFL, committed to a national business footprint, was left with the absurdity of Los Angeles, the nation's second largest market, without a football franchise.

Justice for Davis meant that loyal fans paid the price of the marketplace, not only in the cost of tickets, but also in the potential loss of their beloved team to another city. A freer marketplace for "the game played with a prolate spheroid" meant more money for those who already had money.

Most significantly, Davis' antitrust suit against the NFL was the final installment of his personal vendetta against his fellow NFL club owners and Pete Rozelle. NFL owners had denied Davis the opportunity to relocate because of who he was. Davis fought back because the league's leader was the person he saw as his archenemy. Neither motive was appropriate for invoking the system of sports justice. But Davis was more than willing to put the NFL joint venture at risk. He knew that the games played off the field were rough and nasty, and he had complete confidence that the self-made tough guy from Brooklyn would prevail.

CHAPTER 9

THE TIGHT END, FREEDOM, AND THE ANTITRUST LAWS

I will not permit thirty men to travel four hundred miles to agitate a bag of wind.

ANDREW D. WHITE

Baseball is what we were. Football is what we have become.

MARY MCGRORY

• • • Football began on the nation's college campuses shortly after the end of the Civil War. An amalgam of English rugby and soccer, the game proved very rough. As a result, it was irresistible to the young men who played the sport, even if Cornell University's president, Andrew D. White, disapproved of the pastime. (His "bag of wind" referred to the ball at the center of the mayhem. White resigned from Cornell in 1885. The school would become a football powerhouse by the end of that century.)

It is unclear exactly when football began. Rutgers and Princeton played a contest on November 6, 1869, that some consider the first game of American football, although it was more like soccer since no one picked up the odd-shaped ball. Harvard played McGill in Cambridge in 1874, in a rugby-like game much closer to modern football. By 1876, the boys from Harvard had joined others from Yale, Princeton, and Columbia to form the Intercollegiate Football Association. The elite schools began to recruit a sturdy stock of Midwestern young men to bolster their club teams, and the game was on.

To be a sport, football needed written rules that would be uniformly enforced. Walter Camp, the "Father of American Football," supplied those rules in his 1891 book *American Football*, setting the game firmly on its modern path. Although the rules shifted over time, football was always a violent confrontation to gain and hold territory in an effort to score points at the opponent's goal line.

Professional football also began late in the nineteenth century. Barnstorming teams in western Pennsylvania visited neighboring towns for friendly, if blood-soaked, matches. Participants would do anything to avoid a dreary and dangerous life in the mines or mills, and playing football was one of the few available options. The modern sport emerged from this working-class, immigrant background, even though it was mostly the East Coast colleges that perfected the game. Open professionalism with paid players dates from 1892, when William "Pudge" Huffelfinger of the Alleghany Athletic Association received five hundred dollars to play in a game against the Pittsburgh Athletic Club. On September 3, 1895, teams from

Latrobe and Jeannette in western Pennsylvania played what was considered the first professional game.

On August 20, 1920, representatives of the Akron Pros, Canton Bulldogs, Cleveland Indians, and Dayton Triangles met in a Jordan and Hupmobile automobile showroom in Canton, Ohio, and formed the American Professional Football Conference. On September 17, they were joined by the Hammond Pros and Muncie Flyers of Indiana, the Rochester Jeffersons of New York, and the Rock Island Independents, Decatur Staleys, and Racine Cardinals of Illinois in what was now called the American Professional Football Association. These entrepreneurs, joined later that year by the Buffalo All-Americans, the Chicago Tigers, the Columbus Panhandles, and the Detroit Heralds, formed the first lasting professional circuit of clubs. It would become the National Football League in 1922, although the early all-professional game was a far cry from the business juggernaut we know today.

By the 1950s, professional football began to outstrip the college game for national attention. Many credit the 1958 NFL championship game between the New York Giants and the Baltimore Colts, decided in sudden-death overtime, as the dawn of today's pro football supremacy. America's blue-collar sport was filled with military precision and violence, rivalry and retribution. It attracted hot-blooded participants and a growing cadre of spectators who lived through their heroes' performances on the field each Sunday.

JOHN MACKEY AND A UNION OF FOOTBALL PLAYERS

John Mackey was a premier athlete: All-American in high school football, basketball, and track; All-American in football at Syracuse University; All-Pro in the National Football League over a ten-year career. A Hall of Fame performer for the Baltimore Colts, Mackey revolutionized the way the tight end position was played. He ran with the strength of a running back — "as if he were a bull," the *New York Times* said — and flew down the field like a wide receiver. Once Mackey caught a pass — generally thrown by quarterback Johnny Unitas or Earl Morrall — tacklers fell like blades of grass as he ploughed a swift path to the goal line.

After the merger of the National and American Football Leagues in 1970, John Mackey became president of the National Football League Players Association. In that capacity, he was the named plaintiff in a suit brought against the league—a suit that revolutionized the relationship between professional athletes and club owners in team sports. Mackey used the federal courts and federal law to obtain free agency for NFL players.

The suit seeking player free agency would not have been possible without the financial backing of a union. Members of the NFL's Cleveland and Green Bay teams had formed the first players association in 1956. Unhappy about players' pay and other terms of employment, the association sought to meet with club management to set minimum salaries and make other modest improvements. Management refused to deal with them, and in the first of what would become a series of court cases, the union bought suit seeking to establish that football was a business that "affected interstate commerce" and thus was covered by the nation's antitrust laws. It would take until the 1970s, however, before genuine collective bargaining between the NFL and the NFLPA would emerge, and even then it was a rocky field to traverse with the balance of power tipped heavily toward management.

The unionization of professional athletes has always seemed anomalous to the viewing public. Playing sports for a living appears to be such a dream that players' complaints about their fringe benefits and free agency seems rather petty to fans. How could men earning salaries to play a game throw in their lot with a trade union? It seems preposterous.

Yet the working life of a professional football player, to borrow a phrase from Hobbes' *Leviathan*, can be "nasty, brutish, and short." With an average career span of four or five seasons, followed by the chronic pain of injuries, the possibility of dementia, and the prospect of a shortened life expectancy, a professional football player has many legitimate concerns that cannot be easily assuaged by a few years of high pay. Most importantly, whether the athlete plays or sits or leaves the squad all together—as in all professional sports—is a matter within the total discretion of the coaches, who are selected by management. There is no right to a job or even a right to be treated fairly. Unions are formed from this cauldron of employee uncertainty.

Professional football players are only employees, albeit highly paid in recent years. They play a game quite different from most other sports, and not simply because of the presence of authorized violence. Football is a corporate game of formalized brutality where units of talented, large, and agile men perform choreographed plays in unison. Success depends on how well they execute the plays together. Football is often described as a contest to gain territory, but gaining territory is only the means to an end — to score points by a touchdown or field goal. (No one wins a football game solely by gaining more yards than the opponent or catching more passes.) Baseball, by comparison, is an individualistic sport — pitcher against batter — with teammates that are arguably unnecessary on many specific plays. Football is tougher, more bounded by time, and more welcoming of violence and emotion.

The NFL Players Association never enjoyed the solidarity of its brother organizations in other professional sports, such as baseball. Its strikes, while certainly troublesome to the public, never proved powerful enough to catalyze victory at the negotiating table. How can we explain the difference in strength between the football and baseball unions? The superstars of football, unlike their counterparts in baseball, did not experience the leveling and bonding experience of the minor leagues. Their development system in Division I college football programs brought them much acclaim on campus, even if they could legally receive no compensation other than a free college education. They did not spend seasons traveling on buses from town to town like Single A baseball players.

The baseball players union also enjoyed more experienced executive leadership than its football counterpart. Marvin Miller, an economist who was the longtime executive director of the Major League Baseball Players Association, had worked for years with the Steelworkers Union before coming over to baseball. John Mackey would prove a stalwart president for the football union, but he did not have the familiarity and training with labor relations that Miller brought to the table. Mackey was battle-tested on the field, however, and that brought him significant legitimacy among his troops.

A BRILLIANT TIGHT END

The grandson of a slave — and the son of a Baptist preacher who escaped from South Carolina a few steps ahead of the Ku Klux Klan — John Mackey grew up in a strict home. In the 1950s, his father was a pastor at the Mount Sinai Baptist Church on New York's Long Island. At home, Mackey learned the lessons of respect and trustworthiness. His word was his bond. At Hempstead High School, Mackey learned how to use his developing skills as an athlete. He admired the great Jim Brown, five years his senior, who starred for Manhasset High School, about ten miles to the north. Mackey enjoyed a splendid high school career, including weekly touchdowns for the Hempstead Mustangs and equally impressive performances on the basketball court, and was named the outstanding high school athlete in Nassau County in 1959. He decided to attend Syracuse University and play football on Piety Hill, as had his hero Brown. And like Jim Brown before him, the swift and elusive Mackey would be the only black player on the Orangemen's team.

Mackey succeeded on the ball field by learning to hit the man who had been assigned to hit him. He was a tough runner to bring down. A smart player, he flourished on both offense and defense in college. Described by the *New York Times* as the Orangemen's "famed [and] brilliant right end" and by *Sports Illustrated* as a "superb blocker, defender and pass catcher," Mackey won second team All-American honors after his senior year and was selected in the second round of the 1962 draft by the Baltimore Colts.

It was Mackey's good fortune to play the professional game for eight seasons with perhaps the greatest quarterback in the history of the game, Johnny Unitas. Unitas and Mackey developed a smooth rhythm on the field. They knew each other's moves and that synchronicity proved remarkably successful. As a rookie in 1963, Don Shula's first year as coach of the Colts, Mackey averaged more than twenty yards a catch and made the Pro Bowl. As he matured as a professional, Mackey became known for a menacing forearm, brute force at the line of scrimmage, and a fleet sprint to the goal line.

The city of Baltimore was segregated when Mackey joined the NFL, and racism corroded the professional game. Clubs had secret quotas for the number of black players they could play at any one time, notwithstanding the talent of the player pool. Under Coach Shula, however, Mackey and other black players flourished. Shula valued smart players and Mackey fit that bill. Mackey and Shula learned from each other. Each became a superstar—one on the field, the other on the sidelines.

CREATING A MORE PERFECT UNION

The NFL Players Association was formed in 1959. Each player paid fifty dollars to join. In the early years, it proved woefully ineffective in its efforts to better the work life of players. Involvement in union activity was risky for players. A club's union representatives were almost certain to be traded, benched, or waived—a clear violation of national law that went unredressed. During or after the 1970 bargaining, for example, San Francisco's player representative Kermit Alexander, an outstanding cornerback, was traded to Los Angeles; Pittsburgh's representative Roy Jefferson was traded to Baltimore; Dallas' representative John Wilbur, a starter at guard, was traded to St. Louis; and Miami's representative Dick Westmoreland was traded to Minnesota, then cut.

When the rival American and National Football Leagues merged in 1970, John Gordy resigned as president of the NFL Players Association. His AFL counterpart, Jack Kemp, supported John Mackey's candidacy to be president of the newly merged union. Colts owner Carroll Rosenbloom also urged Mackey to take on the leadership role. (Rosenbloom thought that owners could manipulate Mackey to control the union's activities.) Mackey agreed to become the union's standard bearer, but he would be anything but a pawn of management. Mackey told the press that the union (which he insisted was an "association" and not a "labor union") intended to press for increased pension benefits, a revised option clause, a larger share of product licensing, and improved fringe benefits. He anticipated that owners and players would enjoy "amicable negotiations."

Before the negotiations began, NFL commissioner Pete Rozelle invited Mackey to stay at his luxurious New York City apartment, where he had assembled some club executives, including the outspoken Tex Schramm of the Dallas Cowboys. Schramm cornered Mackey and asked, "Do you want to go down in history as the man who killed the goose that laid the golden egg?" But Mackey would not play Schramm's game. He arose early the next morning and left Rozelle's place before breakfast.

At the first informal discussion session between the two parties, management pressed Mackey to "keep it in the family" and urged the union not to bring in its own lawyer. At the first formal bargaining meeting, however, the owners brought in Ted Kheel, a noted New York City labor lawyer, who told Mackey to sign the draft agreement he had just been handed. Mackey walked out and sought counsel from University of Wisconsin labor-relations professor Nate Feinsinger. Feinsinger recommended a well-known Minneapolis attorney, but Mackey favored a younger lawyer from the Lindquist and Vennum firm, Ed Garvey. Garvey would work for the union for more than a decade, first as its attorney, then as its executive director.

As negotiations progressed in 1970, NFL club owners continued to demonstrate their disdain for the players and their union. Tex Schramm publicly objected to the union's effort to invade what he saw as "management's prerogatives." The owners vowed to show the union who was boss; that summer, they locked the players out of training camp. The union responded that the players were not planning to show up in any case — and would not do so even if owners opened the camps.

John Mackey had become the public face and voice of the players and their union. Perhaps parodying the owners' plea that he "keep it in the family," Mackey told reporters: "This is a family argument. We're not out to win as much as we are to get it settled amicably. You don't try to win in a family squabble. You just try to get it settled."

Mackey understood that owners wanted to sweep players' concerns under the artificial turf, and that management's "family" metaphor was meant to quiet the players. He had no such plan in mind. Already voted the best tight end in the history of football, Mackey had experience on the gridiron that others across the table lacked: "I've got broad shoulders," he told management's negotiators, "and I can take a lot more abuse than I've already had." There would be plenty of abuse, but Mackey proceeded full speed ahead, just as he had done on the field with the pigskin tucked under his arm. Recalling that time, Jack Kemp said that Mackey was "the smartest man in the room." But negotiations stalled when the parties could not agree on a site for the talks. It was Honolulu one week, New York the next, then Bimini, Miami, Minneapolis, Baltimore, Chicago, and Philadelphia.

Calling the players' bluff, the owners decided to open the training camps. At the same time, the owners' strategy was to pander to the players' guilt, seeking the union's capitulation because legendary Green Bay coach Vince Lombardi was dying. The union sent flowers instead. When the owners' lockout ended, the players' strike began. While a few players trickled in to camp, most did not break ranks. In the end, Commissioner Rozelle cajoled the owners into a settlement.

The 1970 strike showed management that the union took itself seriously, but the owners were not convinced that the players association had the staying power to produce significant change. Mackey announced that "There wasn't any winner. We have an agreement, that's the important thing." He realized that his career as a premier player would soon be over. He could not be a union leader and a tight end at the same time.

After the settlement, the union continued to deal with the owners' intransigence and lack of respect. When management attempted to make unilateral changes in the agreement, Mackey responded publicly: "We had hoped to work in cooperation with the owners, but until they begin to live up to their commitments, cooperation will not be possible." Months later, both parties finally signed the deal they had reached.

FREEDOM LITIGATION

Mackey's union found the negotiation process frustrating. Management's lack of respect for the union was apparent, and bargaining did not bring about the fundamental improvements in the labor relations system which the players had sought. As *New York Times* sports columnist Red Smith wrote, the NFL owners still evidenced "a feudal mentality." The owners certainly outplayed the association when it came to public relations, but public relations, after all, were Commissioner Rozelle's specialty. In the public's mind, the players were the greedy, ungrateful villains of the drama.

Because the union's effort to demonstrate economic power through a work stoppage was not convincing to the owners (even though it produced an agreement), Mackey and his fellow players decided to call a different play. Much as Mackey would make adjustments on the field during the course of a game, the union needed to change its strategy and tactics. For assistance in obtaining justice, it turned to the courts.

On May 24, 1972, thirty-two NFL players led by John Mackey filed suit in federal court in Minneapolis against the National Football League and its commissioner, Pete Rozelle. All of the plaintiffs were either union player representatives or free agents. The suit alleged that the NFL clubs had acted collusively, in violation of the nation's antitrust laws, to hold down player salaries by boycotting those players who had completed their contractual obligations. Unlike most other employees, the players' salaries were limited by a collusive arrangement among their employers — the antithesis of a free market. The owners' collusion, the suit alleged, violated the Sherman Antitrust Act, which prohibited "contracts, combinations or conspiracies in restraint of trade." In a free market, players, like other employees, should have been able to work for any club they wished at a price agreed upon by both owner and player. But that was not the way employment operated in the National Football League.

How did the owners accomplish this restraint of trade? They followed the so-called "Rozelle rule," named for the NFL's commissioner. This rule allowed players who had completed their contract option years to declare free agency and seek offers from other NFL clubs for their services. Considering only that aspect of the rule, it was the epitome of open competition. Then came the restraint that killed the free market. Under Article 12.1 (H) of the NFL's constitution and by-laws, any club acquiring a free agent would have to assign one or more of its players to the club losing the free agent or compensate that club with future draft choices. (In professional football, draft choices are very valuable commodities because those players have completed at least three years of college development and demonstrated their football potential.) Under the compensation portion of the rule, if the two clubs could not reach an agreement on compensation, "the Commissioner may name and then award to the former club one or more players . . . of the acquiring club as the Commissioner in his sole discretion deems fair and equitable; any such decision by the Commissioner shall be final and conclusive." Out of 176 cases over twelve years, Rozelle was required to set compensation five times.

Consider the following hypothetical example. Player Jones of the Giants has completed his contract obligations to the club. As a free agent, he can seek employment with any club that he wishes, including the Jets. Under the Rozelle rule, if the Jets sign Jones, then the Jets also have to compensate the Giants with players and/or draft choices of equal value.

The effective result of the rule is to convert free agency into a forced trade between two clubs, which makes the acquisition of any free agent much less appealing. In terms of player value, the acquiring club would have to give up exactly what it was obtaining by signing the free agent. Even if the acquiring club still wanted to proceed because, for example, it needed the particular skills the free agent brought with him, that free agent might receive a significantly lower salary offer than would be the case without the rule, since the club would also have to consider the cost of its obligation to the player's former club. And if the forced trade was not completed, the player's home club need not pay him what he might have obtained in a truly free market.

As a result of the Rozelle rule, a player's bargaining power in the free-agent market was constrained and restricted, and the player's value in the constrained market was undercut. Through the owners' establishment of this rule, a free market for players did not exist. The union claimed that the arrangement violated national antitrust laws which, as we have seen in Al Davis' case, were intended to prevent business competitors from colluding in this manner.

Through collective bargaining in 1968 and 1970, the NFL Players Association had not been able to modify the Rozelle rule's restrictions. The owners insisted that the rule was essential to maintaining competitive balance in the league. Although the collective bargaining agreements did not mention the compensation rule, they did incorporate by reference the NFL constitution and by-laws, which contained the rule. More than 90 percent of NFL players wanted the rule either abolished or substantially modified, but nothing would change in the absence of court intervention.

Mackey's suit was heard by Judge Earl Larson in federal court in Minneapolis in 1975. The players were represented by local attorney Edward Glennon, who would later handle many other cases for the association. John D. French of the major Minneapolis firm of Faegre & Benson was local counsel for the NFL and Rozelle, but the chief defense attorney was Washington's Paul Tagliabue, who in 1989 would succeed Rozelle as NFL commissioner.

The trial began on February 3, 1975, and would take fifty-five court days to complete. John Mackey testified as the first of sixty-three witnesses. "Salary wasn't the most important thing," Mackey explained: "It was pride. They couldn't pay me enough to sit on the bench [and not play]." He insisted that the freedom to play for a club that would use the player on the field was what was at stake. Each club had players who sat on the bench who could start for another club. Mackey's argument was ingenious, but it was also a bit disingenuous. The case really was about money, lots of money.

The owners' primary defense to the union's charges of illegal collusion was that the Rozelle rule was reasonable in light of the clubs' compelling business need to maintain continuity on their teams' rosters and competitive balance in the league, in turn protecting the sport's entertainment value. If there was to be a change in the NFL's pay structure, it should be addressed through collective bargaining—the owners' preferred venue—and not the federal courts. In collective bargaining, the owners believed they held the upper hand. Anything else, they argued, was pure "anarchy."

The owners argued that, without the Rozelle rule, a few very wealthy owners could accumulate all the talent and crush their opponents on the gridiron. The theory was absurd, as NFLPA executive director Ed Garvey explained to the press:

> It presumes irrational behavior on the part of the owners. They are profit maximizers, after all. They are not going to risk making a profit in order to corner the superteam that has no one to play. That argument assumes everyone is a sportsman owner except a few greedy guys.

The "crushing dynasty" theory, as it was called, made no economic sense. George Burman, the center for the Washington Redskins who was working on his Ph.D. in labor economics, explained further: "An important limitation is that no one would be willing to build a dynasty, and keep it, in a dying industry. An NFL franchise now goes for $20 million. What owner would want to see the value of his franchise drop to $3 million or to zero?" Moreover, a league with perennial losers would not be able to sell as attractive a product to the television networks.

Tex Schramm was always ready to respond to the union's public pronouncements. He offered a variation on the crushing dynasty theory: "Certain cities like New York, Los Angeles and Chicago, in that order, would always be favored because they can offer tremendous fringe benefits to a player. Weather and glamour would be important factors in attracting top players to Miami, New Orleans and San Francisco." Schramm's theory suggested that these six clubs would predominate in the absence of the Rozelle rule. But even if that were so, league rules limited each club to fifty-three players. Certainly there would be other good players available to the other clubs. The public, however, saw Pete Rozelle as imbued with Solomonic wisdom and neutrality, rather than as the defender of the owners' wealth and the status quo. It certainly bought the league's rhetoric, but would Judge Larsen?

After the trial, as the court reviewed the record, the owners tried to force the union back to the bargaining table. If the union clearly agreed to the Rozelle rule in negotiations, the league would be insulated from antitrust liability. The union knew that it had little bargaining power until it received a court ruling that could pressure management to revise the Rozelle rule's restrictive standards.

On December 30, 1975, Judge Larson handed the union the legal equivalent of a Super Bowl trophy. He ruled that the Rozelle rule was a *per se* violation of the nation's antitrust laws. The agreement among the member clubs under the Rozelle rule constituted a group boycott. (A boycott can be both an absolute refusal to deal with a third party—here, the players—or an agreement to deal only on certain terms—here, under the provisions of the Rozelle rule.) Judge Larson agreed with the union that this concerted refusal to deal with the players in a free market was precisely the kind of business activity censured by the antitrust laws. In response to the opinion, sports columnist Red Smith opined: "the day is approaching when football . . . must begin treating their employees like people."

On appeal, the Eighth Circuit Court of Appeals in St. Louis upheld the trial court's conclusions, but substantially modified the judge's reasoning. Judge Donald Lay, writing for the majority of a three-judge panel, ruled that the business of professional football had distinctive characteristics that required a special antitrust analysis. The *per se* approach Judge Larson had used did not sufficiently take these distinctive characteristics into account. Companies in business normally seek to expand their market share and even to drive their competitors out of business. In team sports, however, a league's clubs need each other to produce the entertainment product— here, NFL football—that is then sold to spectators and television networks. They need to cooperate in setting rules and schedules, for example. More importantly for purposes of the Rozelle rule, they need to achieve balanced competition among the participating clubs to enhance their product and attract consumers.

In its arguments to the circuit court, the NFL claimed that the Rozelle rule achieved an essential goal by fostering stability. Thus, instead of the *per se* approach followed by the trial judge, Judge Lay determined that it would be preferable to evaluate the Rozelle rule under the "Rule of Reason," first announced by the Supreme Court in 1901, which we saw applied in the Al Davis suit against the NFL. Under the Rule of Reason, the anticompetitive effects of the Rozelle rule would be balanced against its asserted pro-competitive justifications. Ultimately, the court would be the referee in this game, basing its judgment on the record of evidence developed in the trial court.

First, the circuit court examined the anticompetitive effects of the Rozelle rule. It was readily apparent that the rule had the direct effect of depressing player salaries by constraining the price players could receive for their services—either from a club acquiring a free agent or from the home club who wanted to keep that free agent. The rule had exactly the same economic impact as an agreement among rival firms on the salaries they would all pay their workers.

Consider the following hypothetical example. If all the supermarkets in town agreed on what they would pay their employees, that would prevent a produce clerk at one store from receiving a higher salary by working for another store. That kind of agreement among supermarkets would be a "combination" of firms that "restrained trade"; in other words, it would inhibit the marketplace for produce clerks by predetermining their salaries. The salaries would be preset by collusion. Although the Rozelle rule did not set salaries precisely, it made signing a free agent costly to the acquiring club and, as a result, kept a lid on salaries and restrained player movement from club to club.

The owners, however, told the court that they had very good reasons for the Rozelle rule. As its primary "business justification" for the rule, the league cited its need to have balanced competition in order to sell its product. Under pure, unrestricted free agency, players would "flock to cities having natural advantages"; no one would want to play in Green Bay in the winter, despite its great football tradition and the genuine warmth and undying support of its fans. The reallocation of talent would destroy the league's competitive balance and, in turn, diminish the interest of its fan base and the value of the NFL's product in the television marketplace.

The clubs also asserted that the Rozelle rule allowed them to recoup their development and scouting costs when a player moved to another club by obtaining other players or draft choices in exchange. Finally, the league claimed that allowing unrestricted movement of players would undermine the team stability that was needed to provide a quality product to the public. If players could move at will, the NFL product would lose value.

In its opinion of October 18, 1976, the circuit court of appeals found the owners' claims insufficient to outweigh the anticompetitive effects of the Rozelle rule. The court rejected the development costs argument in a summary fashion. All businesses have development costs, and there is nothing special about the NFL in that regard. (In fact, the NFL has a free development system provided by college football.) Concerning the other justifications, the court simply responded that the rule was far too broad. While there might be legitimate concerns about the movement of star players in the prime of their careers, the Rozelle rule applied to all players, not just those whose movement might affect competitive balance. And the rule applied to players throughout their careers, even when their addition to a club could not possibly have an impact on balanced competition.

But the league did have another argument, one that could have (and should have) carried the day. The NFL and the NFLPA had discussed the Rozelle rule during their collective bargaining negotiations. In the 1968 agreement, the NFL's constitution and by-laws, which contained the Rozelle rule, were incorporated into the labor agreement by reference. As part of 1970's basic agreement, the parties negotiated the standard contract all players would sign. That contract also incorporated by reference the same league documents that contained the Rozelle rule. Thus, the league argued, the Rozelle rule was part of the collective bargain reached by the NFL and the NFLPA.

Under existing judicial precedent, if the product of free and open labor negotiations was declared a violation of the antitrust laws, the ruling would offend national labor policy which favored collective negotiations as the method for resolving labor disputes. This was called the "implied labor exemption" to the antitrust laws, the most difficult concept raised in sport law cases involving owners and player unions.

The implied labor exemption was devised by the Supreme Court to address a problem that Congress created, but did not solve. Congress had enacted important laws with directly conflicting purposes. The Sherman Act of 1890 (as amended by the Clayton Act of 1914) compelled business entities to compete in a marketplace unconstrained by private deals among them that would, for example, set the price at which they would sell their products or determine the salary they would pay their employees. The antitrust laws were intended to benefit consumers who would, as a result of firms having to compete for their business, receive better products at lower prices. The laws would also protect employees who might move from firm to firm, seeking better terms and conditions of employment.

Decades later, in 1935, Congress enacted the Wagner Act to achieve a totally different purpose. During the Great Depression, Congress sought to enhance the bargaining power of employees by encouraging unionization and collective bargaining. This statute — combined with other legislation in 1948 and 1957 — set forth the nation's rules on union organization and good-faith negotiations. When a union negotiates with many employers at one time — such as when the NFL Players Association dealt with the various clubs of the NFL — the resulting collective bargaining agreement sets the terms and conditions of employment for all their organized employees. Under the law, employers must negotiate over what are called "mandatory" subjects of bargaining, generally defined as "wages, hours and other terms and conditions of employment." As a result, and by its very nature, a collective bargaining agreement between a union and a multi-employer bargaining unit "restrains trade." Every company covered by the collective bargaining agreement must pay the employees what is required by that contract — no more and no less. Under the multi-employer agreement between the NFL clubs and the players union, for example, a club is not able to attract better players by offering more favorable pension terms or fringe benefit plans than those offered by other clubs. Those terms of employment, and many others, are set for all league players by the provisions of the collective bargaining agreement. (Salaries are left to be determined by individual negotiations between the player, his agent, and his club — also conducted under the terms of the collective bargaining agreement.)

Unlike the antitrust laws, the labor laws are not designed to benefit the ultimate consumers of the product. By collectivizing their economic strength — colluding, if you wish — employees, however, may be able to improve the terms and conditions of their employment. In a multi-employer arrangement, collective bargaining also allows employers in the same market to eliminate competition among themselves on matters addressed in the collective bargaining agreement.

The Sherman Act encourages free competition; the Wagner Act encourages collective restraints of trade. A collision between the statutes was inevitable. How should a court reconcile the pro-competitive policies of the antitrust laws and the anti-competitive policies of the labor laws? The Supreme Court in its 1965 *Jewel Tea* decision (and lower courts in numerous subsequent decisions) explained how courts should go about this difficult job of reconciliation. A collective agreement among employees and employers that would otherwise be an illegal restraint of trade (because it is a contract that restricts the free market) would be immune from antitrust liability if it addressed "mandatory subjects" of bargaining (wages, hours, terms and conditions of employment), if the arrangement was embodied in an agreement reached through genuine collective bargaining, and if the restraint only affected the parties to that agreement.

Applying these complicated tests, the circuit court correctly concluded that the parties' 1968 and 1970 collective agreements *did* incorporate the

Rozelle rule. The rule affected the salaries that players would be paid and, as such, it dealt with a mandatory subject of bargaining. The court decided, however, that since the players association had been a weak entity which could not impose its will in negotiations and did not receive anything in return for conceding on this issue, the Rozelle rule was not the product of bona fide, arms-length bargaining. Thus, under the circuit court's approach, the Rozelle rule should not benefit from the implied labor exemption. The rule would remain a federal antitrust violation.

The court's conclusion on this final and critical point was wrong. It demonstrates a lack of understanding of the way labor negotiations actually operate. Labor law does not promise a union a good bargain at the negotiation table. It promises only that management must bargain "in good faith" about terms and conditions of employment and, as far as we know, management met that standard in 1968 and 1970. A bad deal for the union simply reflected the fact that it did not have much bargaining strength. Power at the bargaining table is a direct reflection of a union's ability to impose a cost on employers through striking. In the case of the NFL Players Association, that strength was weak. Sometimes the best a union can achieve is an agreement that embodies the status quo. Even if that agreement is not favorable to the union or its members, it is certainly the product of genuine collective bargaining.

The Supreme Court's reconciliation of the labor and antitrust laws was intended to foster labor negotiations. It should be applied, however, to results obtained by both strong and weak unions. Although the players union may not have been overjoyed with the results of the 1968 and 1970 negotiations, the parties did reach agreements that maintained the status quo on the Rozelle rule. That should have insulated the rule from antitrust liability under the implied labor exemption.

Although they lost in the circuit court, the owners continued the fight, seeking review in the U.S. Supreme Court. The Court declined to hear the appeal on September 12, 1977. The case had taken more than five years to resolve. But before that final whistle sounded, the parties reached a new collective bargaining agreement.

FUMBLE AT THE GOAL LINE

Sports justice for John Mackey and his fellow football players offered them the right to seek a market return for the services they could provide during their brief careers on the gridiron. They had collectivized their bargaining power into a union without much success, but eventually prevailed in court. Without their union, the players would not have had the resources to sue and win. Without Mackey, the players association would have remained a social club. It is ironic that the ultimate fate of the rights to free agency that they won in court once again depended on the union's strength (or weakness) at the bargaining table. This proved the players' undoing, at least in the short run.

In collective bargaining following their court victory, the players association was hampered by its prior history. Unlike their baseball counterparts, football players had found it difficult to marshal the solidarity needed to support their positions with an effective threat to withhold their services. As a result, the ensuing collective bargaining agreement conceded the court victory in exchange for cash. The union accepted a revised form of the Rozelle rule in exchange for a payment of $13.65 million, to be distributed over ten years among some 3,200 active and former NFL players. Legal fees amounted to $1.5 million. John Mackey's share was $20,000. This result reflected the comparative economic power of labor and management in professional football during those years.

AFTER THE WHISTLE BLOWS

John Mackey left the gridiron when he realized that he could not play football and act as union leader at the same time. The punishment his body had absorbed during his ten years in the league had been costly. He later developed frontotemporal dementia, a progressive degeneration of the temporal and frontal lobes of the brain.

Mackey's chronic pain was not unusual for a professional football player, many of whom also suffered from depression, dementia, and a poor quality of life. A recent study of 2,500 former NFL players by the University of North Carolina showed that they faced a 37 percent higher risk of Alzheimer's disease than other men their age. A 2009 study commissioned by the National Football League determined that former players suffer memory-related diseases at nineteen times the normal rate for men ages thirty through forty. The *San Francisco Chronicle* reported the physical condition of 49ers' heroes Joe Montana and Dwight Clark, twenty-five years after they won their first Super Bowl:

Montana's left knee is essentially shredded. His right eye occasionally sags from nerve damage. His neck is so stiff, he could not turn his head. . . . Clark, also 50, endures sharp pain every time he lifts his arms above his head . . . because of a bent screw in his left shoulder and arthritis in his right shoulder. The simple act of turning his head also is a chore, thanks to all those jarring hits on crossing patterns over the middle.

Football disables its players, and every player knows he is only one play away from the end of his career. The real battle begins, however, after the whistle blows. The average life expectancy of retired football linemen is fifty-five, more than twenty years less than the average male. Every year as a professional football player cuts two to three years off his life expectancy.

In his ten seasons in the professional game, Mackey caught 331 passes for 5,236 yards and 38 touchdowns. He was, as *Sports Illustrated* wrote, "the prototype of the modern tight end." He was also an incomparable leader. Mackey was elected to the Hall of Fame in Canton, Ohio, in 1992, his fifteenth and final year of eligibility. As one of the premier players of the 1960s, who was named in 1971 the all-time best at his position, this slight could only be understood as retribution for his union activism. In the year that Mackey was inducted into the Hall of Fame, Al Davis was also admitted to football's shrine. Mackey was quoted as saying: "They decided to let all the trouble makers in at once." When asked how he was informed of the honor, Mackey responded: "A hotel operator called and said I had been 'indicted.' I panicked and said, 'For what?'" In 2000 the NCAA recognized his greatness by creating the John Mackey Award, presented annually to the collegiate tight end who best exemplifies the play, sportsmanship, academics, and community values of John Mackey.

Mackey's victory in court, even if based on a misreading of prevailing doctrine at the confusing intersection of antitrust and labor law, and even if followed by capitulation in negotiations, had great symbolic value. Although fans still have difficulty empathizing with millionaires who play football, they do understand the human toll of the game. Players acknowledge that, while they knowingly accept the physical risks of violent contact, they genuinely regret the loss of autonomy that can result. Sometimes that autonomy is exchanged for plenty of money and the Faustian deal has the semblance of free choice. At other times, players are treated like fungible property, to be discarded for good reasons or for bad.

Mackey and his union colleagues felt powerless under a system of trade that allowed economic strength to control outcomes. At least in the short run, the court's enforcement of antitrust laws proved that there was a power in the football world other than the club owners. That must have come as a shock to management, and it served as a genuine palliative in the players' locker rooms. However, the law rarely redresses grievances permanently, especially when other available laws favor negotiation instead of litigation. Later work stoppages in 1982 and 1987 proved ineffective in revising the fundamental relationship between owners and players. In 1989, the players took a drastic step — the decertification of their union — in order to bring the game back to court. In 1993, after secret negotiations between NFL owners and players' representatives, the parties reached a new arrangement that allowed free agency but bound each club to a salary cap. Individual players could (and did) move from club to club, but each team's payroll was limited, thus restraining salaries. Owners continue to complain, of course, about the level of salaries. The current rapprochement is only a temporary truce.

CHAPTER 10

T.O. MEETS THE ARBITRATOR

Get your popcorn ready, 'cause I'm gonna put on a show.
TERRELL OWENS

I don't have to worry about what people think of me, whether they hate me or not. People hated Jesus. They threw stones at him and tried to kill him, so how can I complain and worry about what people think?
TERRELL OWENS

• • • Arbitration has changed American sports. In the most famous sports labor arbitration case, arbitrator Peter Seitz ruled in December 1975 that baseball's century-old reserve clause only preserved a club's option to sign a ballplayer for one year after the expiration of his contract. Seitz had tried without success to get Major League Baseball and the MLB Players Association to settle their differences and design a new player reservation system on their own. Ultimately, Seitz had to decide the case himself. He ruled that if the uniform player contract option provision was intended to allow for perpetual renewal, it would have had to spell that out clearly. He granted the union's grievance.

Under Seitz's ruling, free agent players were able to sign with any employer after they played out their option year. Major League Baseball, the losing party in the arbitration, sued to have Seitz's award set aside in court, but the courts enforced the decision. Under prevailing law—as we discussed in Brian Shaw's case—courts will not second-guess an arbitrator. Shaw's case was a rare example of management invoking arbitration against a player. We now focus on a much more typical case, one involving the discipline of a player by his club. We will see how arbitration actually works to resolve a dispute.

TERRELL OWENS

Misbehaving athletes are common in professional sports. Team management normally enjoys the unrestricted right to retain or dismiss a player, as long as it complies with the terms of the standard player contract and the procedures set forth in the collective bargaining agreement. Retaining a disruptive, though productive, player—as the Boston Red Sox did with Manny Ramirez for part of the 2008 season—can shred team cohesiveness. Dismissing a player does not free a club from its obligation to pay his guaranteed salary, however. Trading that player to another club—an option that might free the team from one salary obligation in exchange for another—also risks strengthening a potential opponent. There are times when a club might choose to discipline a recalcitrant player

previous page
When the Philadelphia Eagles suspended Terrell Owens for
misconduct, a labor arbitrator upheld the disciplinary action.
AP Photo / Bradley C. Bower

in the hope, if not the expectation, that a fine or suspension will rehabilitate him.

As a result of a series of incidents in 2005, the Philadelphia Eagles suspended their star receiver, Terrell Owens, who is generally referred to by his initials, T.O. His union, the National Football League Players Association, initiated a grievance protesting this action under the terms of the collective bargaining agreement. Unable to resolve the matter, the union processed the case to arbitration as provided in Article XXVII of its agreement with management.

Owens' performance on the football field in 2004, his first season with the Eagles, had been spectacular. Owens' activities off the field throughout 2005 were just as noteworthy, although not in a positive way. The resulting labor arbitration proceeding in November 2005 riveted the attention of America's sports fans and brought arbitration center stage in the business of sports.

Terrell Eldorado Owens is a magnificent athlete. After playing eight years for the San Francisco 49ers, the talented receiver led his Philadelphia club to the Super Bowl game in February 2005 at Jacksonville's Alltel Stadium. Although the Eagles ultimately fell to the New England Patriots, Owens played splendidly—despite having been severely injured during the season. Until that time, Owens' NFL career had been filled with superlatives. He was a performer destined for enshrinement in the Hall of Fame.

By any measure, Owens was also a genuine character, perhaps even a caricature worthy of a reality show. (In fact, T.O.'s reality show premiered in 2009 on VH-1.) His on-field shenanigans were legendary. In 2000, while playing for the 49ers against the Cowboys in Dallas, Owens celebrated two touchdown catches by dancing on the famous star logo at the fifty-yard line. These celebrations, which Owens said his teammates loved, cost him a week's pay (over $24,000) and a suspension by his club. "I was just out there having fun," he explained. During a Monday night game against the Seattle Seahawks in 2002, Owens scored a touchdown, pulled a Sharpie marker out of his sock, and signed the football. This stunt, which Owens said came to him spontaneously during the game's third quarter, also resulted in a fine. After a touchdown catch in 2006, Owens—now playing for Dallas against the Washington Redskins—lay down in the end zone and pretended to take a nap. He used the football as his pillow. The Cowboys were penalized fifteen yards for the escapade, considered by the referees to be "excessive celebration."

Most of the time, there is a joyous frivolity to Owens' antics, which were enjoyed by his fans and marketed by constant repetition on ESPN's Sports Center and YouTube.com. "I am a cool cat when everyone else is tight," Owens writes in his autobiography. On the other hand, his behavior reveals a person either unwilling or unable to conduct himself within the bounds of traditional and expected norms. He certainly does not subscribe to the prevailing ethos espoused by NFL coaches, such as Tom Landry of the Cowboys, that when you get to the end zone you should act as if you have been there before.

Terrell Owens, like many controversial athletes, blamed the media for misunderstanding him. In 2006, he expressed his version of events in *T.O.*, coauthored with Jason Rosenhaus, the brother of Owens' sports agent Drew Rosenhaus, who played an important role in the 2005 saga. Owens' book showed no remorse and contained an answer for every accusation against him: "I can only be one way—my way."

Born in 1973 in Alexander City, Alabama, about halfway between Montgomery and Birmingham, Owens was raised by his mother and his grandmother. He says that the bullying he endured in "Alex City" gave him the motivation to "be special" and stand his ground. (He later would see the National Football League, its clubs and management, the press, and anyone else who opposed him as similar "bullies" who wanted him to fail.)

Owens attended Benjamin Russell High School, home of the Wildcats, where he lettered in football, basketball, track, and baseball. Despite his high school success, Owens was not recruited by the top college football programs. He eventually starred on the gridiron at the University of Tennessee at Chattanooga and was picked in the third round of the NFL draft by the 49ers.

Owens' performances on the field for San Francisco were often dazzling. On December 17, 2000, against the Chicago Bears, Owens made twenty catches for 283 yards, surpassing the single-game record that had stood for fifty years. Foreshadowing the troubles to come, however, Owens publicly feuded with 49ers quarterback Jeff Garcia and head coach Steve Mariucci. He was upset when the club exercised its contractual right to designate him as their "franchise player," which restricted him from declaring free agency. He also thought he was underpaid.

Owens vowed to leave the 49ers, but his agent, David Joseph, missed the window in which to void the final year of his contract. (Owens blamed himself for trusting Joseph with his business dealings.) The club then traded him to the Baltimore Ravens, but Owens refused to accept the trade. After the players association filed a grievance on his behalf, the case was heard by University of Pennsylvania law professor Stephen Burbank. At the hearing, Burbank gave an indication that he would rule in Owens' favor. That prompted the Ravens, the 49ers, and the Philadelphia Eagles to work out a deal that moved Owens to Philadelphia. Owens told a reporter for the *Philadelphia Inquirer*: "I'd definitely love to come to Philly. Those guys have gotten to the NFC championship game three years in a row. Absolutely no disrespect to the players they have, but there's something out there they need to get them over the hump. I definitely believe I'm that missing piece."

Owens' brief stay in Philadelphia began with mutual expressions of good intentions by the player and club management. Within a year, the Eagles and their owner, Jeffrey Lurie, would wish that Owens had gone missing. As the self-proclaimed savior of the Philadelphia franchise, Owens signed a seven-year, $49 million contract with the Eagles. He received a $2.3 million signing bonus and a $6.2 million roster bonus. The remainder of his contract was not guaranteed, however, which meant that the team could release him at any time. Owens later expressed his dismay when he learned that the Eagles had paid free agent defensive end Jevon Kearse much more by way of guaranteed money.

The relationship between a quarterback and a wide receiver is a critical part of the so-called "West Coast" offense run by Philadelphia's coach Andy Reid. Owens got along well with his quarterback, Donovan McNabb, until the sixth game of the 2004 season. In preparation for that game against the Cleveland Browns, Owens and McNabb worked on one particular play during a week of practice. When Coach Reid called the play during the game, Owens sped downfield, but McNabb went to another receiver, a pass that fell incomplete. Owens could not understand why McNabb had not thrown the ball his way.

Later in the season, in a game against the Giants, it happened again. When Owens returned to the huddle, he said: "I was open. . . . Dude, you missed me." Owens expected McNabb to admit his error, but instead he said: "Shut the fuck up!" McNabb's expression of disrespect in front of their teammates, according to Owens, led to the feud that kept the quarterback and his ace receiver from effectively communicating ever again. McNabb had been "like family" to Owens, but the guy "turned out to be someone else." The Owens-McNabb spat corroded the morale of the team and the prospects for the franchise.

Owens saw McNabb as the reincarnation of his childhood bullies, as well as a failed quarterback motivated by jealousy for Owens' stardom. He could not simply shrug it off. The "insult in the huddle" began the slide that ended Owens' tenure in Philadelphia. Shortly thereafter, Owens was injured with a broken leg and a serious ankle sprain. For most players, the surgery that followed would have meant the end of their season. Owens, however, miraculously recovered ("God had cleared me to play"), and he was ready to go full speed by the time the Eagles faced the New England Patriots in the 2005 Super Bowl.

Owens played brilliantly in that game, although the Eagles came up short. Although he had risked re-injuring his leg and ankle — and perhaps ending his playing career — some in the media made negative comments about him. Owens thought he deserved a reward for his performance and felt underappreciated by his team. In April 2005, Owens hired a new agent, Drew Rosenhaus, known to be an aggressive representative, then informed the press that, because he had "outperformed" his existing contract, the Eagles would need to offer him a more lucrative arrangement, one consistent with his status as a premier receiver. Although the media reported that Owens had originally signed a seven-year contract, he had actually signed a series of one-year deals (rather than the multi-year guaranteed contract common in baseball and basketball). The Eagles could decide to void the remaining years and roster bonuses at any time. Owens, on the other hand, was bound to the club for as long as it wanted him, up to seven full seasons.

Rosenhaus crunched the numbers and determined that, based on the first two years of his Philadelphia contract, Owens' pay was not among the top ten receivers in the league, and certainly not an appropriate contract for the "ultimate player." His higher-paying seasons were loaded at the back end of his contract years. If his performance declined, the Eagles could release him before those seasons arrived. Owens formally demanded that the Eagles rewrite his contract. "Just give me what I deserve," he insisted, expressing concerns about being able to "feed his family."

Owens insisted that the total value of his series of one-year contracts reflect his higher level of accomplishment: "That's not being selfish. That's not being greedy. Right is right, and wrong is wrong." Owens wanted a "fair contract" which would pay him what he was worth. It was true that Owens had had an outstanding 2004–2005 season; he caught seventy-seven passes for 1,200 yards and fourteen touchdowns, leading the club in each category. As was its right, however, the club refused to rewrite his contract, concerned that the precedent would encourage other players to seek better deals after a good season.

Up to this point in 2005, the Owens' dispute was typical of many similar controversies in professional sports. Through negotiation, player agents and club representatives attempt to project the monetary value of a player's future contributions to the club's success. That projection is embodied in a contract. When a player underachieves (and management considers that he is overpaid), the terms favor the player. But the club benefits when a player blossoms into an underpaid, overachieving star. Management may attempt to revise downward the salary of underperforming players; similarly, a player may seek to increase his rate of pay following a particularly meritorious season. If there is a signed and guaranteed contract in place, neither side has the right to demand that it be changed. In the NFL, however, multi-year contracts are typically not guaranteed; the club can always free itself from what it thinks is an unfair deal by cutting the player.

The history of professional sports is filled with stories of players who tried to improve their compensation by threatening to withhold their services. Some have had to carry through on their threats in order to obtain better terms. There are player holdouts in football every year. It has almost become a tradition, both for high draft choices and veteran players. For example, in the season that Owens threatened to hold out, at least a dozen other significant football players also warned they would withhold their services unless their demands were met.

Terrell Owens did more than threaten to holdout, however. He announced that, unless he got his way, he would disrupt the club's preparation for the 2005 season by behaving badly. That was a promise Owens would keep. He would demonstrate that no club rules applied to him as long as he thought his Eagles contract remained "unfair." Without receiving an indication that the owner would act "in good faith" toward him,

Owens skipped the voluntary off-season program, then the mandatory mini-camp in late April, explaining that he did not want to risk injury. His appearance at the scheduled summer training camp would depend on the renegotiation of his contract.

Owens was powerless to compel the Eagles to renegotiate, however. Unlike other athletes whose cases we have discussed, Owens could not go to court to seek outside intervention to improve his circumstances. His contract had been negotiated fairly by competent representation, and he was bound to keep his promises, even if it now seemed he had received a bad deal. Frustrated by the Eagles' intransigence, he used the only methods he had available. He would force the Eagles to pay attention to his concerns by acting out.

On April 12, 2005, Owens told ESPN reporter Len Pasquarelli that he had done everything the club had asked him to do, even playing in the Super Bowl when injured. He added: "[I] wasn't the one who got tired in the Super Bowl," an apparent shot at his quarterback, Donovan McNabb. (In his postseason book Owens admits that he should have apologized for this comment, "but I couldn't bring myself to do it, and I refused to consider any point of view other than my own.")

Few wide receivers in NFL history have been as productive on the field as Owens, but no player before Owens had so systematically undermined a club's morale and cohesiveness in an effort to increase his pay. Owens knew that if he did not report to training camp, the club could fine him and even require him to repay his signing bonus. He eventually did report, but said that, while he was there, he would "not be happy." He felt disrespected by management's "bullies" who were in positions of authority. And he was proud of the fact that he had spoken his mind.

Owens did not, and would not, surrender what he called his "iron will." He continued to avoid talking with McNabb. He missed mandatory autograph sessions, claiming he needed to get further rehabilitation treatments. He was insubordinate to his supervisor, offensive coordinator Brad Childress, and thought Childress was being antagonistic when he said "Hi Terrell." Owens told Childress not to talk to him unless he talked to him first. When he attended team meetings, Owens refused to open his playbook. He took offense when head coach Andy Reid, in exasperation, finally told Owens to "just shut up." Owens responded that he was a grown man, and that it was Reid who should shut up.

After the start of the preseason, the Eagles sent Owens home for a week, although at no loss of salary. (Players are not paid their regular salary until the first game of the regular season.) The club wrote to him, hoping that he would return to camp "with renewed attitude and focus." He did return, but with the same attitude he had left with, determined to show the Eagles that he "couldn't be broken no matter what they did." To Owens, it was both a matter of respect and a contest for control.

During the week of his suspension, at halftime of an ESPN national preseason game, Owens told two reporters, Michael Wilbon and Bob Ryan, that he had no desire to talk to McNabb and he didn't think he and McNabb could play together. He described Coach Reid as a "controlling guy. He wants to be the main guy." Realizing that the Eagles were not going to budge on his demands, however, Owens vowed that he would return to summer training camp "as a professional."

During the 2005 regular season, Owens continued his periodic tantrums and misbehaviors. At times, he also failed to exercise common sense. For example, he "paid tribute" to his friend Michael Irvin by wearing his Cowboys jersey on the team plane after the Eagles lost to Dallas, 33–10.

During an Eagles home game against the San Diego Chargers in week seven, Owens scored his one hundredth career touchdown, a milestone previously reached by only five NFL receivers. He was shocked that the club did nothing during the game to celebrate this remarkable accomplishment, an omission Owens took "as a slap in the face."

On November 3, in what turned out to be the final act in this allegorical saga, Owens gave an interview to a young friend on ESPN, Graham Bensinger, which inflamed the Eagles and led directly to a four-game suspension. Earlier that day, Owens had had a physical confrontation with former Eagles defensive end Hugh Douglas, who yelled profanities at him in the locker room. Although Douglas was no longer an active player, the club had hired him as a "team ambassador" to work with roster players. The two men exchanged blows.

Still smarting from the fight, Owens reported for the ESPN interview as scheduled. Exuding supreme personal confidence and claiming to be honest and truthful, he again attacked his quarterback and said the Eagles organization "lacked class." He questioned the integrity of the Philadelphia club and said he felt "disrespected." After enumerating his complaints, he summarized the future: "I expect the worst [and] if you align expectations with reality, you will never be disappointed." The response from the club was immediate.

Andy Reid ordered Owens to apologize to the team or be suspended. Owens rejected the direct order, and issued a statement to the media instead. Reid was adamant. Owens then said he was willing to read a statement to his fellow players, but he would not apologize to McNabb. Reid insisted that he apologize to McNabb or he would sit out the next game. Owens felt bullied once again and refused to comply.

On November 5, 2005, after many documented warnings about his conduct, the club suspended Owens for four weeks and docked him four weeks' pay. It also informed him that, while his pay of $191,176 a game would resume when the suspension ended, he would be placed on the inactive list and would not play for or practice with the club for the remainder of the season.

Following his suspension, Owens' differences with the club moved from demands (which the Eagles had refused) to adjudication. Owens claimed that he was never warned he could be suspended for his transgressions. He wanted another chance, but the club's patience had run out. Owens felt insulted, angry, and hurt. In addition, he had now been penalized almost $800,000.

Did the club have the right to discipline Owens? This was a matter of interpreting the club's and the player's rights under the provisions of two contracts. Under the terms of Owens' standard player contract and the collective bargaining agreement between the NFL and the NFL Players Association, the club could suspend him without pay for up to four weeks, but only if it had "just cause" for the discipline. But Owens' case presented a second, unprecedented issue. Was it a violation of the agreement for the Eagles to bench Owens after his suspension and bar him from practice sessions, even though the club was paying his full salary?

In a simple contract dispute, parties may file suit in state or federal court. Under the collective bargaining agreement between the NFL and the NFL Players Association, a dispute involving player discipline should be resolved through the labor arbitration process. The grievance, which the players association filed on behalf of Owens, would be heard by the permanent arbitrator, who had been mutually appointed by the union and the league. Unlike a court trial, the proceeding would be private, informal, and expeditious. The NFL-NFLPA arbitrator was an experienced neutral who knew the business of football and had adjudicated disputes between the parties for many years. His decision on Terrell Owens' grievance would be final and binding.

THE ARBITRATOR

Grievance and arbitration procedures are included in virtually every collective bargaining agreement in every unionized industry across the country. About three hundred private arbitrators, all of whom are elected members of the National Academy of Arbitrators, hear approximately 90 percent of all the cases brought to arbitration. Normally these arbitrators go about their jobs out of the glare of the media. However, nothing involving Terrell Owens could avoid the media's attention.

Arbitrator Richard I. Bloch of Washington, D.C., a premier and universally praised neutral, had served for years as the permanent arbitrator in professional football, selected jointly by the commissioner's office and the players association. Bloch understood the parties' relationship, the internal rules that controlled their rights and responsibilities, and the context of their long-standing and sometimes stormy relationship. He was skilled in running arbitration hearings and issuing thoughtful and timely opinions. Under the contract's procedures, the arbitrator's award would be final and binding on all parties. The Owens case would present Bloch with one of his greatest challenges. The case was set for hearing on November 18, 2005, in a meeting room at an airport hotel near Philadelphia.

Rich Bloch is among the very best labor arbitrators in the country. A graduate of Dartmouth College, where he was a star hockey goalie, and the University of Michigan Law School, Bloch also earned a master's degree from Michigan. He practiced for a year with a major law firm before turning to academia, teaching full-time, then part-time, at law schools in Michigan and the District of Columbia.

Like all sports arbitrators, Bloch has extensive experience in a wide variety of fields, not just in the business of sports. He has been a permanent arbitrator in the steel industry, in mining, television, tire manufacturing, and for various airlines. He currently is the permanent arbitrator for the National Hockey League. Bloch would bring forty years of experience as a trusted and respected neutral to the Owens case. There could be no more qualified person to hear the dispute.

The night before the scheduled hearing, with all interested parties in town, Bloch tried to achieve a voluntary settlement. He brought Owens and his agent, along with representatives of the players association, the NFL, and the club, to a hotel suite that he had reserved under an assumed name to avoid the media. An experienced mediator as well as an arbitrator, Bloch tried to help the parties find common ground. However, this case might have had too high a public profile to allow for a mediated settlement. Settling by mediation requires both sides to give something, and that was not going to happen. Although Bloch's efforts failed to produce an agreement, all parties agreed that the meeting should be kept absolutely confidential.

Bloch soon learned that the Owens case would be an explosive experience. Before the next day's hearing, radio bulletins began reporting the failed attempt to settle. Someone had breached confidentiality. The next day, while the parties prepared to present their evidence and arguments, Bloch watched as helicopters from the local television stations circled the hotel.

Bloch's written decision describes in great detail the facts that led the Eagles to discipline Terrell Owens, then forbid him to play or practice with the club for the remainder of the season. As is common in all disciplinary cases, management bore the burden of proving it had just cause for the suspension. Bloch also had to decide whether the power to bench Owens after the suspension fell within management's rights. The parties' collective bargaining agreement capped disciplinary suspensions at four weeks. If Owens' benching was a continuation of discipline, it would violate this contractual ceiling.

The evidence presented during a very long day of arbitration detailed Owens' campaign to force the Eagles to renegotiate. Bloch heard how Owens sought improvements in his contract by announcing to the press that he would engage in a pattern of disruptive behavior. The details included his refusal to report to mandatory spring practice, his press comments disparaging the club and his teammates (in particular, Donovan McNabb), his refusal to communicate with coaches and players during summer camp, and his failure to meet his contractual obligation to sign autographs.

The club presented compelling evidence that Owens was warned repeatedly about the consequences of his misconduct, a fact conspicuously (and perhaps conveniently) omitted from Owens' book about the same events.

Head coach Andy Reid had signed a series of letters to Owens, specifying each of his transgressions as they occurred, and warning him of the consequences if they continued. While Reid is a well-respected NFL coach, it is apparent from the letters' contents that team lawyers also were involved in their composition. While the club might have hoped that these repeated warnings would encourage Owens to rethink his attitude and meet his responsibilities, they also served to establish that the club would suspended him if his misbehavior did not cease.

Bloch heard how Owens continued his campaign of harassment and insubordination. The club showed tolerance, and Reid continued to send warning letters. After the ESPN interview on November 3, when Owens referred to the Eagles as an organization without class and reiterated his criticism of McNabb, the club was forced to take action.

Owens had arrived at the arbitration hearing with a dream team of superb attorneys, led by NFLPA general counsel Dick Berthelsen and chief outside counsel Jeffrey Kessler. The league was represented by Daniel Nash, a noted management attorney from the Washington office of Akin, Gump, and David Gardi, labor relations counsel for the NFL's management council. Management's key witness was Andy Reid, who explained the events of that year. (Owens thought the arbitrator "looked giddy" upon meeting the coach.)

Owens remained unrepentant to the end. At the arbitration hearing, he told Bloch he had done nothing wrong and still did not believe it was necessary for a wide receiver to talk with his quarterback. Bloch thought he might have misheard what Owens had said. He asked Owens to repeat his answer. Owens complied.

Within five days — a remarkably short period of time — Bloch issued his opinion resolving the dispute. His first task had been to decide whether the club had just cause to discipline Owens for four weeks. The record showed that Owens orchestrated a media circus accompanied by outright insubordination. There was no question that Owens had been on notice that he would be subject to discipline if his conduct continued. Bloch summarized Owens' misbehavior and its impact:

> Terrell Owens' stature as a compelling athlete and outspoken public figure contributed meaningfully to the destructive power of his actions. Despite all attempts by the Club to persuade him to modulate his pos-

ture and his posturing, he persisted in broadcasting his dissatisfaction and in stirring and stoking the growing attention and dissent around him. In so doing, he engaged in conduct that was manifestly detrimental to the Club.

Needless to say, Owens did not agree with Bloch's conclusion. He later wrote that he thought the case had been a "lock" in his favor. In dealing with the Eagles and the media, he had merely been exercising his freedom of speech—and was wronged in the process. (The First Amendment, of course, acts only as a limitation on governments, not football teams, but no one has ever suggested that Owens was a constitutional scholar.) The thirteen-hour hearing, according to Owens, demonstrated without question that he had not received due process, equal treatment, or progressive discipline, and that he suffered double jeopardy. Much to Owens' apparent surprise, Bloch did not see it that way.

Although the players association claimed that a four-week suspension was "overkill," Bloch concluded that the extent of penalty was commensurate with the player's misconduct. Describing Owens' behavior, Bloch wrote "These are remarkable circumstances and unparalleled detrimental misconduct." The club had placed Owens on notice, warned him, counseled him, and finally suspended him. Owens, Bloch wrote, could have avoided these consequences at any time by stopping his misconduct and changing his attitude.

The players association brought Bloch's attention to other sports arbitration cases it thought comparable, in particular a baseball case involving Atlanta pitcher John Rocker. The Braves disciplined Rocker based on an interview that he gave to *Sports Illustrated*, in which he disparaged virtually every minority group in the country. Baseball arbitrator Shyam Das found Rocker's discipline was too onerous and, while upholding the right of a club to discipline based on a player's off-duty misconduct, he reduced the penalty. Bloch noted a difference in Rocker's case, as Rocker's conduct reflected poorly on the player only and did not disparage his club, as Owens' had done. In addition, there was no specific rule governing Rocker's alleged violations. Owens, on the other hand, knew exactly what was required of him and consciously violated those rules.

Regarding the effective removal of Owens from the club for the remainder of the season, Bloch decided that this management action was not discipline because the player continued to receive his salary. In the business of sports, management traditionally reserves the right to determine who shall play or practice with the team. A club could rightfully consider Owens' potential for disruption in deciding whether he should be involved in team activities. The arbitrator did not have the power to order the Eagles to allow Owens to practice. Such a ruling would have compounded the injury Owens had already inflicted on the club.

Bloch must have known that his decisions in such a high-profile case would risk his multi-year tenure as football's permanent arbitrator. Shortly after the issuance of this award, the players association removed Bloch from his position, as was its right under the collective bargaining agreement. The union's general counsel, Richard Berthelsen, told the press:

> His ruling . . . ignores the obligation a club has to either provide employment to a player or allow him to play somewhere else. We are confident that we put in a winning case at the hearing last Friday, and we still believe Terrell Owens had a right to a legitimate reinstatement.

The player association's executive director, the late Gene Upshaw, added that Bloch "will no longer be an arbitrator in any more of our cases." Bloch continues to hear and resolve disputes in other professional sports and in industries throughout the country.

Owens was proud that he lost only the case and not his dignity. But, in a subsequent arbitration, he also lost a considerable sum of money. In addition to the pay for his four-week suspension, he was ordered to return $1.725 million of his $2.3 million signing bonus to the Eagles. Owens was sure that the people in power were against him. He thought that he deserved another chance, and he would get one down in Texas.

POSTSCRIPT

The Terrell Owens case demonstrates the importance of the arbitration process in the sports business. In a matter of days, the dispute was resolved and both parties knew their rights under contract. The arbitrator upheld a club's right to impose the highest level of discipline allowed under the collective bargaining agreement, and therefore the Eagles obtained justice through arbitration, as the Celtics had in Brian Shaw's case. Terrell Owens, however, finished the season without obtaining any measure of what he considered justice. His use of what lawyers call "self help" certainly left him worse off. Not only was he underpaid (in his mind) for his services in the 2005 season, he also lost millions of dollars in the process. In his book Owens excoriated the arbitrator: "The man robbed me without a gun! It was the perfect crime."

After the 2005 season, the Eagles granted Owens his wish and freed him to sign with other clubs. In March 2006, Owens signed a lucrative three-year, $25 million contract with the Dallas Cowboys and continued his high level of play, at least for a while. The Cowboys were so pleased that they threw out the last year of the contract and signed him, in June 2008, to a new four-year contract worth $34 million with a $12 million signing bonus. The disruptive Terrell Owens returned during the 2008 season, however, as he publicly criticized the failure of Tony Romo, the Cowboys' quarterback, to throw enough passes in his direction.

Owens' stay in Dallas lasted until March 2009, when the Cowboys released him. "America's Team," as the Cowboys like to call their club, could not countenance Owens' behavior. He had publicly criticized the club's offensive coordinator, Jason Garrett. He had accused Romo of colluding with tight end Jason Witten in drawing up plays behind Owens' back. Once again, he had become a distraction. Considering Owens' attitude, course of conduct, and failing productivity—after thirteen years in the NFL, he was in his mid-thirties—the Cowboys decided to move "in another direction."

Owens moved in a new direction as well. Two days after being released by Dallas, the receiver signed with the Buffalo Bills for one year at $6.5 million. He also laid the groundwork for his next round of controversy:

> I'm going to be the same person that I was the last three years with the Cowboys. When I'm on the football field, I'm a passionate guy. I demand a lot from myself and from the guys around me. I'm sure those guys and some of the guys around the league and in the locker room all know that whatever is being said out there, it's not accurate.

Obviously, neither time nor discipline have changed Owens' ways.

JUSTICE FOR ALL

Justice is the crowning glory of the virtues.
CICERO

This ain't fun. But you watch me, I'll get it done.
JACKIE ROBINSON

• • • These stories of sports justice at work tell tales of both courageous and outrageous participants in athletics and the sports business. Renee Richards and Al Davis used access to the courts to protect their statutory rights. John Mackey led the NFL Players Association during its formative years and used federal antitrust statutes to grant players free agency, only to watch the hard-won victory lost at the negotiation table. Some of the participants in this arena have attracted public attention; others have played their roles out of the limelight. All sought justice before courts or arbitrators because they could not find justice within existing sports organizations.

The most remarkable example of modern sports justice, however, did not involve a court, an arbitrator, or the invocation of statutory law. It involved a business decision made by an enlightened and profit-minded general manager and a courageous and talented ballplayer. All other examples of sports justice pale by comparison. I refer of course to the announcement on April 10, 1947, by Branch Rickey, the general manager of the Brooklyn Dodgers, that Jackie Robinson would play for the club.

Rickey, a University of Michigan–trained lawyer who played and coached professional baseball, understood what few other sports businessmen of his time appreciated: the business of baseball would flourish in the postwar years if it was integrated. Jackie Robinson, an extraordinary athlete and a great hero for his times and ours, proved to be the right person for beginning this enormous task. The Robinson-Rickey partnership changed the National Game and, in turn, changed America.

Rickey explained to the press why he had signed Robinson: "I signed him because I knew of no reason why I shouldn't." Baseball was about winning ballgames, and Robinson was very good at what he did on the field. Many baseball insiders were quick to criticize Rickey's move. Hall of Famer Rogers Hornsby explained that a "mixed baseball team" wouldn't work because "ballplayers on the road live much closer together." When asked what he might do if he found resentment among Dodger players to Robinson's acquisition, Rickey responded: "I should be sorry to find resentment, but if I did I would then call upon an ally of mine — time."

previous page
Jackie Robinson and Branch Rickey changed baseball forever, without the help of the courts, an arbitrator, or the law.
AP Photo

Albert "Happy" Chandler, the Kentucky-born commissioner of baseball who took the reins in 1945 (after Kenesaw Mountain Landis died in office), was both governor of, and later senator from, a southern state that was segregated by law. In such states, youngsters of different races were assigned to attend different public schools. Public facilities, hospitals, restaurants, churches — even cemeteries — were designated by race. This legal architecture of apartheid was supported by a social system that mandated separation.

Commissioner Landis had been an adamant opponent of integration. Among major league club owners, there had been a longstanding "gentlemen's agreement" to exclude persons of color. Landis shared the prejudices of his time and snuffed out any effort made by the occasional renegade owner, such as Bill Veeck, to breach the color line.

Happy Chandler, however, bravely offered his support as Rickey and Robinson made history. All of the club owners except the Dodgers' voted against Rickey's earth-shaking proposition. With Chandler's acquiescence, Rickey proceeded anyway. Turned out of office by the other club owners, Chandler returned to Kentucky to serve another term as governor.

JACKIE ROBINSON

All sports fans know the story of Jackie Robinson. A brilliant athlete in four sports at the University of California, Los Angeles, Robinson was a star in the making. While serving in the Army during World War II, Robinson rose from private to lieutenant. In October 1945, Rickey signed Robinson to play for the Montreal Royals, the Dodgers' premier farm club in the International League. He led that league in batting with a .349 average, stole forty bases, and was the best fielding second baseman in the league. On April 10, 1947, Brooklyn purchased Robinson's contract from Montreal. He signed the history-making contract the next day, becoming the first black ballplayer of the modern era. He soon became a fixture in the Dodgers lineup.

Rickey had cautioned Robinson about what lay ahead, and Robinson followed Rickey's admonition that he "not fight back" when the racial prejudice of his teammates, his opponents, and the fans turned their noble experiment into a personal ordeal. Off the field, he kept to himself.

Seven years before the U.S. Supreme Court would rule that segregation in the public schools was a violation of the Equal Protection Clause of the

Fourteenth Amendment, the decision of these two remarkable men, Robinson and Rickey, changed baseball and, in turn, helped change American life. It is difficult to overestimate the importance of Robinson to the history of sport, of baseball, and of America. The subject of race in the postwar period was, to use Arthur Daley's phrase from the *New York Times*, "as easy to handle as a fistful of fish-hooks."

Although Robinson received a mixed reaction from his teammates and a negative one from most members of opposing clubs, he persevered. Rickey was not alone in his commitment to progress. Manager Leo Durocher informed his Dodgers team:

> I do not care if the guy is yellow or black, or if he has stripes like a fuckin' zebra. I'm the manager of this team, and I say he plays. What's more, I say he can make us all rich. And if any of you cannot use the money, I will see that you are all traded.

The Rickey-Robinson revolution and its aftermath did make money for baseball. Black Americans came to the games in droves as, one by one, the sixteen clubs added black players to their rosters. It took more than a decade for every team to add at least one player of color. The Red Sox were the last, signing Pumpsie Green to the Boston squad in 1959. It was fitting that Boston be the very last in line, because the Red Sox had rejected an early opportunity to acquire Robinson. Robinson had a tryout at Fenway Park on April 16, 1945, before he signed with Rickey's Brooklyn organization. It is said that then-owner Tom Yawkey, seeing Robinson from the stands, screamed: "Get that nigger off the field." Yawkey's prejudice cost the Sox in reputation, revenue, and team performance.

The Robinson-Rickey triumph shows that sports justice sometimes comes from within a sport, without need to invoke the intervention of outside institutions. Every business, whether related to sport or not, makes decisions and takes risks. Some pay off and some do not, but the most efficient way to effect change is to do so internally. Would the PGA Tour, the U.S. Open, or the National Football League have changed without the involvement of the courts? It seems unlikely, but who would have dreamed that Major League Baseball, that bastion of Southern prejudice, would lead America on its march toward justice for all? Change can be difficult, but avoiding change may prove costly or even fatal.

THE FUTURE OF SPORTS JUSTICE

The movement for sports justice does not end with the transformative victories of a disabled golfer, a transgendered tennis player, and a team of female gymnasts from Brown University. Some barriers to the right to play remain firmly in place. In 2009, for example, an Israeli female tennis player was barred from participating in a tournament in an Arab country. The Sri Lankan cricket team was attacked by terrorists in Lahore, Pakistan. The gender of a young South African runner, Caster Semenya, was questioned after she blew away the field in the women's 800 meters at the International Association of Athletics Federation's track and field world championship. Age-old prejudices remain firmly in place despite occasional personal victories.

Sport and justice can only be analyzed and evaluated in context. Neither exist in a bubble, unaffected by society's problems. We can take pride in the trend of increasing access to sports, but we must be vigilant to protect our successes lest they fade from view.

After writing four books on the law, economics, and social history of baseball, it was a major challenge to collect a new library of non-baseball books dealing with the business of sports. While not as rich as the baseball literature, there are excellent nonfiction texts on football, basketball, and golf. Hockey is a little thin in terms of scholarly resources, but there is much in the popular press about the game on ice.

The nature of research has changed in the last decade. For this book, I was able to use the online archives of *Sports Illustrated*, the bible of the games we love. Similarly, the *New York Times* online resource is invaluable. Researching anything online requires significant care. One website frequently copies an error from another, so it is best to find contemporary media sources whenever possible. (Because the narratives in this book all involve cases decided in the past forty years, I was able to follow this rule.) Google's collection of books is incredibly valuable. The full court decisions discussed are available online and in any law library, and I have included citations in each chapter note below.

Much of the book is based on the course in sports law that I have taught since the mid-1980s, at various law schools where I have served as dean and faculty member. Some of the insights came from my students as we discussed the cases and placed them in context. Other ideas came from my colleagues in the sports law and sports management fields, including Paul Weiler, Stephen Greyser, Gary Roberts, and Stephen Ross.

INTRODUCTION: SPORTS AND THE LAW

Michael Novak's *The Joy of Sports* stands as the definitive theoretical work on the nature of sports. Although originally published in 1976, a time when few university scholars were writing about sports, it remains in print.

Curt Flood's antitrust suit against baseball, *Flood v. Kuhn*, 407 U.S. 258 (1972), includes Blackmun's remarkable list of baseball players. Inadvertently, Blackmun left Mel Ott off his list, a decision he deeply regretted (Roger Abrams, "Blackmun's List," *Virginia Sports and Entertainment Law Journal* 6 [2007]: 181–205).

Jonah Lehrer's new book on decision making, *How We Decide*, is a splendid introduction to research on the brain and the analysis of decisions in various contexts, including sports.

The 2009 Wisconsin Supreme Court decision involving the cheerleader can be found at *Noffke v. Bakke*, 315 Wis.2d 350, 760 N.W.2d 156 (2009); it interprets Wis. Stat. § 895.525(4m)(a) (2005–06).

CHAPTER 1: STAY OUT OF MY COURT

The *Hackbart* decision is included in many sports law casebooks as an example of how courts address the compensation of injuries suffered in professional sports. Judge Matsch's discussion of judicial abstention makes the case far more important and more interesting than a simple assumption of risk/consent case based on events on the field of play. The district court opinion can be read at *Hackbart v. Cincinnati Bengals and Clark*, 435 F. Supp. 352 (D. CO 1977). It was reversed on appeal, as explained in the text, in *Hackbart v. Cincinnati Bengals and Clark*, 601 F.2d 516 (10th Cir., 1979). The Supreme Court refused to grant certiorari to hear the matter: *Cincinnati Bengals, Inc. v. Hackbart*, 444 U.S. 931 (1979).

Robert Janis' interview with Dale Hackbart can be accessed at www.extremeskins.com.

CHAPTER 2: SWING FOR THE GREEN, IF YOU CAN

Casey Martin's saga is told by Tom Cunneff in *Walk a Mile in My Shoes: The Casey Martin Story*, but the book ends at 1998, before the appellate decision. The media quickly recognized the poignancy of his quest for justice and followed the narrative carefully. No case in sport law has provoked such a storm of criticism as Martin's triumph. Most who have suffered through a game of golf — amateur or professional — find Casey Martin appealing as a person, but consider his victory in the Supreme Court quite appalling. Each year, this case stimulates the best discussion in my course. The Supreme Court opinions can be found at *PGA Tour, Inc. v. Casey Martin*, 532 U.S. 661 (2001).

John Feinstein is America's finest author on golf and many other sports. His *Tales from Q School* presents a splendid picture of life on the fringes of the PGA Tour and provides a context for understanding why a golf cart might appear to make such a difference.

CHAPTER 3: GENDER IDENTITY IN A CHANGING WORLD

To understand the importance of Renee Richards' case, you must confront the context of gender identity, issues not well appreciated when she played tennis, but now the basis for a growing literature. Richards tells the story from her own perspective in *Second Serve* and its sequel *No Way Renee: The Second Half of My Notorious Life*. Susan Stryker's recent book, *Transgender History*, proved quite helpful.

The New York trial court's opinion can be found at *Renee Richards v. U.S. Tennis Association*, 400 N.Y.S.2d 267 (1977).

CHAPTER 4: THE IDEAL OF AMATEURISM

There are numerous sources critical of the NCAA's regulation of college sports, including that of Walter Byers, whose often scathing attack on his own organization in *Unsportsmanlike Conduct: Exploiting College Athletes* is quite surprising. Andy Zimbalist is one of the finest academic commentators on amateur and professional sports; his *Unpaid Professionals: Commercialism and Conflict in Big-Time College Sports* is first-rate. The NCAA manuals are available online, which is useful because they have grown too heavy to carry around.

The Colorado Court of Appeals decision denying Bloom's claim can be found at *Jeremy Bloom v. NCAA*, 93 P.3d 621 (2004). Counsel for Bloom supplied me with copies of the litigation papers in the case, which are otherwise available through the clerk of court's office. A good place to learn about mogul skiing is Dan DiPiro's book, *Everything the Instructors Never Told You About Mogul Skiing*.

CHAPTER 5: SPORTS ARBITRATION AND ENFORCING PROMISES

Dan Collins' arbitration opinion in Brian Shaw's case is not publicly available, but is discussed in some detail by Judge Breyer in his opinion for the First Circuit Court of Appeals, *Boston Celtics v. Brian Shaw*, 908 F.2d 1041 (1 Cir 1990). The press, in particular the *Boston Globe*, followed the Celtics-Shaw story in some detail.

There are two major resources for information about labor arbitration. Professor Ted St. Antoine and other elected members of the National Academy of Arbitrators wrote the thoughtful book, *The Common Law of the Workplace: The Views of Arbitrators*. Frank and Edna Elkouri's tome, *How Arbitration Works*, is now in its sixth edition, with the assistance of Alan Miles Ruben. I discussed the operation of sports arbitration in *Legal Bases: Baseball and the Law*.

CHAPTER 6: GENDER EQUITY ON THE PARALLEL BARS

Title IX has inspired a vast literature and some very active and interesting blogs, such as http://title-ix.blogspot.com. By transforming college sports, the statute (and accompanying regulations) created an active group of male athletes who felt abused by its success, even though all studies show that the number of men's varsity teams has increased, rather than shrunk. Welch Suggs' *A Place on the Team: The Triumph and Tragedy of Title IX* is a good place to begin investigating this field. Lynette Labinger tells the story of the Brown University women in "Title IX and Athletics: A Discussion of Brown University v. Cohen by Plaintiff's Counsel," published in the *Rutgers Women's Rights Law Reporter* in 1998. There are many published federal district and circuit court opinions covering this litigation, but the best one to read is Judge Selya's decision in *Cohen v. Brown University*, 991 F.2d 888 (1993).

Jennifer Sey's well-written autobiography, *Chalked Up: Inside Elite Gymnastics' Merciless Coaching, Overzealous Parents, Eating Disorders, and Elusive Olympic Dreams*, will give you a sense of the training and performance regimens of the young girls who devote themselves to gymnastics. It seems a nasty business, but if the women at Brown University wanted to swing, bounce, and jump, the law would protect them.

CHAPTER 7: STICKS ARE SWINGING, BUT IS IT A CRIME?

Ted Green's co-authored autobiography, *High Stick*, is representative of the "gee whiz" genre of sports writing. It also is a revealing portrait of a man who played his national game with pride and without too much concern for his physical well-being. A much more literate narrative by Hockey Hall of Famer Ken Dryden, *The Game*, adds to the mosaic of a game that serves as Canada's social touchstone.

Green's criminal case can be found at *Regina v. Green*, 16 D.L.R.3d 137 (1970). The case of his co-participant in icy assault, Wayne Maki, can be found at *Regina v. Maki*, 10 C.R.N.S. 268 (1970).

CHAPTER 8: AL DAVIS, PETE ROZELLE, AND FRANCHISE FREE AGENCY

The best book about Al Davis is an unflattering narrative by Mark Ribowsky, *Slick: The Silver & Black Life of Al Davis*. *Sports Illustrated* followed Davis' career from his first days in Oakland to his current position as a senior statesmen of our national game. Davis effectively used the press to tell his side of every controversy, and there have been many.

His antitrust battle against the National Football League and Pete Rozelle resulted in many published court opinions. The most important is the Ninth Circuit decision in *Los Angeles Memorial Coliseum Commission v. NFL*, 726 F.2d 1381 (9 Cir. 1984), which upheld the lower court's finding of an antitrust violation and made the Raiders a franchise free agent.

The U.S. Supreme Court visited the "single entity" question during the 2009–2010 term in a case brought by an apparel manufacturer, American Needle, against the National Football League, claiming an antitrust violation.

CHAPTER 9: THE TIGHT END, FREEDOM, AND THE ANTITRUST LAWS

John Mackey tells his own story in *Blazing Trails: Coming of Age in Football's Golden Era*, a better-than-average athlete autobiography. His exploits on and off the field were regularly chronicled in the *New York Times* and in *Sports Illustrated*, in particular the collective bargaining with Rozelle and the owners. Mackey's court victory achieving free agency for players can be found in *John Mackey v. National Football League*, 543 F.2d 606 (8 Cir. 1976).

The history of professional football can be found in many sources. ESPN's Sal Paolantonio's *How Football Explains America*, is the most recent.

CHAPTER 10: T.O. MEETS THE ARBITRATOR

The American public has been subject to a daily dose of Terrell Owens in recent years. His 2009 signing with the Buffalo Bills meant that the show would continue, at least for a while. The self-titled autobiography, *T.O.*, relates his side of the various controversies. Labor arbitration opinions in the sports business are rarely available to the public, but because of Owens' prominence, Rich Block's arbitration opinion is available online at http://sports.espn.go.com/nfl/news/story?id=2234819.

The labor arbitration sources listed in the notes to chapter 6 apply to this chapter as well.

CONCLUSION: JUSTICE FOR ALL

The classic text on Jackie Robinson is the late Jules Tygiel's *Baseball's Great Experiment: Jackie Robinson and His Legacy*. It certainly takes much more than a short chapter to do justice to the Robinson-Rickey story, and Tygiel's monumental work is a great resource for readers interested in the whole story. I devote a chapter to Branch Rickey in *Legal Bases: Baseball and the Law*, which also discusses his creation of the farm system despite the bitter opposition of Commissioner Landis.

BIBLIOGRAPHY

Abrams, Roger I. *Legal Bases: Baseball and the Law*. Philadelphia: Temple University Press, 1998.

———. *The Money Pitch: Baseball Free Agency and Salary Arbitration*. Philadelphia: Temple University Press, 2000.

———. *The First World Series and the Baseball Fanatics of 1903*. Boston: Northeastern University Press, 2003.

———. *The Dark Side of the Diamond: Gambling, Violence, Drugs and Alcoholism in the National Pastime*. Burlington, MA: Rounder Books, 2007.

Ashe, Arthur. *Days of Grace*. New York: Random House, 1993.

Blake, James. *Breaking Back: How I Lost Everything and Won Back My Life*. New York: HarperCollins, 2007.

Bragg, Paul, and Patricia Bragg. *Super Power Breathing: For Super Energy*. Santa Barbara, California: Health Science, 1999.

Byers, Walter. *Unsportsmanlike Conduct: Exploiting College Athletes*. Ann Arbor: The University of Michigan Press, 1995.

Cogan, Karen D., and Peter Vidmar. *Gymnastics*. Morgantown, WV: Fitness Information Technology, 2000.

Cunneff, Tom. *Walk a Mile in My Shoes: The Casey Martin Story*. Nashville: Rutledge Hill Press, 1998.

Day, Frederick J. *Clubhouse Lawyer: Law in the World of Sports*. New York: iUniverse Star, 2002.

———. *Sports and Courts: An Introduction to Principles of Law and Legal Theory Using Cases from Professional Sports*. New York: iUniverse Star, 2002.

Dryden, Ken. *The Game*. Toronto: Wiley & Sons, 1983.

Dunning, Eric, and Dominic Malcolm. *Sport: Critical Concepts in Sociology*. New York: Routledge, 2003.

DiPiro, Dan. *Everything the Instructors Never Told You About Mogul Skiing*. Bloomington, IN: Authorhouse, 2005.

Elkouri, Frank, Edna Elkouri, and Alan Miles Ruben. *How Arbitration Works*. Sixth edition. Washington, DC: BNA Books, 2003.

Falk, David. *The Bald Truth: Secrets of Success from the Locker Room to the Board Room*. New York: Simon & Schuster, 2009.

Falk, Gerhard. *Football and the American Identity*. New York: Haworth Press, 2005.

Feinstein, John. *A Good Walk Spoiled*. New York: Little Brown and Company, 1995.

———. *The Majors: In Pursuit of Golf's Holy Grail*. New York: Little Brown and Co., 1999.

———. *The Punch: One Night, Two Lives and the Fight That Changed Basketball Forever*. New York: Little Brown and Co., 2002.

———. *Next Man Up: A Year Behind the Lines in Today's NFL*. New York: Little Brown and Co., 2005.

———. *Tales from Q School*. New York: Little Brown and Co., 2007.

Feinstein, John, and Red Auerbach. *Let Me Tell You a Story: A Lifetime in the Game*. New York: Little Brown and Co., 2004.

Fountain, Charles. *Under the March Sun: The Story of Spring Training*. New York: Oxford University Press, 2009.

Gallwey, W. Timothy. *The Inner Game of Tennis: The Classic Guide to the Mental Side of Peak Performance*. New York: Random House, 1974.

Gilbert, Brad, and Steve Jamison. *Winning Ugly: Mental Warfare in Tennis — Tennis from a Master*. New York: Simon & Schuster, 1993.

Green, Ted, and Al Hirshberg. *High Stick*. New York: Dodd, Mead & Co., 1971.

Lehrer, Jonah. *How We Decide*. Boston: Houghton Mifflin Harcourt, 2009.

Lewis, Chris. *The Scoreboard Always Lies: A Year Behind the Scenes on the PGA Tour*. New York: Free Press, 2007.

Lewis, Michael. *The Blind Side: Evolution of a Game*. New York: W.W. Norton & Co., 2006.

MacCambridge, Michael. *America's Game*. New York: Random House, 2005.

Mackey, John, and Thom Loverro. *Blazing Trails: Coming of Age in Football's Golden Era*. Chicago: Triumph Books, 2003.

McDonagh, Eileen, and Laura Pappano. *Playing with the Boys: Why Separate Is Not Equal in Sports*. New York: Oxford University Press, 2008.

Novak, Michael. *The Joy of Sports*. Lanham, MD: Madison Books, 1976.

Owens, Terrell, and Jason Rosenhaus. *T.O.* New York: Simon & Schuster, 2006.

Paolantonio, Sal. *How Football Explains America*. Chicago: Triumph Books, 2008.

Pier, Arthur Stanwood. *The Story of Harvard*. Boston: Little, Brown, and Co., 1913.

Pope, S. W. *Patriotic Games: Sporting Traditions in the American Imagination 1876–1926*. New York: Oxford University Press, 1997.

Richards, Renee. *Second Serve: The Renee Richards Story.* New York: Stein and Day, 1983.

———. *No Way Renee: The Second Half of My Notorious Life.* New York: Simon and Schuster, 2008.

Ribowsky, Mark. *Slick: The Silver & Black Life of Al Davis.* New York: Macmillan, 1991.

Ross, Stephen F., and Stefan Szymanski. *Fans of the World Unite! A Manifesto for Sports Consumers.* Stanford, CA: Stanford University Press, 2008.

Russell, Gordon W. *Aggression in the Sports World: A Social Psychological Perspective.* New York: Oxford University Press, 2008.

Seib, Philip. *The Player: Christy Mathewson, Baseball and the American Century.* New York: Four Walls Eight Windows, 2003.

Sey, Jennifer. *Chalked Up: Inside Elite Gymnastics' Merciless Coaching, Overzealous Parents, Eating Disorders, and Elusive Olympic Dreams.* New York: Harper Collins, 2008.

Shirley, Paul. *Can I Keep My Jersey? 11 Teams, 5 Countries and 4 Years in My Life as a Basketball Vagabond.* New York: Random House, 2007.

Shulman, James L., and William G. Bowen. *The Game of Life.* Princeton, NJ: Princeton University Press, 2001.

St. Antoine, Theodore, editor. *The Common Law of the Workplace: The Views of Arbitrators* (National Academy of Arbitrators). Arlington, VA: BNA Books, 2005.

Stryker, Susan. *Transgender History.* Berkeley, CA: Perseus Book Group, 2008.

Suggs, Welch. *A Place on the Team: The Triumph and Tragedy of Title IX.* Princeton, NJ: Princeton University Press, 2005.

Szymanski, Stefan. *Playbooks and Checkbooks: An Introduction to the Economics of Modern Sports.* Princeton, NJ: Princeton University Press, 2009.

Thelin, John R. *Games Colleges Play: Scandal and Reform in Intercollegiate Athletics.* Baltimore: The Johns Hopkins University Press, 1994.

Tygiel, Jules. *Baseball's Great Experiment: Jackie Robinson and His Legacy.* New York: Oxford University Press, 1983.

Ware, Susan. *Title IX: A Brief History with Documents.* Boston: St. Martin's Press, 2007.

Yost, Mark. *Tailgating, Sacks and Salary Caps.* Chicago: Kaplan Publishing, 2006.

Zimbalist, Andrew. *Unpaid Professionals: Commercialism and Conflict in Big-Time College Sports.* Princeton, NJ: Princeton University Press, 1999.

———. *May the Best Team Win.* Washington: The Brookings Institution, 2003.

INDEX